Creating Competence
from Chaos

A Comprehensive Guide to Home-Based Services

A NORTON PROFESSIONAL BOOK

Creating Competence from Chaos

A Comprehensive Guide to Home-Based Services

Marion Lindblad-Goldberg

Martha Morrison Dore

Lenora Stern

W. W. Norton & Company
New York • London

Library of Congress Cataloging-in-Publication Data

Lindblad-Goldberg, Marion.
    Creating competence from chaos : a comprehensive guide to home
-based services / Marion Lindblad-Goldberg, Martha Morrison Dore,
Lenora Stern.
        p.   cm.
    "A Norton professional book."
    Includes bibliographical references and index.
    ISBN 0-393-70264-2
    1. Home-based mental health services for children. I. Dore,
Martha Morrison, 1944–   . II. Stern, Lenora. III. Title.
RJ502.4.L56   1988
362.2'4'083—dc21   98-20695 CIP

W. W. Norton & Company, Inc., 500 Fifth Avenue, New York, N.Y. 10110
http://www.wwnorton.com
W. W. Norton & Company Ltd., 10 Coptic Street, London WC1A 1PU

1 2 3 4 5 6 7 8 9 0

To the families of Pennsylvania
whom we have been privileged to serve

CONTENTS

ACKNOWLEDGMENTS

THIS BOOK DEVELOPED from our involvement with Pennsylvania's family-based mental health services initiative implemented in 1988. The vision for Pennsylvania to develop a comprehensive system of care designed to keep children in their own homes and their communities was supported by Karen Snider, former Secretary, Department of Public Welfare; Ford Thompson, former Deputy Secretary, Office of Mental Health; Constance Dellmuth, former Director, Bureau of Children's Services; and Patricia Serra, former Mental Health Specialist, Bureau of Children's Services.

The Philadelphia Child Guidance Family Therapy Training Center's faculty put flesh on the skeletal paper descriptions of the mental health home-based programs by consulting with program directors on how to actualize service implementation from an eco-systemic perspective. In many ways the development of this book benefited from the years of lively and critical discussion among the Center's faculty. Throughout the book, the voices and clinical wisdom of these talented professionals are evident: Andy Fussner, Gordon Hodas, Ann Itzkowitz, Wayne Jones, Ruth Sefarbi, and Iolie Walbridge. Two faculty members, Gordon Hodas and Iolie Walbridge, were particularly helpful in reviewing several chapters. Continual encouragement was provided by administrative support staff, Wendy Siegel and Janice Savage.

Pennsylvania's family-based mental health program directors and their staff were collaborative partners in teaching us how to shape the training curriculum and evaluation plan to satisfy their needs. Their insights and experiences helped us to define the unique aspects of in-home therapy and the challenges faced in clinical work and supervision. We wish to thank the therapists, Patricia Buch, Joan Cashion, Sarah Gardner, Hope Graves, Rick Haley, Nell Jackson, Cory Jex, Liane Kuhns, Sue Richards, Chris Telfer, Rosemarie Witt, and the supervisors, Bruce Buchannan and C. Wayne Jones, who contributed case material. Strong appreciation is expressed to Patricia Buch for her specific reflections on in-home practice. We want to highlight the special contributions of the following program directors who contributed their ideas regarding the development, administration, and evaluation of mental health in-home programs: Cynthia Archacki-Stone, Jeff Blau, D. J. Dunlap, Helene Elko, Kris Ericson, Clarice Ford, Mike Graziano, Jim Houser, Deanna Linn, Sue Richards, Michael Sowers, and Ellen Wolf. We found their suggestions valuable and are profoundly grateful for their assistance.

We would also like to acknowledge the efforts of the many home-based program directors and their staffs in helping us collect data essential to evaluating the program's effectiveness—and beg their forgiveness for the constant barrage of phone calls asking for yet another data form. Special thanks goes also to Elana Yaron and Hadass Shaffer, research assistants; without their competence and dedication to the data-gathering task the evaluation would have been incomplete. We would also like to acknowledge the guidance and direction of those whose work in evaluating home-based and family preservation programs guided us. The wisdom and advice of colleagues like Peter Pecora, Mark Fraser, Kristine Nelson, Jacqueline McCroskey, Scott Henggeler, Marianne Berry, and Kathleen Wells was essential to our success in this endeavor.

Glenda Fine, Joyce Borden, and Christina Corp, professional parents and key leaders from the statewide parent advocacy network, focused our consciousness on the parents' perspective as consumers of this new service. Special recognition is given to the late Joyce Borden who taught us the true meaning of working with parents as partners. As an adjunct faculty member of the Family Therapy Training Center, she exemplified the wisdom that parents know best what their children need and therefore are the most important teachers to service providers. We hope that our readers hear her voice throughout the book's descriptions of clinical practice.

Certainly much of the book's clarity was made possible through the supportive editing efforts of our editor, Susan Munro, and her staff at W. W. Norton. We deeply appreciate their encouragement and guidance.

Most of all we want to thank our families and friends for understanding our preoccupation with "the book" and encouraging our efforts. We are grateful to Karin Yanoff for her editorial wisdom, Dara Goldberg for her literary quest, and David Goldberg for making our communication in the computer age possible. We are especially indebted to Martin Goldberg for his advice, patience, and expertise in designing figures and tables.

INTRODUCTION

After cutting his wrists during a devil worship ritual, Peter was hospitalized at the age of fifteen years. Following his parents' divorce five years earlier, he had required emergency psychiatric hospitalization on four occasions. Poor school performance due to a severe learning disability and subsequent truancy eventually led to a brief placement in a child welfare group home. His single-parent mother felt she could no longer control Peter's behavior, despite weekly outpatient therapy at a mental health center. Frustrated and desperate, mother was considering placing Peter in a residential psychiatric facility.

THE LACK OF adequate mental health services for children and adolescents with emotional, behavioral, or mental problems like those seen in Peter's story is a common problem. Too frequently these children are referred from one child-serving system to another with minimal attempts to collaborate across systems. Yet severe emotional and behavioral problems that lead to out-of-home placements are often found in children served by multiple helpers such as mental health, child welfare, juvenile justice, and education.

In 1985, funding from the National Institute of Mental Health's Child and Adolescent Service System Program (CASSP) provided an opportunity for Pennsylvania to examine the needs of children and families from a mental health practice perspective. As the CASSP Director for Pennsylvania's Department of Public Welfare, Office of Mental Health, Bureau of Children's Services, one of the authors, Lenora Stern, began asking mental health consumers and providers such questions as: Where are the gaps in services within local communities? Do services need to be modified or adapted to meet the special needs of children and their families? The resounding response was a need for services for *both* families and children, designed to improve the functioning of children *and* help families better cope with their child's special needs. There was also a desire that such services be readily accessible to families, that they be delivered in families' homes and communities.

Lenora envisioned what an ideal mental health home-based services model would look like and how it would be funded. Delivered in the family's home and involving parents as partners, these services would try to improve child and family functioning through family therapy, creating collaborative links between appropriate community and family resources, and providing family support funds for concrete services such as transportation, respite care, or emergencies. While child welfare had sponsored Pennsylvania's in-home "family preservation" programs targeted to children at risk of placement because of abuse and neglect, these new mental health home-based programs would serve children at risk for out-of-home placement due to a diagnosis of severe mental illness or emotional or behavioral disorders. The new home-based services would also be used to reunite children with their natural or substitute care families following discharge from inpatient hospitals or psychiatric residential placements.

Another proposed innovative feature of the Pennsylvania model would be to adhere to a unifying ecosystemic model as a theoretical and practical basis for developing the statewide mental health home-based services, training, and research initiatives. An ecosystemic model implies that individual functioning is inextricably linked to environment. Treating a symptomatic child within this model meant working with the family, the home setting, and the family's community network. Establishing statewide services in Pennsylvania within an ecosystemic model would also mean working with each of the 67 counties and their resources to support the new home-based programs. Office of Mental Health staff believed that their goals of coherence and consistency of the program model throughout the state, quality control of staff development, and effective treatment outcome would be furthered through joint efforts in training and evaluation, implemented in 1988 by two of the book's authors, Marion Lindblad-Goldberg, Director of the Family Therapy Training Center, and Martha Dore, Senior Research Consultant, both from the Philadelphia Child Guidance Center. Training from an ecosystemic framework would target county and program administrators as well as the home-based staff. Ecosystemic-based research would measure changes in the child's and the family's functioning in addition to problem resolution.

***

We exchanged polite, professional conversations as we each searched for directional signs to guide us to the Morgantown, West Virginia, airport. None of us would admit being lost. The previous day we had met each other for the first time as we embarked on "home visits" to the agency sites housing Pennsylvania's new mental health home-based programs. After visiting agencies in the northwestern part of the state, we had rented a car to drive to sites in the southwestern counties. A scheduled deadline in Philadelphia led us to search for the closest airport in a desolate rural area within the bordering state of West Virginia. Each of us was immersed in her own thoughts about the daunting challenge that faced us. How would we take what was on paper and put into practice a major statewide paradigm shift in children's mental health services? How would we promote competence in clinical practice that could potentially bring hope and effective treatment outcome to families on the brink of dissolution, given the morass of bureaucratic chaos endemic to this new endeavor? The driver, Marion, found herself on a flat strip of concrete pavement that seemed unusual for the terrain. A man dressed in an orange jumpsuit was standing on the edge of the pavement. She sighed with relief at finding an indigenous helper who could perhaps offer directions. Rolling down the window, she was just about to ask for the way to the airport when the man yelled, "Lady, get off the runway!"

This hilarious moment of shared human fragility allowed us to shed our professional masks and bond us as friends and adventurers in the creation of a vision. The episode also became a future metaphor for the collaboratie relationships that home-based therapists would form with families who helped them to know when they were off course and on the "runway."

***

Over the past ten years, mental health home-based programs across Pennsylvania have treated over 35,000 families with children at risk. Over 600 professional and paraprofessional practitioners have been trained in ecosystemic in-home therapy by Marion and the faculty at Philadelphia Child Guidance's Family Therapy Training Center. Martha's research and evaluation team has collected data on child and family functioning, problem resolution, and post-treatment outcomes up to one year on nearly 2,000 families. These data indicate significant changes in family interaction, child psychosocial functioning, and problem resolution for families who completed home-based services.

The impetus for this book came from numerous national and international consultation requests generated from those interested in the Pennsylvania model. The requests generally took the form of "how to" questions from those who were developing or implementing mental health home-based programs or from other child-serving home-based initiatives seeking to strengthen the mental health component within their area (i.e., child welfare, juvenile justice, education, health, drug and alcohol, etc.). Policymakers and program developers wanted to know the details of program design, how to make a program work, and how to evaluate results. Supervisors wanted to know how to supervise and develop staff skills within this new off-site treatment context. Both professional and paraprofessional practitioners, as well as academicians in social work, psychology, marital and family therapy, counseling, juvenile corrections, psychiatric nursing, and community child psychiatry wanted to know how home-based services work and what mental health issues would be encountered.

Children with significant mental health problems are known to all of us who are committed to helping families at risk. *Creating Competence from Chaos* seeks to present a mental health home-based approach to strengthening these vulnerable families that is grounded in ecosystemic thinking and practice. The values underlying this treatment model are shared by other professionals who believe that a family's needs are best met through individually tailored, family-centered, community based, culturally competent, and outcome-oriented services. By identifying what works in all aspects of developing and implementing home-based services from a mental health perspective, our goal is to provide the field with a practical, comprehensive resource that will be stimulating and useful.

We believe there is much practical information in the chapters to follow that can be widely used across disciplines and fields of practice with high risk families to inform readers regarding home-based services from an ecosystemic perspective. This book begins with a historical overview of the development of home-based services in children's mental health and then moves on to describe the elementary theoretical foundations of family interventions in home-based practice. We believe that therapists doing in-home therapy need to be grounded in the general principles of family development and a working knowledge of systems and structural theory. Further, assessment and treatment planning with families and community agencies require knowing how to distinguish between families experiencing a destabilizing but time-limited developmental crisis and families whose coping efforts are repetitively thwarted. Emphasis is given to the methods of developing a supportive context for home-based programs within a state, community, and agency, since successful in-home therapy is intrinsically linked to these contexts. Key elements of home-based practice are described; these involve building collaborative relationships with families and other helpers, working in the family's home, and implementing specific assessment and treatment planning tools with families and agencies.

Clinical challenges represent the heart of in-home therapy, and so we pay particular attention to specific interventions with families whose children are depressed, suicidal, hyperactive or impulsive, oppositional, aggressive, out-of-control, and violent. Case vignettes provide illustrative examples of how the home-based therapist develops assessment hypotheses and interventions to confront these challenges. The distinguishing features of off-site supervision and training are examined carefully because we believe these efforts are essential to developing the practitioner's skills. There is a significant need to evaluate treatment outcome for mental health home-based services in a managed care environment and to conduct efficacy research. Therefore, we provide information on how to develop and implement a research and evaluation protocol. We conclude with a set of appendices that provide information infrequently requested by home-based programs.

By describing the pragmatics faced by home-based service providers, our goal is to stimulate creativity in work with families rather than to reinvent the wheel. This book has been written with the hope that the ideas will expand the mental health perspective in the delivery of home-based services.

Creating Competence
from Chaos

A Comprehensive Guide to Home-Based Services

CHAPTER 1

Home-Based Services in Child Mental Health: An Overview

When my son was born, it was as if I'd emerged in New York City. Every day, every hour, was like a screeching, horn-blowing nightmare. It was howling, sleepless nights with a baby like that—like New York City—never seemed to sleep, never paused. There were many gray and stormy days. No interest in rocking and scant patience for lullabies.

—Churchill, 1995

Chuck has influenced our family deeply since the beginning of his life. Each of the siblings in his or her own way has noticed that Chuck was different from the rest of us. . . . We guarded and watched him more than we would another sibling. . . . We adapted to his frequent tantrums. He could always get a reaction from one of us.

—Tingley, 1995

It was very difficult and frustrating to watch our son deteriorate. As he deteriorated, our dreams for him shattered. At a young age my son had been tested through the schools. His test scores were very high. At one point we were told, "You've got a genius." . . . After my son's first [psychiatric] hospitalization we were told that he would probably not complete high school. We could forget about college completely.

—Rinkin, 1995

EVERY DAY, in juvenile and family courts across America, bewildered, frustrated, and emotionally exhausted parents and other family members sit on hard wooden benches or in long, uncomfortable pews awaiting a judge's decision whether to place a child in the care and custody of the state. These are not uncaring parents who have abused or neglected their children in some way. They have not battered or beaten them, nor have they starved their children for love and affection. On the contrary, they are often parents who are deeply and wholly committed to nurturing their children as best they know how.

But something has gone terribly wrong. And now these families find themselves petitioning the court to place their children in a psychiatric facility or a residential treatment center or a special group home for seriously emotionally disturbed children— somewhere, anywhere—that might help bring back the youngster they once knew as a smiling, eager six-year old, begging Dad to play catch and pasting together lacy valentines for Mom—somewhere, anywhere—that can take this sullen, hostile, drug-addled teenager who refuses to go to school and stays out all night, looting and stealing to support her habit, or this frightened, withdrawn 12-year-old with his sudden violent rages and vicious attacks on siblings and neighborhood pets, and restore to the parents the children they cherished.

Petitioning the state to take custody of one's child in order to get help for that child is a terribly painful step for most parents. It seems to signify utter failure as a parent. It forces parents to place their trust in an institution, the state, which may or may not respond in the child's best interests. And, as many parents have discovered, the battle to secure appropriate services for their child has only *begun* at the point of placement, yet their legal standing to participate in treatment decision-making is severely curtailed. The child may be placed in a residential program many hundreds of miles from family and community, restricting the family's ability to visit frequently and straining family ties to the point of breaking. Further, families are seldom offered any assistance in dealing with their own feelings of embarrassment, frustration, and despair. Nor are they taught better strategies for coping with the behavior of a child with emotional and behavioral problems. It is no wonder that family members often distance themselves from a child with serious emotional disturbance, withdrawing the support and encouragement such a child so desperately needs.

It is also no wonder that families sometimes become abusive or even break apart under the strain of caring for a disturbed child. Such a child's demands for time and attention often result in neglect of other family members' emotional needs. And the behavior problems of a child with serious emotional disturbance frequently preclude the family outings and activities that build family unity and enhance the functioning of the family system. As one mother of a child with a serious emotional disability poignantly put it:

Make no mistake about it—these children *do* make their parents crazy. Parents can't take them to the store because the kids will immediately force their parents to chase them up and down the aisles. Parents can't take their children to friends' homes to visit. The adults won't have a chance to visit in peace because the kids will get into all of the cupboards and drawers, knock things over, and just generally bounce off the walls. . . . Inevitably, parents withdraw to their own homes, isolated because of their inability to cope with their children's behaviors anywhere else. . . . (Melton, 1989, p. 11)

What, then, are the alternatives to this scenario of family desperation, placement, and social and emotional withdrawal? One alternative is to offer families the support and guidance they need *before* they throw their hands up in despair.

Family-focused interventions have been recognized as an important adjunct to treatment of mental health problems in children since the child guidance movement first began in the 1920s (Fauber & Long, 1991). Recent developments in child mental health research and practice, as well as changes in public policy, have increased attention on the family as the locus of service provision (DeChillo, Koren, & Schultze, 1994; Friesen & Koroloff, 1990; Heflinger & Bickman, 1996; Lourie & Katz-Leavy, 1991). This increased attention to families' needs has given rise to a new form of treatment in the children's mental health continuum: *home-based services* (Diamond, Serrano, Dickey, & Sonis, 1996; Dore, 1993; Evans & Boothroyd, 1997; Henggeler et al., 1997)

Rather than treating the family as an adjunct to child treatment, home-based services target the family as the primary recipient of mental health care (Friesen & Koroloff, 1990). Unlike family therapy models, however, which treat the family as the locus of the child's *pathology*, home-based services focus on expanding the family's available internal and external *resources* to nurture and

care for a child with serious emotional disturbance (deKemp & Van
Acker, 1997; Heflinger & Bickman, 1996; Lindblad-Goldberg &
Dore, 1989). While practitioners engaged in home-based services
recognize and address any dysfunction in the family system that
is likely to interfere with a family's ability to maintain and nurture
a seriously emotionally disturbed child, attention is also given
to establishing relationships between the family and community
services, organizations, and institutions that can support and enhance their efforts. The home-based services treatment model reflects current research on the influence of family interaction and
functioning on child development (Dore & Pereira, in press).

RESEARCH ON FAMILIES AND THE
MENTAL HEALTH OF CHILDREN

Over the past two decades longitudinal and cross-sectional studies have contributed significantly to the knowledge base for developing mental health treatments for children, including home-based
services (Birmaher et al., 1996; Kutash & Rivera, 1995; Tuma,
1989). Researchers have identified a number of factors that increase
the probability of emotional disturbances in children, many of
which occur within the family system. Such internal family factors
(listed in Table 1.1) are repeatedly found to be associated with
emotional and behavioral disorders in children. Contextual factors,
such as poverty, single-parent status, low educational attainment
by parents, large family size, and minority group status, also appear
to increase a child's vulnerability to psychological distress
(Comer & Hill, 1985; Rutter, 1987; Tuma, 1989; Werner, 1989).

It is not one or even two but a combination of these factors that
substantially increases the probability of child psychopathology
(Garmezy, 1987; Williams, Anderson, McGee, & Silva, 1990).
It is also important to note that there are children whose own
neurobiology or biochemistry makes them vulnerable to severe
emotional or behavioral disorders without any apparent risk factors in their lives (Hooper & Tramontana, 1997). Many of these
children are difficult almost from birth; others seem to function
normally until puberty, when the stresses of major biochemical
and biological changes apparently trigger latent vulnerabilities to
mental disorder. Currently it is believed that children's genetic and

Table 1.1
FACTORS THAT INCREASE THE PROBABILITY OF EMOTIONAL DISTURBANCE IN CHILDREN

Marital Conflict and Violence	Substance Abuse	Parental Mental Illness	Child Abuse and Neglect	Poor Parenting Practices
Kashani, Daniel, Dandoy, & Holcomb, 1992	Dore, Kauffman, Nelson-Zlupko, & Granfort, 1996	Downey & Coyne, 1990	Carlson, Furby, Armstrong, & Shales, 1997	Belsky, Woodworth, & Crnic, 1996
McCloskey, Figuerdo, & Koss, 1995	West & Prinz, 1987	Jensen, Bloedau, Degroot, Ussery, & Davis, 1990	Flisher et al., 1997	Bronstein, Clauson, Stoll, & Abrams, 1993
Reid & Crisafulli, 1990		Seifer & Dickstein, 1993	Malinosky-Rummell & Hansen, 1993	Gardner, 1989
Spaccarelli, Sandler & Roosa, 1994		Radke-Yarrow, Nottelmann, Martinez Fox, & Belmont, 1992	Manly, Cicchetti, & Barnett, 1994	Pettit, Bates, & Dodge, 1997
		Rutter & Quinton, 1984		

temperamental vulnerabilities range along a continuum to severe emotional disorder, and that the kinds of environmental and family stressors described above serve to heighten this vulnerability (Dadds, 1995; Diamond et al., 1996).

What attributes enable some children to overcome the familial and environmental factors that place them at high risk of emotional disturbance? Current research on resilience and stress-resistance in children has identified a number of factors that seem to innoculate seemingly resilient children against the effects of a hazardous environment: having a moderate temperament, a warm, nurturing relationship with at least one stable caregiver, and the presence of a modicum of social support (Garmezy, 1987; Holahan & Moos, 1987; Rutter, 1987; Werner, 1989).

One recent study of outcomes for children of drug-addicted mothers highlights the interactive effects of these variables that support resilience (Johnson, Glassman, Fiks, & Rosen, 1990). Children exposed to drugs prenatally were evaluated neurologically at three years of age, using the Merrill-Palmer Scale of Mental Tests, and with regard to overall psychosocial development. Their outcome measures were then grouped statistically into three cohorts. The major predictor of resilience evidenced by the highest functioning cohort was a nurturant and responsive home environment. It was not simply the presence of a single involved caregiver, as almost all the children in the study had at least one such person in their lives, but the positive interaction of family and environmental factors with characteristics of the individual child that predicted more positive child outcomes (Johnson et al., 1990). All of these children lived in adverse environments filled with interpersonal violence and drug-related activity; those who thrived had families able to moderate the effects of the environment on their children.

Other research supports the mediating effects of responsive parenting on outcomes for children (Fauber & Long, 1991; Goodyer, 1990; Pettit, Bates, & Dodge, 1997). The rich body of research on attachment in infancy illustrates the beneficial effects of competent early caregiving (Ainsworth, 1985; Bowlby, 1988; Crittenden, 1985), while studies of the interactions between abusive parents and their children support findings of a relationship between coercive parenting practices and negative developmental outcomes for children (Aber, Allen, Carlson, & Cicchetti, 1989).

Research shows that mothers' responsiveness and affectional involvement with their children are highly predictive of child social/ emotional functioning over time (Goodman & Brumley, 1990). Studies of maternal depression and its effects on mothers' interactions with their children highlight this finding. These studies identify severe inhibition in depressed mothers' social-emotional responsiveness to their children (Gordon, Burge, Hammen, Adrian, Jaenicke, & Hiroto, 1989; Rutter & Quinton, 1984). Such mothers frequently appear almost unaware of their children's presence and are clearly unable to protect them from effects of noxious environments (Gelfand & Teti, 1990).

Research on Family Systems

Family systems researchers have looked beyond the parent-child dyad to seek correlates of child psychopathology in various patterns of family interaction (Anderson & Henry, 1994; Blatt & Homann, 1992; Chiariello & Orvaschel, 1995; Dadds, Barrett, Rapee, & Ryan, 1996; Fristad & Clayton, 1991; Ge, Best, Conger, & Simons, 1996; Leadbetter, Bishop, & Raver, 1996). This research is based on family systems theory of the recursive nature of family interactions(Combrinck-Graham, 1989). Patterns of family interaction are developed and maintained as normal coping responses to the everyday stresses and strains of meeting the family's systemic maintenance needs as well as the psychosocial needs of individual members. Over time, however, these patterns may become stereotyped and inflexible, no longer serving an adaptive function for the changing demands on the family system. Or, the family may develop maladaptive or dysfunctional patterns in response to overwhelming system-wide stress, such as that generated by efforts to care for a child with severe emotional or behavioral problems. In either circumstance, one or more individuals in the family soon exhibit symptoms of the system's distress and may be identified as needing therapeutic intervention.

The effects of conflict in the marital dyad on the functioning of children in the family is one of the most frequently researched family interaction patterns (Amato & Keith, 1991; Barber & Eccles, 1992; Borrine, Handal, Brown, & Searight, 1991; Reid & Crisafulli, 1990). Studies of the post-divorce functioning of children have identified a pre-divorce history of severe marital conflict as highly correlated with long-term maladjustment (Borrine et al., 1991; Shaw & Emery, 1987). Researchers examining the relationship between marital discord and dysfunctional parenting practices have concluded that, in addition to the direct effects of conflict within the family system on child well-being, such conflict also has indirect effects through its disruption of normative parenting (Fauber et al., 1990). In one such study, aggression in very young children was related to problems in parenting which, in turn, were highly correlated with marital conflict (Jouriles, Pfiffner, & O'Leary, 1988).

In addition to research on events in the marital subsystem and their relationship to child functioning, attention also has been given to other patterns of system interaction in families of children with emotional or behavioral problems. Gilbert, Christensen, and Margolin (1984) compared the intrasystem alliances of families of children treated in mental health clinics with those of families whose children did not have identified emotional or behavioral problems. Treated families were characterized by weak levels of mutual support among all family members, weak marital alliances, and conflicted relationships between the mother and the emotionally disturbed child in these families. In addition, both parents tended to have more positive relationships with other children in the family.

Using a sample of college students, Teyber (1983) examined intrafamilial alliances and their relationship to child psychosocial adjustment. Half of the subjects reported that the marital dyad was the primary dyad in their families of origin; the other half reported the primacy of another dyad (parent/child, sib/sib, grandparent/parent, grandparent/child). On tests of psychosocial adjustment, females who rated the marital dyad as primary in their families were found to be better adjusted than those who did not. This finding did not hold for males in the sample, however. The author interpreted these results in conjunction with another finding in his study: that fathers in primary marital dyad families were perceived by their children as more emotionally accessible. Teyber cited prior studies showing that emotional inaccessibility of fathers affects personality development in daughters more than in sons. He concluded that his findings underscore the importance of recognizing and addressing family alliances in the treatment of malad-justed children.

To test a basic assumption of family systems theory that cross-generational coalitions are associated with child symptomatology, Mann and his colleagues (1990) studied the relationship between cross-generational family alliances and adolescent antisocial behavior. On one indicator, involving higher verbal activity with one parent (mother) and higher rates of conflict-hostility with the other (father), delinquents demonstrated more such alliances than did a control group of nondelinquent peers (Mann, Borduin, Henggeler, & Blaske, 1990). Parents of delinquents also demonstrated lower rates of positive martial dyadic alliance than parents of nondelinquents and exhibited less mutual support and more conflict and hostility. These findings lend additional support to the association between specific family interaction patterns and child functioning.

Research on Family Stress and Coping

While few researchers have directly observed the patterns of stress and coping in families of seriously emotionally disturbed children, studies of coping responses in families caring for children with physical or cognitive disabilities are extensive. This work provides solid support for family-focused home-based interventions. Most such studies have found clear associations between positive adaptation to caring for a special-needs child and specific family factors. These include *supportive relationships between family members*, especially in the marital subsystem (Friedrich, Wilturner, & Cohen, 1985; Trute, 1990); *open and direct communication* (Hampson, Hulgus, Beavers, & Beavers, 1988); and *high levels of social support* (Schilling, Gilchrist, & Schinke, 1984; Trute & Hauch, 1988; Unger & Powell, 1980).

Other studies have identified the influence of environmental factors on families coping with special-needs children (Crnic, Friedrich, & Greenberg, 1983; Kazak, 1986). Supportive community agents, such as schools, religious institutions, medical personnel, and social organizations, have been found to positively affect the response of the family system to extraordinary caregiving demands (Schilling et al., 1984; Suelzle & Keenan, 1981; Unger & Powell,

1980). This research speaks to an important component of home-based mental health services for children: its focus on family interaction with external systems.

THERAPEUTIC APPROACHES TO WORKING WITH FAMILIES

Family-focused home-based treatment for mental health problems in children reflects an amalgam of two parallel, infrequently intersecting, fields. One field is the family therapy movement, which has gained increasing momentum since the 1960s. The other is family social services, which developed in response to problems presented by distressed families in the public social service and child welfare systems. The historical development of each of these efforts has been thoroughly explored elsewhere in the literature and will not be replicated here; instead, the contributions of both to the development of home-based children's mental health services will be explored.

Family Therapy

Although there are various schools of family therapy, each with its own understanding of family dynamics and methods for facilitating family-level change, nearly all share the common theoretical base of systems theory. Whereas psychodynamically-oriented therapy seeks modification of internal personality structure, family therapy focuses on changing dysfunctional transactions among members of the family system. Family therapists understand problems presented by individual family members as reflecting dilemmas confronting the system as a whole. Such dilemmas arise from the family system's inability to evolve and adapt to changing internal and external demands. The therapist's role is to observe and identify maladaptive patterns relative to the presenting problem and to enable family members to adopt more productive, mutually satisfying transactions. Productive transactions allow for normal growth and development of all family members as well as the family unit itself.

Systems-based family therapy tends to be time-limited and goal-directed. Outcome goals are established by the family with help from the therapist, as are the steps to be taken to achieve those goals. Systemic approaches reject the concept of individual pathology and search for strengths and resources within the family to utilize in the process of change. Treatment tends to be proactive rather than reactive, with the therapist moving quickly to initiate changes in family transactions rather than waiting for insights regarding causal agents to emerge. Family members are helped to create new patterns of interaction with one another as a way of stimulating change.

Family Social Services

In contrast to the well-defined application of systems theory in family therapy, family social services evolved more or less atheoretically in response to perceived needs of families served by family and child welfare agencies. Since most professionals providing family social services are identified as social workers, it is possible to look to the early days of that profession when "friendly visitors" first gave attention to troubled families. As Broderick and Schrader (1981) noted in their history of marital and family therapy, social workers were the first professionals to focus attention on the family as a unit and on the interrelationships among family members. They quote Mary Richmond, a social work pioneer and early theoretician, who wrote in 1917 of the need to rebuild families and to observe members "acting and reacting upon one another" (Broderick & Schrader, 1981).

Since Richmond's time, social work has emphasized the "helping relationship" as the vehicle for bringing about change in clients. In the 1930s and 1940s, psychodynamic theory gave family social workers a framework for interpreting the behavior of individual family members but contributed little to their understanding of how to intervene with the family as a whole. Family social workers recognized, as had their predecessors, the "friendly visitors," the impact of adverse environments and institutions on families, but they lacked tools for effecting changes in these transactions at the case level. For decades family social workers sought interventions that would initiate real and long-lasting change in distressed and dysfunctional families. More often than not, they found themselves removing vulnerable children from harm's way, forming helping relationships that seemed only to encourage long-term dependency, or limiting their efforts to meeting families' immediate needs for concrete services such as food, clothing, and housing as they intervened in crisis after crisis. The St. Paul Family Project, initiated in 1957 to identify more effective ways of helping highly disorganized and dysfunctional families, was a landmark effort to enhance the efficacy of family social services interventions (Maybanks & Bryce, 1979).

As family social workers in the 1960s and 1970s increasingly recognized the importance of focusing attention on the family unit and bolstering its caregiving capacities, demonstration projects across the country were developed to keep fragile families together and prevent out-of-home placement of children. Like the St. Paul Family Project, these efforts usually included some combination of intensive counseling (most often, of parents), concrete services, and development of support networks (McGowan & Meezan, 1983; Stehno, 1986).

HOME-BASED SERVICES ACROSS
CHILD-SERVING SYSTEMS

By the early 1970s changes that had taken place with regard to the care and treatment of institutionalized adults had influenced children's services as well. The principles of deinstitutionalization, normalization, and community-based care were applied to child and youth services through litigation and advocacy by parents and patient-rights activists (Dore & Guberman-Kennedy, 1981). All that remained was to shape public policy, through state and federal legislation, reflecting judicial decisions regarding the right of children to treatment in the least restrictive, most normal settings possible. What followed over the next two decades was a series of laws passed by Congress that has defined the contemporary context for children's mental health services.

The Juvenile Justice System

One of the first pieces of legislation was the 1974 Juvenile Justice and Delinquency Prevention Act, which proscribed housing juveniles in adult facilities and mandated treatment of "status of-fenders" in community settings (Schwartz, Jackson-Beeck, & Anderson, 1984). Status offenders are children and youth whose offenses, such as running away or violating curfew, would not be considered offenses at all if committed by adults. In the mental health system, these youth are often diagnosed as having conduct disorders. The mandate of community-based care for status offenders focused significant attention on the home-based management of difficult, acting-out children. A number of family-level intervention models, regarded as highly effective with conduct-disordered youth, were developed in response (Alexander, Barton, Schiavo, & Parsons, 1976; Parsons & Alexander, 1973).

Patterson's (1982) work with families of delinquent boys was seminal in developing approaches to treating delinquency in a home and family context. He identified patterns of interaction between parents and children that reinforce and exacerbate antisocial behavior. Helping parents learn alternative ways of interacting with their adolescents has been a focus of family-focused home-based interventions since this research (Miller & Prinz, 1990).

Alexander, Parsons, and their colleagues (1973, 1976) developed their functional family therapy model using behavioral techniques to modify interactions in families of acting-out youth. One study supporting this model involved treatment of serious juvenile offenders with multiple offenses that included misdemeanors and felonies (Gordon, Arbuthnot, Gustafson, & McGreen, 1988). A two-year follow-up comparing recidivism rates of youth receiving functional family therapy with a group of offenders receiving standard probation services revealed that the standard services group had significantly higher recidivism rates (as measured in charges resulting in a court hearing) (Gordon et al., 1988).

"Multisystemic therapy" is the name given to an intervention model that combines principles of systemic family therapy and behavioral therapy to treat juvenile offenders in a home- and community-based context (Schoenwald, Scherer, & Brondino, 1997). Like family social services, multisystemic therapy recognizes the need to intervene in transactions between the family and other systems as well as those within the family itself. In comparison studies this treatment model has proved efficacious in preventing out-of-home placement of juvenile offenders in justice facilities (Borduin et al., 1995; Henggeler et al., 1993; Henggeler, Melton, & Smith, 1992).

The Child Welfare System

Public policy mandating home- and community-based care has also influenced the child welfare system. As a result of the 1980 Adoption Assistance and Child Welfare Reform Act (PL 96–272), whose provisions were greatly enhanced by the Family Preservation and Support Act of 1993 (PL 103–66), state child welfare authorities were mandated to keep children and youth in their own homes whenever possible, rather than placing them in foster care (Early & Hawkins, 1994). PL 96–272 called for judicial determination of "reasonable efforts" to prevent out-of-home placement of children (Sudia, 1986). The Family Preservation and Support Act provided states with funding to develop and implement services to preserve families and prevent child placement. Such services are family-focused and home-based; they fall under the rubrics of "family preservation," "family support," and "family reunification" services (Berry, 1997; Cole & Duva, 1990).

In 1985, in response to the required "reasonable efforts" to prevent family dissolution and child placement, the Edna McConnell Clark Foundation, a long-time supporter of voluntary child welfare services, published a widely-disseminated, often-cited pamphlet entitled "Keeping Families Together: The Case for Family Preservation." An emotional introduction by poet Maya Angelou called for an end to removing children from their birth families, only to have them languish for years in the foster-care system. In this pamphlet the Clark Foundation proposed that "Homebuilders"—a home-based program developed in the early 1970s in Tacoma, Washington—be adopted nationally as the model for family preservation services. Subsequently, under the leadership of Peter Forsythe, director of its "Program for Children," the Clark Foundation focused its considerable resources on influencing inclusion of the Homebuilders family preservation model in state and national legislation (Adams, 1994; Forsythe, 1992). By the mid-1990s, most states had passed some form of legislation requiring provision of preventive child welfare services; many specified services closely reflecting the Homebuilders model.

Homebuilders is based on crisis intervention theory, social systems theory, and social learning theory (Barth, 1988). It is a short-term, four-to-six-week treatment program that provides round-the-clock availability of therapists with small caseloads to maximize responsiveness to families in crisis (Kinney, Haapala, & Booth, 1991). Family members, especially parents, are taught new skills with which to manage interpersonal transactions as well as personal stress (Kinney et al., 1991). Treatment takes place primarily in the family home or, alternatively, in community settings such as schools and community centers. The expressed philosophy of Homebuilders is that children belong with their biological families and that most families, with support and direction, are willing and able to learn better ways of caring for their children (Kinney et al., 1991).

Early outcome evaluations of Homebuilders programs seemed to indicate that this model was highly effective in preventing out-of-home placement of children in families at imminent risk of dissolution (Pecora, Fraser, & Haapala, 1992). In one study of Homebuilders programs serving 446 families in Utah and Washington, Pecora and his colleagues (1992) found that 93% of children judged to be at imminent risk of placement were still with their families after Homebuilders' interventions. These researchers followed a smaller subsample of treated families and a matched comparison group of untreated families over a 12-month period post-treatment. Eighty-five percent of the children in the comparison group had gone into foster care, as opposed to 44% in the treated group (Pecora, Fraser, & Haapala, 1991). Other studies appeared to confirm these findings of Homebuilders' effectiveness (Bath, Richey, & Haapala, 1992; Theiman & Dail 1992; Yuan & Struckman-Johnson, 1991).

To many in the child welfare field, Homebuilders is the prototypical family preservation model, yet the term "family preservation services" actually includes a wide variety of program models and mix of services (Nelson, 1997). Berry (1997) identified several characteristics that all family preservation services have in common:

1. an emphasis on family strengths as opposed to deficits
2. provision of services in the family home and community settings
3. family-focused and family-centered service provision
4. crisis-oriented service delivery
5. short-term intensive intervention

Some of these alternative home-based models implemented in child welfare settings are short-term and crisis-oriented, like Homebuilders; still others draw more directly on family systems theory and traditional family social services models (Berry, 1997; Morton & Grigsby 1993; Nelson, 1997; Schwartz, AuClaire, & Harris, 1991). Outcome studies of these models show mixed results in preventing child placement (Bath & Haapala, 1995; Littell, 1995). One major study of a state-wide family preservation effort in Illinois found no differences in placement rates between families receiving preservation services based on a family-systems model and those receiving the usual child welfare services (Schuerman, Rzepnicki, & Littell, 1994). This study is noteworthy as one of the few using random assignment to treatment and control groups.

Even though the Illinois researchers attempted to address the flaws of previous studies of family preservation services, their own study had serious limitations (Epstein, 1997). These include violation of random assignment, questionable reliability of instruments used to collect data, and failure to demonstrate treatment integrity (whether clients actually received services as specified in the treatment model). Family preservation researchers are attempting to address these and other limitations of existing studies, and to identify more clearly those families who can truly benefit from family-focused home-based services in the child welfare system (Bath & Haapala, 1993; Berry, 1997; Wells & Freer, 1994).

Mental Health Needs Across Child-Serving Systems

Increasingly, research is demonstrating that children in the child welfare and juvenile justice systems show symptoms of serious emotional disturbances at rates similar to those of children receiving services in the mental health system (Edens & Otto, 1997; Famularo, Kinscherff, & Fenton, 1992; Stein, Evans, Mazumdar, & Rae-Grant, 1996; Trupin, Tarico, Low, Jemelka, & McClellan, 1993). Indeed, there is growing evidence that the factors that truly differentiate children across service systems are often age, race, and socioeconomic status: Poorer and younger children enter the child welfare system, older and minority youth enter the juvenile justice system, and nonminority youth with more economic resources enter the mental health system (Barth, Courtney, Berrick, & Albert, 1994; Benjamin, 1997; Westendorp, Brink, Roberson, & Ortiz, 1986).

Studies of children in the child welfare system have historically found high percentages with diagnosable mental disorders (Stein et al., 1996; Trupin et al., 1993). A five-year study by Fanshel and Shinn (1978) identified serious psychological problems in 24% of a sample of children in the New York City foster-care system. Another early study of New York foster children found that 35% evidenced marked-to-severe impairment in psychosocial functioning in psychiatric evaluations (Swire & Kavalar, 1978). And, in a study of children in foster care in Tennessee, nearly half displayed evidence of serious difficulties on the Child Behavior Checklist, a parent-report measure of problem behaviors (McIntyre & Keesler, 1986).

More recent studies of the mental health status of foster children seem to indicate that the emotional problems and needs of these children are greater than ever, validating the informal observations of child welfare workers and clinicians who work with this population. In one random sample of 50 Canadian foster children in the care of an urban child welfare agency, 62% were observed to have some form of mental disorder as indicated by scores in the psychopathological range on two or more of the standardized assessments used in this study (Thompson & Fuhr, 1992). It is noteworthy that nine children originally sampled were rejected because their caseworkers felt they were too disturbed even to be tested.

In another recent study, in Washington State, Trupin et al. (1993) tested 191 children, ages 3 to 18, randomly selected from that state's protective services caseload. Findings were compared with those from children in the state's mental health facilities. Seventy-two percent of the children in the child welfare sample were indistinguishable from those in psychiatric care on a composite functioning score. In Sacramento, California, researchers screening children entering out-of-home care in that city's child welfare system found that 68% demonstrated significant difficulties in one or more of the domains of psychosocial functioning assessed (Urquiza, Wirtz, Peterson, & Singer, 1994).

Studies of children and youth in the juvenile justice system show similarly high levels of emotional disturbance. When administrators of facilities for adjudicated delinquents were asked what proportion of youth in their facilities they considered to be severely emotionally disturbed, they responded that 17% of their charges could be so described, with an additional 36% identified as moderately disturbed (Young, Dore, & Pappenfort, 1988). Some estimates have placed the prevalence of serious emotional disturbance among juvenile offenders as high as 60% (Rotenberg, 1997). A Virginia study found that 8–10% of that state's incarcerated youth were severely emotionally disturbed, while another 40% were moderately disturbed (Rotenberg, 1997). In all, 75% of youth in Virginia's detention facilities exhibited symptoms of at least one diagnosable mental disorder.

This evidence of a significant number of children and youth with serious emotional disturbances in all child-serving systems—each mandated by public policy to deliver services in the least restrictive, most normalized environment possible—underscores the importance of developing family-focused home-based approaches to addressing the mental health needs of children.

Home-Based Care in Children's Mental Health Services

Arguably the legislation having the most profound and lasting influence on home-based care of children with serious emotional disturbance is Public Law 94–142, the Education for All Handicapped Children Act. Passed by Congress after very little debate in 1975, this legislation mandated public schools to provide educational programs in the most normal setting possible for all children, no matter what their special physical, mental, or emotional needs (Goldberg, 1982). It took at least a decade for many school systems to comply, and some of the law's provisions regarding services to seriously emotionally disturbed children are still being tested in the courts. Nevertheless, P. L. 94–142 has enabled scores of children and youth, who formerly required residential care, to remain in their own homes and communities (Salend, 1990). Children age four and older with serious emotional disturbances are now entitled to a free, appropriate public education alongside their normally functioning peers. As a result, however, families are asked to cope with and manage children whose problems and behaviors can place extraordinary demands on resources within and outside of the family system.

Another significant piece of legislation, Public Law 99–457, passed in 1988, mandates early identification and treatment of special needs children under age four, including those with emotional and behavioral difficulties, and contains a significant focus on families (Meisels, 1989). Both this legislation and the earlier P. L. 94–142 recognize parents as the primary caregivers for their children. However, unlike the earlier law, P. L. 99–457 makes the family, rather than the child, the focus of service delivery (Ooms, 1990). This law emphasizes building the family's capacity to care for and nurture a child with special needs, as well as recognizing the family's need for community support in this endeavor. As the most recent federal effort to translate the principles of normalization, least restrictive environment, and community-based care into children's services, P. L. 99–457 reflects the clearest public policy statement yet of home-based service delivery (Woody, Woody, & Greenberg, 1991).

With over a decade of federal mental health legislation providing a context, the Child and Adolescent Service System Program (CASSP), initiated by the National Institute of Mental Health in 1984, provided the impetus for development of home-based services in the child mental health system (Lourie & Katz-Leavy, 1991). The CASSP initiative grew out of concern for the limited range of mental health services for children available in most communities and the failure of the major child-serving systems—mental health, child welfare, juvenile justice, and education—to collaborate in providing services to children with serious emotional disturbance wherever they were found (Stockdill, 1991).

It is clear from the previous discussion that family-focused home-based interventions are not unique to the children's mental health system. Indeed, present public policy, research on child development and psychopathology, and current practice technologies support family-level approaches to child treatment irrespective of system of origin. In the mental health system the CASSP initiative encouraged states to develop a continuum of children's services ranging from least to most intrusive. *Intrusiveness* is defined as the degree of impact on normal activities of everyday life. Family-focused home-based services are conceptualized as more intrusive than outpatient treatment and less intrusive than day treatment or partial hospitalization, as measured in number and duration of clinical contacts per week (Dore, Wilkinson, & Sonis, 1992).

As the name suggests, home-based children's mental health services are primarily provided in the family home; however, they may be delivered in other natural community settings as well, including schools, recreation centers, and even fast-food outlets. According to Stroul and Goldman (1990), despite differences in approaches to service delivery, all models of family-focused home-based services have the following goals in common:

1. to preserve the integrity of the family and to prevent unnecessary out-of-home placement
2. to link the child and family with appropriate community agencies and individuals in order to create an ongoing community support system
3. to strengthen the family's coping skills and capacity for functioning effectively in the community (p. 66)

Taking its cue from the fields of mental retardation and physical disability, where parents have long been active advocates for family-centered supportive services, CASSP has increasingly incorporated a philosophy of "families as partners" in all phases of service planning and implementation (DeChillo, Koren, & Schultze, 1994). Home-based services reflect this philosophy by focusing treatment interventions on the family as a whole, by engaging family members in all aspects of treatment planning, and by shaping services to meet each family's unique needs (Friesen & Koroloff, 1990).

Home-based children's mental health services are not limited to family therapy but include a range of supportive and educational services as well. In this way, the home-based model incorporates practice principles and knowledge from both family therapy and family social services. This treatment model incorporates current research on family stress and coping (Burr, Klein, & Associates, 1994; Hobfoll & Spielberger, 1992) as well as new understandings of family ecology (Gilgun, 1996; Harrison, Wilson, Pine, Chan, & Buriel, 1990). Working with families to develop an ongoing network of social and community supports is a central goal in home-based services. According to one qualitative study, parent advocacy groups are an especially effective method of empowering parents (Fine & Borden, 1989). Such groups provide a continuing source of mutual aid, education, and acknowledgment for parents caring for seriously emotionally disturbed children (Friesen & Koroloff, 1990) and are an integral component of home-based services.

Effectiveness of Home-Based Services

Research on outcomes of home-based services in child mental health is more limited than the previously described family preservation research in the child welfare system. Because home-based services are only one type in an array of children's mental health services, and admittedly not the least expensive, this form of treatment has not garnered the attention and resources that has spurred family preservation research. Most currently available studies of home-based children's mental health services (1) describe treated populations, (2) are matched comparison studies, or (3) are explorations of service delivery (deKemp & Van Acker, 1997; Dore et al., 1992; Henggeler et al., 1997; Liddle, 1995; Seelig, Goldman-Hall, & Jerrell, 1992; Werrbach, 1992; Zarski & Fluharty, 1992). Discussions of the effectiveness of home-based children's mental health services often draw heavily from research on family preservation services with child welfare populations (Kutash & Rivera, 1995), despite significant differences in the context and focus of service delivery in these two child-serving systems (Dore, 1991a). Preventing the imminent placement of a child—the most frequently measured outcome in child welfare—may not be the most meaningful measure of effectiveness in children's mental health services. Improvement in the psychosocial functioning of a child with serious emotional disturbance, as well as enhancement of a family's internal and external resources for caring for such a child, are more relevant indicators of treatment success. Some even believe that a brief psychiatric placement, or respite, may have a salutary effect on treatment, as contrasted with foster-care placement or the detention of a delinquent, which almost always signals a breakdown in the treatment process.

At this time there are no well-controlled studies of family-focused home-based services in child mental health similar to those that have emerged from the juvenile justice and child welfare arenas. As family therapy researchers have discovered, studies of treatment models based on ecological and systems theories are more difficult to carry out due to the theoretical circularity of cause and effect and the absence of well-standardized instruments measuring change in family systems. There is also the difficulty of measuring changes in families' relationships with external systems and of differentiating those changes within external systems that, in turn, have an impact on family caregiving. There are also inherent problems in conducting studies outside of clinical settings where uncontrollable varibables may wreak havoc on well-developed research protocols (Henggeler et al., 1997).

However, despite these obstacles, a growing body of research *is* demonstrating the effectiveness of this form of mental health care in enhancing child and family functioning and preventing crisis-driven psychiatric hospitalizations of children (Dore, 1991b; Evans & Boothroyd, 1997; Verwaaijen & Van Acker, 1993; Zarski & Fluharty, 1992). Home-based models are increasingly employed in child mental health practice. Since 1988 Pennsylvania has allocated a substantial portion of its children's mental health budget to developing a system of home-based services statewide (Dore, 1991b). Texas has initiated a demonstration project utilizing family-focused home-based children's mental health services at five sites (Toprac & Rouse, 1993). New York has developed and tested its own model of home- and community-based supportive treatment for families who have children with serious emotional disturbances (Evans & Boothroyd, 1997).

Family-focused home-based programs are funded in Maine by a cooperative agreement between the Departments of Human Services and Mental Health (Werrbach, 1992). Similarly, Tennessee's family-focused home-based programs are funded jointly by that state's mental health and child welfare agencies (Ooms & Beck, 1990), as are programs in Virginia, Ohio, and Kentucky (Knitzer,

1989). In addition to these state-sponsored programs, home-based services have been added to the continuum of child mental health services offered by individual public and voluntary outpatient psychiatric clinics and residential treatment centers nationally and internationally (Heying, 1985; Kagan & Schlossberg, 1989; Liddle, 1995; Seelig et al., 1992; Verwaaijen & Van Acker, 1993; Zarski & Fluharty, 1992).

Family-focused home-based services are becoming an increasing presence in the continuum of children's mental health care. Parents have expressed the need for services for the whole family, not just the child with severe emotional problems (Tarico, Low, Trupin, & Forsyth-Stephens, 1989). Thus, enhanced understanding of the theory and practice of this approach to serving seriously emotionally disturbed children and their families is imperative. In the following chapter we explore the theoretical underpinnings of family intervention in home-based practice.

CHAPTER 2

The Theoretical Foundations of Family Interventions in Home-Based Practice

> Just at the very moment we attempt to take a step . . . we can suddenly
> feel that the chasm is insurmountable.
>
> —David Whyte, 1994

HOME-BASED PRACTICE potentially exposes the therapist to the seven "C"s: chaos, crisis, cross-system complexity, cultural sensitivity, collaboration, competence, and change. Riding in the "boat" of a multiproblem family requires a delicate balance of connecting to family members while challenging the way they operate. It is easy to lose your footing and overreact to the cracks and defects in the boat's structure rather than focusing on its resiliency. While therapists need to "sit" in the family's boat from time to time, they must maintain a sense of equilibrium.

A clear theoretical model for clinical practice helps therapists navigate the extreme complexities of home-based work without resorting to unfocused "flare gun" techniques that create the illusion of help but net nothing more than a superficial fizzle. For example, a predictable reflex to a family's crisis is often precipitously to remove a troubled child from the home rather than using the crisis to promote change within the family. Another common technique is to respond to every expressed problem with an immediate referral to an external service rather than working with the family's own internal resources. Reliance on theory serves to anchor the therapists so that they don't drift aimlessly but are positioned

24

solidly, binoculars in hand, as they search for relevant data. Theory allows therapists to prioritize and screen data by answering the two most challenging questions posed by home-based clinicians:

- "What information should I pay attention to?"
- "How do I organize the information in assessment and practice?"

Theory also helps therapists position themselves in relation to the family. Theory provides the navigational coordinates for the therapeutic map guiding the therapist's attention—to know *where* to be, with *which* of the family members, at *what* point in time during the family's treatment.

The following list highlights the theoretical assumptions we will discuss in this chapter. When taken together, these assumptions serve as an anchor for the therapist in "staying put" despite the rough waves of the family ecosystems:

- All behavior is a form of communication within a defined cultural context.
- Symptoms occur within the context of social interactions.
- Causality is a circular, not linear, phenomenon.
- Families are evolving multibodied systems that continually regulate their internal structure, rules, and roles in response to developmental and environmental changes.
- Adaptive functioning is determined by the fit of a family's structure to the functional demands made upon it from within and beyond the system.
- Family members relate to each other in patterned ways that are observable and predictable.
- Repetitive patterns created by family roles and rules evolve in an interlocking, complementary fashion.
- Family members develop a preferred degree of emotional and functional levels of proximity and distance in relating to one another.
- Families are hierarchically organized, with unwritten rules for interactions between and within subsystems.

- Inadequate hierarchical structure and boundaries maintain symptomatic behavior.
- Family patterns are replicated in the surrounding ecosystems.
- Individuals are inherently competent, although rigid interactional patterns can inhibit the expression of that competence.
- Change in family structure contributes to change in the behavior of individual members.
- Promoting alternative transactional patterns broadens the flexibility and competence of individuals and subunits in the family and its ecosystems.
- Families are their own best resource for change.

ECOSYSTEMIC STRUCTURAL FAMILY THERAPY

An ecosystemic model is the theoretical foundation for the home-based practice issues explored throughout this book. Ecosystemic structural family therapy provides a systemic biopsychosocial framework for understanding individuals (child, adolescent, adult) in the context of social system dynamics. The original model of structural family therapy developed by Dr. Salvador Minuchin at the Philadelphia Child Guidance Center was based on the assumption that emotional and behavioral problems of individuals are sustained through patterns of interaction within the family. The goal of treatment was to evaluate and change family patterns of behavior that maintained the presenting symptom(s) (Minuchin, 1974; Minuchin & Fishman, 1981) by bringing absent patterns into existence (Colapinto, 1983, 1991). For example, if an observed pattern of emotional distance in a father-son relationship maintained the boy's symptom of depression, a therapist might focus a therapeutic session on creating an experience of emotional closeness within the relationship.

Clinical practice stemming from the original structural family therapy model has been modified through the years both by staff at the Philadelphia Child Guidance Center and by faculty in the Philadelphia Child Guidance Family Therapy Training Center. Currently called "ecosystemic structural family therapy," the theoretical underpinnings of structural family therapy remain. However, refinements of the original model emphasize the changing trends in the mental health field and subsequent implications for clinical practice that have occurred since the 1970s and 1980s. For example, early contributors to the structural family therapy model recognized the importance of looking beyond the immediate family to the "eco-systems" (Auerswald, 1968, 1971; Minuchin, 1970, 1974) influencing family life. Consequently, "eco-structural" approaches (Aponte, 1970) that combined the resources of family and agency members (e.g., school personnel, child welfare workers) in a therapy session were not uncommon. However, treatment trends for families at risk since the 1980s have led to further enlarging the treatment context by including all essential informal helpers (e.g., clergy, friends, etc.) and formal systems in both the treatment planning and implementation processes. Viewed as collaborative partners, these formal and informal system representatives offer their special perspectives and expertises to the therapeutic decision-making efforts.

Another trend initiated by both consumers and funders of mental health services requires that services to high-risk families be delivered in the least restrictive setting, such as the child's home or community. This recognition of the benefits of home and community-delivered services has helped to justify the kinds of home-based approaches described in this book. Meeting the needs of children and their families in these natural settings often requires more resources than formal mental health service agencies alone can provide. Thus the resources of both informal helpers and formal child service systems are necessary for beneficial treatment strategies.

The value placed on forming collaborative partnerships and achieving consumer satisfaction has also influenced the relationship between the therapist and the family. The mystique and hierarchical position that were typically ascribed to the therapist in relation to the family have equalized in the last two decades. Today's parent-professional partnership more directly recognizes and capitalizes on the respective expertise of both therapist and family. This means that parents are asked what they want for themselves and their children. Within this collaborative relationship, the therapist serves as a catalyst to facilitate actualization of the parents' goal by helping the parents access a variety of resources. For example, a parent requesting psychoeducational testing for her child toward the goal of obtaining an appropriate school placement will be given this information, as would another parent requesting information on parent education classes. Family therapy is provided only if the parent endorses this modality as the best way to reach his or her stated goal. In some cases the discussion between parents and professionals leads to a combination of treatment interventions.

In the past, the structural family therapy model did not emphasize comprehensive clinical assessment before treatment intervention. The focus of structural therapists in an initial family interview was typically on (1) the assessment of family relationships in relation to the child's symptoms, and (2) the implementation of immediate change-producing strategies in the session. Exploration of the child's functioning across all social contexts and gathering historical information were minimized during the initial interview. Further assessment tended to occur in subsequent sessions.

The era of managed care has had an indisputable impact on clinical practice. At the end of an initial interview, the clinician must be able to justify the need for treatment of the adult, child, or adolescent to a third-party payor. Problems, goals, and objectives must be observable (sometimes measurable) and linked directly to changes in the client's current functioning. In this same era of managed care, the values of "best practice" in public mental health have also emerged. These values are espoused by professionals who believe that a child or adolescent's mental health needs are best met through individually tailored, family-centered, community-based, culturally competent, and outcome-oriented services. A thorough, culturally relevant evaluation and assessment is needed so that appropriate services can be determined. The whole child must be understood, not just the child with specific behavioral or emotional symptoms. This commitment to work with strengths and to understand context applies also to the child's family and community supports. A comprehensive biopsychosocial assessment of the child or adolescent within significant social contexts should occur at both the macro and micro levels (Hodas, 1997). At the macro level, assessment focuses on the needs of the family in relation to its resources and those of the extended family, indigenous helpers, and the community. At the micro level, the symptoms, needs, and strengths of the child are carefully explored and relevant historical information is obtained.

A holistic developmental approach to assessment is valued. Addressing the child's emotional and behavioral symptoms is not sufficient; the child's social and physical needs must also be taken into account. Thus, the child's assessment should include a description of both strengths and needs in all areas of functioning as demonstrated within the family, peer group, school, and community. A comprehensive assessment not only provides a thorough rationale for authorized treatment but ideally identifies more resources in the individual, family, and helping systems, increasing the probability that rapid change will occur and endure.

Finally, the current ecosystemic structural family therapy model pays more overt attention to the specific assessment and change strategies related to emotional relationships within families than the original model. Minuchin's (1974) identification of a continuum of family interconnectedness is a key concept in structural family therapy. The extremes of this continuum reflect excessive physical/emotional distance or togetherness between family members. Minuchin used the word *boundary* in discussing the parameters of interpersonal physical and psychological relatedness among family members. Wood (1985) discussed the variability that occurs both within and between families in regard to the quality and quantity of emotional sharing that takes place. Green and Werner (1996) emphasized that healthy families demonstrate a high degree of "closeness-caregiving," including characteristics such as "warmth, nurturance, time together, physical intimacy (affection), and consistency." The importance of emotional bonding has also been supported by attachment theory, which emphasizes the need for a "goodness of fit" between parental nurturance and the child's unique developmental characteristics (Bowlby, 1983, 1988). Thus, in addition to assessing the family relationships characterized by hierarchy and patterns of proximity/distance, as in Minuchin's original conceptualization, the ecosystemic therapist explicitly explores and "maps" the relationships that reflect emotional bonding and attachment versus those lacking consistent nurturing and supportive behaviors. The theoretical principles underlying the current family therapy approach, which are drawn from general systems theory, structural theory, and developmental theory, provide the conceptual foundation for therapists' organization of clinical data into meaningful assessment hypotheses and treatment interventions. The following information is for those home-based practitioners who are not familiar with ecosystemic structural family theory.

THINKING SYSTEMICALLY

Since computers were introduced in the fifties, the volume of information produced has been overwhelming. "Thinking systemically" emerged in response to this abundance of information. To approach a problem from a systematic perspective meant dealing with data in a new way. Rather than focusing on content per se, emphasis shifted to the process governing the content. In contrast to seeking Descartian cause-and-effect connections between bits of information, systems thinking highlights the underlying principles of organization that give data meaning.

For our purposes as home-based therapists, specific aspects of systems theory are useful. Family therapy operates from the assumption that individual experience and behavior always takes place in a social context or system. The family is the most significant and enduring of these social systems. The family is more than a collection of individuals; it is the individuals *plus* their interactions. All the individual members of the family, from infants to the oldest members, are part of this interacting system. Each member initiates behavior *toward* others and responds to behaviors *from* others. Since the individual is part of an interdependent family system, his or her behavior cannot be considered independently from the family context.

An ecological perspective emphasizes that the family system is still part of a larger context (Auerswald, 1968). Thus, home-based treatment goes beyond the family and addresses the family's interaction with the community. Use of the term "ecosystemic" reflects a view of the family as an open social system—a multibodied organism that exists in a state of perpetual exchange with the environment surrounding it. The behavior of individuals and families represents interactive adaptations to ecological demands. A nonadaptive fit between a family and its environment will impair family functioning. The ecosystems surrounding the family influence the family and, in a reciprocal fashion, families influence the ecosystems that encompass them. Thus, a family's life is influenced by such ecosystems as ethnicity, social class, the particular culture of their community (urban, rural, suburban), the involved helper agencies, governmental social policies, and the pervading values of the time period.

The most outstanding characteristic of systems thinking is the concept of circular causality. Observing the family as an interactive system reveals the many circular feedback loops of communications and behaviors among members. From this perspective, it is difficult to assign responsibility, blame, or causality to any one individual in the family. An example: During a home-based visit with the Jones family, the mother told her ten-year-old son to sit in his chair. The father, who was allied with the son, patted the couch, indicating that the boy should sit there. The boy proceeded to defy his mother and sat on the couch. In this family's system, the feedback from father to son conveyed that it was acceptable, even desirable, to disobey mother. Who is to blame? Is the boy's disobedience the mother's fault since she did not insist that her son sit in his chair? Is the father responsible because he encouraged his son to sit on the couch? Can the son be blamed for responding to his father's nonverbal feedback rather than to his mother's verbal directive? The sequence of events is circular; each family member regulated the other members' behaviors, while at the same time responding to those behaviors.

If we observed the Jones family over time, we might find repeated examples of the sequence of behaviors described above. Like pieces of a puzzle, each family member's behavior interlocks in the total family system in a predictable pattern. After many repetitions of the same sequence, it would almost appear that the family was following a prescribed rule, given the predictability of the pattern. Identifying the "rules" that govern these sequences of behavioral interaction is called "structuralism." The overall pattern, or the invisible set of rules, that governs transactions among family members as they engage in the daily rituals of family life is called the "family structure" (Minuchin, 1974). There are patterns that involve the behavior of the individual subsystems within the family and those governing the family's behavior as a subsystem in relation to extrafamilial subsystems.

Sometimes patterns in the family also exist in the ecosystems surrounding the family. This *isomorphism* or parallel process occurs when micropatterns of the family correspond to macropatterns of the larger ecosystem, meaning that the two patterns have similar processes in their respective systems (Bateson, 1979). A home-based therapist will attempt to ascertain what is similar about the processes of a particular family and a particular helping agency. How are the central interactive patterns of each contained in the other? The example above describes a repetitive pattern found in the Jones family: Mother directs son; father negates mother's directive and encourages disobedience by supporting the boy's alliance to him. This same pattern might well be replicated in a helping agency to whom the Joneses turn for help. In the session at the agency, for example, the mother complains to the therapist about her son's behavior. The boy tells the therapist that his mother doesn't understand him. Father remains silent. The therapist colludes with the boy and is subtly critical of the mother's point of view. The boy becomes disrespectful toward the mother in the session. Here the therapist has unwittingly repeated the same pattern that exists between mother, father, and son.

The Development of Family Structure: Interlocking Subsystems

Many families are composed of three emotionally connected generations that evolve over time as multibodied organisms. It is important to remember that all the subsystems comprising a three-generational family are linked, so that whatever happens in one part of the family has effects on the other parts. Ideally, the goals or functions of the family are to support the growth, individuation, and sense of belonging of the members. These goals are accomplished through the natural emergence of *subsystems* (individuals, dyads, triads, etc.), the formation of which is determined by a variety of factors (generation, gender, interests, needs, function.) Some of the basic subsystems in a family include: the individual, spouses, parent(s),* parent-child(ren), siblings, in-laws, grandparents, grandchildren, aunts, uncles, nieces, nephews, cousins, and unique groupings based on specific interests (e.g., the athletes versus the computer experts).

---

*The term *parent* throughout this book refers to the biological or adoptive mother or father or the legal guardian or the responsible caregiver of the child, including a foster parent(s).

The smallest subsystem within a family is the individual. A family with children forms in one of two ways. One family formation occurs when two individuals come together, commit themselves to an ongoing relationship that results in cohabitation, marriage, or remarriage and make the decision to give birth or to raise a nonbiological child. The second way a family forms is when an individual chooses to give birth to a child or adopt a child through legal adoption procedures or informal arrangements. Thus, the family system may include adult partners plus a child, or a single parent and child, or an extended family system that incorporates the child and, if present, the parent and the adult partner.

It is important to remember that individuals in families are simultaneously a "whole" unto themselves and a "part" of some other, superordinate whole. For example, a man is simultaneously a male individual, a son, and perhaps a brother, uncle, husband, partner, and/or father. A woman is a female individual, a daughter, and possibly a sister, aunt, wife, partner, and/or mother. Once two individuals become a couple another subsystem forms. If the relationship is legalized through marriage, the original subsystem composed of each of the partner's parents now becomes in-laws as well. The partner's siblings become further differentiated as brothers-in-law or sisters-in-law.

With the birth or adoption of a child, the following subsystems develop: parent(s)-child, grandparents, aunts, uncles, cousins, nieces, nephews. The birth of a second child (or more) creates the subsystems of children and siblings. If divorce and remarriage occur, the subsystems of stepparent(s)-child(ren) and stepsiblings or half-siblings develop.

Each individual belongs to more than one subsystem within a family. In each subsystem varying skills for living are learned and individuals experience differing affective relationships, levels of power, and patterns of closeness/distance. When family members are overidentified with membership in one of the subsystems, their functioning in another subsystem is limited. Sometimes this multiple subsystem membership can lead to complications and becomes a source of problems, particularly with regard to loyalty issues. For example: Should I be more a daughter to my parents or a wife to my husband? Am I spending too much time as a parent to my child and not enough time as a spouse to my husband?

Boundaries and Parameters

In assessing families, home-based workers need to know whether the family's organization enables essential family tasks to be accomplished. Is there good communication among family members? Are children receiving the necessary parental support for optimal growth? Do husband and wife nurture and support each other? Does excessive involvement between family members diminish the family's ability to seek information and support from outside resources? Conversely, does the isolation of family members result in excessive dependency on resources outside the family? Mastering the concept of boundary functioning within families will help practitioners in their assessment of these issues. Each subsystem in the family has different developmental tasks to accomplish and functions to perform throughout the family's development. A well-functioning family will have clear rules that govern which members comprise a particular subsystem and how they are to function in that subsystem. Like any effective organization, family members need to know who is in charge and how tasks will be accomplished.

The rules that define who can participate in a subsystem and how members will behave in that set of relationships are called *boundaries* (Minuchin, 1974). Boundaries regulate the amount and kind of information that flows from one subsystem to another. Additionally, boundaries help define and achieve the separateness between the subunits of the total system, thereby permitting subsystem functions to be performed. Unlike the skin that serves as a boundary around the human organism, the "skin" surrounding the family system and its subparts is initially invisible. Over time, however, family boundaries can be observed in the family's regularly recurring transactions (Umbarger, 1983).

Boundaries—or rule-governed transactions—define implicitly and sometimes explicitly who participates and how that participation is to be expressed in the transactional behavior associated with the subsystem. Who can act as a parent and give parental directives in the family? Is it the mother and father? Is it the mother and grandmother? Is it the mother, father, and oldest offspring? Who is defined as a child and therefore required to obey parental directives? Is it solely the preschooler or does it include the older adolescent? *Diffuse* boundaries create lack of clarity as to who should participate in a subsystem, allowing subsequent intrusion by non-subsystem members; conversely, *rigid* boundaries hinder contact with and the flow of information among other family members. *Clear* boundaries designate unambiguously who participates in various family roles (i.e., parent-child; husband-wife) and protect the specific functions of a particular subsystem, while allowing for adaptive interchange with other subsystems.

Proximity/Distance

How family members operate within a particular subsystem varies depending on several parameters. The first is that of *proximity/distance*, which is always relative to the developmental stage of the individuals involved and the values of the family's culture. (The developmental implications of this parameter will be discussed later in the chapter.) Minuchin (1974) has described the parameter of proximity/distance as a boundary dimension ranging from enmeshed to disengaged and encompassing a normal range. The enmeshed family system is characterized by extreme interpersonal responsivity of individual members to each other and to their primary subsystem. The behavior of one member will immediately affect the others, and small changes in the behavior of one will reverberate strongly through the system. Stress in an individual member resonates quickly to other members of the system. One member's attempts to change elicits immediate resistance in others. Rapid shifts in both the focus of transaction and affective tone occur. Almost all interpersonal transactions contain repetitive power conflicts that are often avoided by conflict-detouring through the symptom bearer. While the boundaries between members of an enmeshed subsystem are diffuse, resulting in a blurring of functions and poor differentiation, the outer boundary of the subsystem is rigid, creating greater distance from other parts of the family and extrafamilial resources. Enmeshment is associated with a heightened sense of belonging and a strong commitment to rules of family loyalty, which concomitantly curtails the individual's attempt to develop autonomy.

The disengaged family system is characterized by rigid internal subsystem boundaries that hinder adaptive interchange among family members. However, the outer boundary of the family in relation to the external world is diffuse, permitting constant intrusions into the family's life from outsiders and unregulated access by family members to the outside. Disengaged families tolerate too wide a range of individual variations and autonomy among members, creating a skewed sense of independence in children. Feelings of family loyalty and belonging are limited, and in response to this vortex family members are invariably drawn to reference groups in the outside world. The actions or stresses of individual members do not lead to strong repercussions; reactions from others come slowly and seem to fall into a vacuum. Monologues are common in these families and members have long intervals in which they appear to move in isolated orbits unrelated to each other. The family's socializing functions of control, guidance, and support are reduced.

Hierarchy

Whereas the parameter of proximity/distance emphasizes interpersonal boundaries, hierarchy refers to the power differential among family members as evidenced by generational boundaries, culturally-determined boundaries (Falicov, 1988), and gender-imposed boundaries (Goldner, 1988). Societal, cultural, and familial rules establish who is primary in status and power and who is secondary. When people interact in a family, they are not interacting as peers but as individuals in different generations, representing different cultural norms and gender expectations, and performing different functions. Most commonly, there are three generations in families and, therefore, three levels of power: grandparents, parents, and children. Families are not democracies; someone needs to be in charge. A well-functioning family must have clearly defined lines of authority and responsibility.

It should be noted that, even within generations, subsystems can have different levels of power. Within the marital subsystem, for example, the social fact of gender inequality or a family's cultural values may lead to male domination. Women may attempt to balance marital gender inequality by assuming more power within the parental subsystem. Children within sibling systems have different levels of power depending on their age, gender and skills, the family's cultural values, and the nature of the parent-child relationship.

Homeostasis, Evolution, Growth

As evolving living systems, families are faced with the difficult task of maintaining the stability of their functional patterns while dealing with extrafamilial challenges and internal family issues such as handling conflict, making decisions, and living together comfortably. The press to maintain the status quo is termed *homeostasis*. When behavior departs from the expected range of a family's patterns, corrective feedback loops reestablish the family's preferred patterns. While maintaining some sort of continuity and balance is adaptive, symptoms in family members may reflect the family's way of maintaining equilibrium in the face of a new circumstance that requires change. It is the inability to change and maintain the balance at the same time that often causes families to seek treatment.

Like all living organisms, the family system has a tendency toward both maintenance and *evolution*. Evolution may occur when internal or external demands for change challenge the structure of the family system. The two major internal demands for change are either developmental changes (when members of each generation make a transition into a new stage) or compositional changes (i.e., an established member enters or leaves). External events, such as job loss, relocation, etc., may require adaptational changes as well. It is important to remember that challenges to individual members in one generation affect movement in the other generations. Thus, families are frequently in a state of unstable equilibrium, and at certain points developmental challenges to individual family members or extrafamilial stressors push the family into crisis. A crisis state, activated by stressors demanding new and unfamiliar responses by family members, requires an expenditure of energy that temporarily moves the family away from homeostasis. Though disintegration in the face of severe crisis is possible, the family system also has the potential to create new patterns that are more appropriate to the changed circumstances (Prigogine, 1973). We call this ability to respond to the challenges of living "family growth." The home-based therapist essentially helps families create alternative possibilities that enhance their responses to new circumstances. The therapist's task is to observe the family structure and assess which aspects of it are functional and which are impeding the development of these alternative possibilities.

The Evolving Family: Developmental Tasks, Boundaries, and Adaptive versus Nonadaptive Patterns

Home-based therapists assess and treat families at various stages of development. It is important to identify whether couples, parents, children, or grandparents have mastered essential development tasks or are struggling with these issues. Minuchin and Fishman (1981) described a child-focused developmental model of the traditional nuclear family encompassing the stages of couple formation, family with young children, family with middle-years children, adolescent children, and grown children. Between these stages are "crisis" periods of transition, in which new rules and functional interactional patterns need to be developed to accomplish the essential developmental tasks. While the sequence of biological events in a family's life cycle is universal, cultural variations occur in the definition of development (i.e., growth in empathy and connection versus growth in individualism), timing of life-cycle phases, developmental tasks, rituals, and solutions to life-cycle predicaments, particularly in families with extended family systems (Falicov, 1988). Given the extent of cultural variability, it is best to explore how and when a developmental task is dealt with relative to a family's cultural norms. DiNicola's (1997) creative and comprehensive discussion of culture as a major organizing principle in a family's life and an individual's mental health can serve as a useful reference. If the family is conceptualized as a three-generational system, the reciprocal nature of developmental tasks for individual family members at each generational level becomes evident. Here developmental movement in one generation is reciprocally linked to movement in the other two, creating a "family life spiral" with no first or last stages (Combrinck-Graham, 1985).

Couples

Couple formation is the most critical building block in families of many cultures. The shaping of this unit will have an impact on the family's entire future. The functional couple's adaptation in nuclear families requires the development of a boundary or set of rules that protects the integrity of this new unit. The process of developing this boundary is based on the partners' primary commitment to each other, which presumes a shifting of each partner's commitment from his or her family of origin (Jordan, Kraus, & Ware, 1993). Privacy and freedom from intrusions of in-laws or others while simultaneously maintaining affirmative relationships with significant others are essential to the couple's development. One primary psychological task for couples is to develop emotional bonding or intimacy. This critical process occurs when couples learn how to negotiate conflict through communication and provide nurturance to each other by offering support, positive regard, and a mutually desired sexual connection. Blending expectations and values learned in two different families of origin is a difficult process and requires a boundary that permits respect for each other as individuals as well as the couple entity.

The couple subsystem develops during the phase of the nuclear family life spiral associated with differentiation and individuation of family members in all generations (i.e., late mid-life transition of parents, late retirement issues of grandparents). If parents or grandparents from either family of origin are having difficulty achieving their developmental tasks, they may pressure the man to be more of a son or grandson than a husband; conversely, the loyalty demands on the woman are to be more a daughter or granddaughter than a wife or partner. Consequently, the primary bond between the couple may be compromised.

Additionally, maladaptive patterns can form within the couple subsystem as they negotiate patterns of proximity/distance and power issues. Balancing separateness and attachment is always a challenge, and especially so when individual needs and cultural norms vary. The relationship may feel too intimate to one partner, who will "back off" to achieve a state of comfort. The complementary response of the other partner may be to pursue the distancing partner and cling to him or her because the distance is not tolerable. Separateness requires each partner to experience herself or himself as different from the other. Partners who fear separateness feel they must have similar thoughts and feelings as well as share all activities and interests, typically becoming so fused in their relationship that individual identity is sacrificed. In contrast, partners who share few activities, interests, and feelings may each create a strong sense of "I-ness" but never a shared identity as "we."

Negotiating the allocation of power is another crucial developmental task for couples. Decisions must be made daily, and partners inevitably have differing points of view. In healthy, egalitarian relationships, both members share the power or take turns being in control of the course of the relationship. Marital difficulties are evident in couples who are more apt to exhibit fixed, rigid patterns based on *complementary* or *symmetrical* interactions (Bateson, 1972; Watzlawick, Weakland, & Fisch, 1967). In the complementary, one-up/one-down couple, one partner seeks control and the other yields to it. There is pronounced inequality between partners and a process of progressive escalations whereby the partners become increasingly unequal. Eventually, one partner may harm the other, or one of them may develop physical or emotional symptoms. In symmetrical relationships partners compete for control of how the relationship will be defined; neither party can let the other win. Over time, symmetrical couples who play a continual game of "tit for tat" typically escalate those games into battles that are unresolvable. The development of symptoms in partners in such unbalanced relationships can be viewed as expressing a need for homeostatic mechanisms that will somehow regulate the boundary and power dynamics of their interpersonal transactions. In this manner individual symptoms may serve an important role in relation to the couple's functioning and/or in relation to in-laws, parents, or grandparents.

Birth of Children

The first child's birth creates a state of disequilibrium for the nuclear three-generational family requiring a rapid reorganization of boundaries and hierarchy as new transactional units are formed—the parent(s), parent-child, grandparents, grandparent-grandchild, aunt-niece, uncle-nephew, etc. The creation of a new generation is often a period of rebuilding and renegotiating previous relationships and brings the family closer together than in the previous stage involving the couple's development (Combrinck-Graham, 1985). The relationship between spouses must be differentiated; now both a marital and a parental relationship must be managed simultaneously. While the partners need to continue their functions, tasks in the new subsystems of parents and parent-child must be mastered as well. These tasks include the provision of nurturance, socialization, and eventually, encouragement of autonomy in the developing child. Whereas in-laws may have respected the boundary of the developing couple, the new role of grandparents may lead to boundary violations that impact the functions of the newly formed parental subsystem.

The shift from the couple dyad to the triad of parent-parent-child may produce a disruption in the partners' mutual experience of affection and intimacy (Russell, 1974). For example, research has demonstrated the relation between the birth of children and physical exhaustion and lack of interest in sex in wives (Hobbs, 1965; Hobbs & Wimbish, 1977). However, the influence of the new parenting role on the couple dyad is obviously not always negative. Frequent incidents of shared pleasure between spouses during parenting activities are related to high levels of maternal and paternal involvement. Interestingly, in a reciprocal fashion, these patterns of parenting relate to a higher degree of competence in the infant's exploratory behavior that, in turn, relates to greater spousal harmony (Belsky, 1979). Additionally, the effects of the infant's unique temperament on the parental subsystem may be mediated by the quality of the couple's relationship (Belsky, 1981).

Siblings

As additional children are born or stepsiblings are added, a sibling unit is created that further socializes the child in the areas of conflict resolution and assertiveness skills, as well as aiding in the process of identity formation. While expanding and adapting to the developmental tasks of a second or third child, family members must make changes in their habitual strategies, roles, and allocation of privileges. Parent(s) must become more economical in the manner in which various tasks of child care and household maintenance are performed. First-born children lose their privileged position of being simultaneously the oldest, youngest, and "only." Parental attention, previously abundant, is reduced and a new role in relation to the parent(s) must be secured (Kreppner, Paulsen, & Schuetze, 1982). Older siblings may emphasize their areas of superior developmental competence relative to younger sibs, either by assuming a parental role or becoming an unequal rival. Some may also increase their requests/demands for attention from parents as a way of decreasing parental attention to a sibling. Others may retreat to solitary play, allowing parents to have private time with the new sibling.

How parents handle interaction between siblings may set the stage for adaptive versus maladaptive patterns of alliance in the family. Parents may establish individual alliances with each child to protect siblings from each other. For example, the oldest child may become "mother's child" and the next sibling "father's child." A very different pattern results when parents remain firm in their expectation that an older child must learn to adjust to a new sibling. For example, the older sibling's demand for parental help regarding the younger sibling's intrusiveness into his or her space is met by the parents' insistence that the older sibling work out the problem without parental involvement. Allowing siblings the opportunity to establish autonomous relationships leads to the development of the primary generational subsystems of "parents" and "children."

Further subsystem differentiation by parents based on individual characteristics occurs when a sibling is about two years old (Kreppner et al., 1982). For example, at this point a parent may distinguish the two sons as "clumsy" versus "athletic" rather than as "our big boy" versus "our baby." When parents elaborate these distinguishing sibling characteristics over the years, they may become an enduring feature of the individual's identity. In contrast, healthy families do not rigidly impose a child's role or identity early in life but allow for flexibility and change as the child grows. Enmeshed families tend to lump children together (i.e., "the kids"), rather than emphasize each child's unique differences.

According to Bank and Kahn (1982), "the sibling bond is a connection between the selves, at both the intimate and the public levels, of siblings; it is a 'fitting' together of two people's identities" (p. 15). A sibling can serve as a reference point to experience one's individual identity. Whether the relationship is positive or negative, sibling familiarity evokes a feeling of constancy and predictability. This is particularly important when a parental relationship is unreliable, abusive, or neglectful (Colapinto, 1995). When parents are emotionally or physically unavailable, siblings will turn to each other for nurturance or may even use fighting as a way of experiencing connection. In some family situations a sibling may take on some of the role and responsibilities of a parent. This can often be an adaptive behavior in single-parent families or families having many children. In extreme situations, however, where parents have abdicated their parenting roles, the responsibilities may be too great, given the child's developmental level. While these "parentified" (Goldenthal, 1996) children may gain a feeling of competence by engaging in adult-like activities, they lose the camaraderie and nurturance that operates within the sibling peer group.

Parent(s)-Child Relationship

The parent-child dyad or parent-parent-child triad is the most significant context in shaping the child's development within the nuclear family. The patterns that form within this subsystem determine whether or not the child will experience symptomatic behavior throughout his or her lifetime. Within extended family systems, however, other adult family members may be equally important in contributing to the child's development.

Beginning at birth, the infant's constitutional and maturational characteristics influence the formation of early relationship patterns with parental figures, and parental characteristics, in turn, have an impact on the developing child. The concept of "goodness of fit" refers to the adaptive match between parental and infant temperaments (Thomas, Chess, & Birch, 1968). Given individual differences between parent and child, the central question is: Will the fit of behaviors be "good enough" (Bowlby, 1983, 1988) for secure attachment patterns to form, so that care and protection will occur across the life cycle?

Before forming attachments, infants must possess the ability to "self-regulate"—to achieve harmony with their internal world and to engage the outer world (Greenspan, 1992). If regulatory processes are ineffective, infants may be hyposensitive or hypersensitive to their sensations and perceptions. Reactions to caregivers can vary on a continuum from a tendency to withdraw or become hyperexcitable under stress to actual avoidance. The variability demonstrated by infants regarding attachment behaviors has been well described by Greenspan: There are those who have the capability of "rich, deep, multisensory emotional investment with caregivers to [those who show] total lack of or nonaffective, shallow, impersonal involvement" (1992, p. 733).

Adaptive or maladaptive relationship patterns of proximity/distance, hierarchy, and emotional bonding form within the emerging parent-child subsystem, depending on the degree of accommodation to individual differences of parent to child and child to parent. If caregivers are sensitive to the baby's feedback, in spite of his or her unique temperament, they will alter their preferred style of communication in order to create a pleasurable involvement with the child. For example, a verbal mother with a high-pitched, loud voice, noticing her baby's low threshold for sound, will lower and soften her speaking style.

Parents who maintain too much emotional distance from their infant do not develop the appropriate sensitivity to their child's cues. This pattern is typical in "failure to thrive" infants. Parents who are unavailable for whatever reason— emotional ambivalence, depression, addiction, etc.—will ignore the infant's communications. A rigid boundary then develops between parent and child, prohibiting the flow of emotional and functional communications crucial to the child's growth. This boundary is termed "disengagement" because it is developmentally inappropriate to the needs of the child. In contrast, parents who are overly reactive to every nuance of their child's behavior create an overly diffuse boundary between parent and child. The child is experienced as an extension of the parent's sense of self and the parent takes it personally if the child does not accommodate to *his* or *her* behavior. Within this pattern, parents are often overly intrusive, controlling, fearful of the developing child's autonomy, and will project their own feelings onto the child. In a sense these parents expect the child to give *them* a feeling of well-being.

As children mature, the boundary between parent(s) and child must be adjusted to reflect each individual's developmental needs. The measure of proximity/distance as enmeshed, disengaged, or clear cannot be ascertained without knowing the developmental needs of each family member as well as a family's cultural values. While parents and children will be much more closely involved when the child is very young, that same degree of proximity would be inappropriate in a traditional American family as the child moves from the middle years into preadolescence and adolescence. Allowing more permission for autonomy in developing children means being able to maintain greater parent-child distance. This requires a change in the implicit rules that have governed previous transactions. Some changes are incremental, evolve gradually over time, and reflect increased autonomy. This is typified by a child's learning new skills. For example, when a preschooler is learning to fasten his or her coat, a parent must learn to delay the hurried "let's-get-going-fast!" approach and wait for the child to grapple with acquiring this new skill. Parents of adolescents may encounter a similar situation when they create opportunities for the teenager to practice driving skills. Other changes are experienced by the family as more abrupt, as when a family member suddenly leaves. When the young adult leaves home for college, military service, work, or marriage, major role shifts will occur within the family.

These role shifts reflect the reorganization of boundaries within the parent(s)-child subsystem. As children become more involved in the world of school and peers, not only does more distance develop between parent and child, but changes also occur in the child's regulatory power within this unit. The child's increasing competence allows for more status in the family decision-making process. Over time, as the child moves through adolescence into young adulthood, he or she may share power equally with the parents.

There are commonly described maladaptive family patterns that reflect disturbances in the regulation of boundary parameters. In assessing these patterns, one cannot ignore cultural values that encourage the expression of proximity over distance (or vice versa) or promote hierarchical arrangements differing from mainstream culture. For example, a cultural preference for family interdependence over individual autonomy may be functional unless there are clear indications that individual or societal adaptation has been adversely affected (Falicov, 1988). Also, while cross-generational coalitions (e.g., father and son unite against mother) would be incompatible with middle-class American family values (e.g., marital cohesion, egalitarian power distribution between spouses, boundaries between parents and children), the same coalition process might not be viewed as dysfunctional within another culture (Falicov & Brudner-White, 1983).

When a boundary between parent and child is inappropriate to the child or adolescent's developmental level, an unresolved family issue is often the hidden cause. For example, when a nine-year-old child was being treated as if she were but three years old, it turned out that the effects of a family trauma involving the crib death of an infant sibling occurring six years previous remained unacknowledged. On the other hand, a nine-year-old being treated like a 15-year-old might suggest that the family desperately needs another adult in the system to help it function. When children are treated as younger than their years, there is usually too much closeness between parent and child. In contrast, when a child is treated like a young adult, excessive distancing between parent and child is typically observable. In those instances when parents allow their children to "parent" *them* by controlling or nurturing them, there has been a complete reversal of power in the generational hierarchy.

Another problematic pattern occurs when adult dyads—either in spouse or parental roles—sidestep conflicts by focusing on the child. Instead of arguing between themselves, the adults employ one of two strategies. With behaviorally disturbed children, the adults may band together, scapegoat the "bad" child, and attempt behavioral control maneuvers that are typically inconsistent. In families having children whose problems are more internalized, the adults may become overly solicitous and protective toward their "troubled" child. One of the most destructive family patterns occurs when conflicted parents separately attempt to enlist the child's sympathy or support against one another. This pattern of triangulation places the child in an intense bind between the two parents.

A family's difficulties in enacting the normal transitional changes may become apparent only when a family member develops a symptom. For example, an adolescent son's increased movement away from the family through peer involvement may threaten the closeness between mother and son that has protected the distance between wife and husband. As conflicts between wife and husband begin to escalate, the son may become socially withdrawn, thus reestablishing the family's previous pattern. While symptoms may initially serve an adaptive function by returning the family to more familiar ways of relating, eventually the symptom's function no longer works—at which point families may seek treatment.

Dislocation and Stress

While all families deal with the challenges presented by developmental transitions of family members, families referred for home-based services typically have histories of numerous and severe dislocations. According to Montalvo (1982), "Dislocation is the experience of having lost one's place in relation to other people. It is the result of fractured relationships, of major shifts in the ties among people one depends or relies upon" (p. 278). The breakdown of relationships and loss of continuity within families is experienced in a multitude of circumstances: marital separation, divorce, cohabitation, remarriage, death, immigration and acculturation, severe medical events such as developmental handicaps, physical and emotional illnesses, hospitalizations, substance abuse, physical neglect, emotional and/or physical abuse, sexual abuse, and placement of children or adults outside of the home. These dislocations are generally present in more than one generation; consequently, intergenerational legacies of emotional and physical disconnection are prevalent. Conversely, losses can also increase the emotional cohesion between the family of origin and the family of procreation. In some traumatized families, family generations cannot facilitate or accept the separation involved in nontraumatic transitions unless they feel confident that separation will not lead to "more death, whether literal or symbolic" (Jordan, Kraus, & Ware, 1993).

Even in families that appear to be enmeshed, family members may be strangers to one another and everyone may experience a lack of connectedness. The fear of separation and growth prevents members from establishing alternative relationships. When concern is expressed, it may take the form of self-destructive behaviors or symptoms that symbolize the breakdown in relationships.

External stressors from the family's ecosystem can also produce discontinuity in the flow of a family's functioning. Examining the contexts of work, school, neighborhood, and community may reveal significant job loss, financial problems, inadequate housing, relocations, and/or multiple agency or institutional involvement. The feeling of being an integral, functional part of a community is often absent. Families may experience the pain of isolation in rural areas and the fear of crime in urban areas. Helpers from the professional community may create additional, if inadvertent, stress when viewed as "intruders" or when they perpetuate the family's feelings of betrayal, mistrust, anger, and helplessness by not responding to a family's specific concerns, abdicating responsibility, or triangulating the family between conflicted agencies.

All families inevitably experience stress in their attempts to cope with developmental and societal demands. Stress is probably best understood as a product of the interaction between a particular situation and a family's capacity to deal with it (Eckenrode & Gore, 1981; Lindblad-Goldberg & Dukes, 1988). Lindblad-Goldberg (1989) has proposed a link between stressful life circumstances and adaptive functioning that is related to a family's resources, its members' appraisal of stress, their coping responses to stress, and availability of a social network of support. How a family experiences stress is a product of the interactions between and among the following elements: (1) the characteristics of the stressful situation (frequency and magnitude of the event); (2) the family's definition of the event (positive, negative, or neutral); (3) characteristics of the social support system (amount of support and reciprocity within one's social network); and (4) a family's internal resources (family members' coping philosophy, sense of well-being, health status, problem-solving skills, and level of family organization).

Adaptive functioning is the outcome when the family *and* social context share resources to create change. For example, a depressed, single-parent mother with five children became overwhelmed when her washing machine broke. The in-home worker encouraged the mother to organize her children so that the clothes were washed in the tub and hung outside. Additionally, the worker prompted the mother to reach out to her brother for help. The brother came the next day and repaired the machine. Evolving belief systems develop within the family and social network that motivate what Antonovsky (1979) has described as the desire for a "sense of coherence." In his words,

The sense of coherence is a global orientation that expresses the extent to which one has a pervasive, enduring though dynamic feeling of confidence that one's internal and external environments are predictable and that there is a high probability that things will work out as well as can be reasonably expected. (p. 123)

In families experiencing severe dislocations and numerous extrafamilial stressors, there is little sense of coherence and a defeating sense of powerlessness, which is sometimes mirrored by agency helpers. For example, a single parent, living in an isolated rural area, desperately wants to improve her family's financial stability and her self-esteem by getting a job, but neither the mother nor the home-based worker can locate essential child care resources. Mutual frustration breeds poor self-concept with irritability, withdrawal, and scapegoating at times of stress and tension. Individuals experience themselves as failures when they are unable to solve problems and help each other. Consequently, everyone withdraws and a feeling of disconnection and hopelessness prevails.

CREATING A STRENGTHS-BASED PRACTICE

Home-based therapists can be a source of hope, challenging the stereotyped reality of the family and pointing to alternatives not yet tried. Families referred for home-based services are often like icebergs. What can be seen is only the frozen tip that surfaces above the troubled water. Beneath the water is a vast reservoir containing other moments in the family's life, perhaps times when the family was doing well and enjoyed pleasurable exchanges. By recognizing and identifying areas of strength in the family without minimizing areas of difficulty and pain, a strengths-based approach breaks with the tradition of hunting for pathology and pointing it out. Problems are seen as resulting not from an individual's flaws but from the absence of essential adaptive patterns in the family and/or community. When adaptive patterns emerge within the family, the strengths of all family members become visible (Minuchin & Nichols, 1993).

Searching for strengths in families comes from the assumption that competence is inherent in all families. Like the miner panning for gold, one needs the conviction that embedded within rigid rock patterns are threads of gold. To extract the gold, the pattern must first be shattered. Knowing that families have the internal capacity to heal themselves and to develop their own patterns of helping behavior, the therapist's goal is to "repower" them in a change process. If the family cannot find reasons to hope for change, then it is the therapist's job to elicit those reasons by engaging family members in cooperative work. The therapist organizes treatment with the goal of catalyzing families in the direction of their own evolution.

An ecosystemic, strengths-based approach includes the expectation that competence is inherent in other systems as well, such as the family culture and the agency culture. Consequently, agencies and other cultures are viewed as potential "partners" in the treatment process, not adversaries.

Still another critical therapeutic attitude is one of viewing families as having the solutions to problems rather than subtly blaming them for causing the problems. To view the family as an adversary only reinforces symptoms and distance. Framing a positive perspective is essential. One can view a family who goes from professional to professional as exhibiting traits of ambivalence, mistrust, resistance or persistence, resilience, and dedication to obtaining help for family members. In contrast, when families isolate themselves from outside resources, they may be protecting members from perceived pain or danger rather than exhibiting irresponsibility or neglect.

We have seen how the ecosystemic model forms the theoretical basis for family interventions in home-based practice. Chapter 3 will discuss how this model is pragmatically applied in planning and developing home-based programs.

CHAPTER 3

Planning and Developing
Home-Based Services

Only a few achieve the colossal task of holding together . . . the clarity
of their vision. . . . they are artists of the living.

—Claremont de Castillejo, 1974

ESTABLISHING EFFECTIVE mental health home-based service programs requires support at the state, regional, county, and provider levels. While many programs are spawned by public and private outpatient agencies and residential treatment centers, some states have created home-based service initiatives statewide. In this chapter, we will talk about how one state, Pennsylvania, created a statewide mental health home-based service initiative in 1988 by first creating a context wherein these new programs could flourish.

CREATING A CONTEXT FOR
FAMILY-CENTERED SERVICES

As mentioned in chapter 1, the 1984 federal CASSP initiative was interpreted in Pennsylvania as an opportunity to develop a shared belief system and collaborative partnerships among the child-serving systems—namely, mental health, child welfare, mental retardation, juvenile justice, drug and alcohol, education, health care, and vocational rehabilitation. There were four steps taken to accomplish these goals. First, the state reiterated and endorsed the CASSP values and philosophy that would underlie all services

51

for children and adolescents (Bureau of Children's Services, 1995). One key value emphasized family-centered services wherein families would be viewed as partners, not just in the stages of decision-making throughout the assessment and treatment planning process, but in all policy-making groups at the state and local levels as well. Following our ecosystemic model outlined in chapter 2, we embraced a definition of family that included foster parents, siblings, grandparents, and other relatives and other adults who demonstrated commitment to a child with serious emotional disturbance. Values identified as cornerstones for the proposed services included:

- respect for the unique cultural variation of each family
- the importance of creating individualized, strengths-based child-centered services that would be developmentally sensitive to the emotional, behavioral, social, and physical needs of each child
- the importance of a community-based services approach that would utilize both formal and informal resources to promote the child's functioning in the community through services delivered in the least restrictive setting and in the least intrusive manner to the child and family
- the importance of creating a collaborative service-planning process between all relevant child-serving systems and the family

Endorsing these CASSP values created a major paradigmatic shift in all the state's child-serving systems, which had traditionally been oriented toward serving the child independent of the family and social contexts. Endorsing the value of "individualized community-based services that would serve children in the least restrictive environment" led eventually to a new concept of wraparound services in child mental health service delivery (Hodas, 1996a). Historically, families and children had to fit their needs to existing services. As a family's needs became more complex, their service options should have become more individualized—but, more often, the very opposite occurred. Individualizing services to meet specific child and family needs and "wrapping" these services around the child and family greatly increased the possibility that a family could keep their child at home.

The second step taken by the state of Pennsylvania in developing its CASSP services initiative was to identify the key collaborative partners whose resources would be utilized in developing programs for children and their families. Partners at the state level and in the state departments included mental health, mental retardation, Medicaid, child welfare, juvenile justice, regular and special education, vocational rehabilitation for adolescents, drug and alcohol treatment services, a statewide parent advocacy network, and statewide professional and provider groups. Before developing and expanding new services within the state departments, a third step created management approaches to ensure that a collaborative process of communication would occur across these departments at the state, regional, and county levels. A community organizing management approach was used to develop communication channels among key partners in county, regional, and state offices. A sponsorship model was used to encourage dialogue from the state level down to the local provider level, and from the provider level back up to the state level. This type of communication network facilitated a flow of feedback, which clarified how providers could implement the new values and also helped to define the kind of state support needed by providers.

This horizontal and vertical feedback process was essential in co-evolving a shared understanding among the key partners about the meaning of the CASSP-inspired values. While it sounded easy to say that services should be "family focused," the interpretation of this value differed depending upon whether the service provider was a mental health professional, educator, child welfare supervisor, or juvenile justice probation officer. The beliefs unique to each child service system were challenged during the collaborative process. Agreement was achieved quickly for some values; others were discussed for as long as 18 months before consensus was reached. The core conflict centered around those children who were connected with more than one service system. For example, a child who had mental health problems, needed special education, had done something illegal, and whose parents had been reported for abuse to child welfare evoked a "ping-pong dynamic" among the child service system partners. "It's *your* case, Mental Health.

It's not my case," responded Education, Juvenile Justice, and Child Welfare. Two guiding ecosystemic principles evolved, which were critical in resolving this core conflict:

- No single child service system would be responsible for all the care and treatment of a particular child.
- The child and the family would be the responsibility of a collaborating group of community servers whose creed would be: "The child belongs to the family; the family is a part of a community; the service systems are part of the community. Therefore we all share responsibility for providing services that will help this family."

The fourth step in Pennsylvania's program was to develop and implement the new services that would incorporate the CASSP values. Since one of the largest gaps in service delivery was the lack of mental health home-based services, this became the "pilot" service that would implement the new values regarding what should constitute "best practice" in relation to treating children with mental health needs. State funds were available for only ten programs, and each program would be expected to work in conjunction with an interagency advisory council. The first year, agencies and organizations interested in providing this new type of service were asked to submit proposals in response to a statewide RFP. Applicants were required to submit letters from the other child service systems in their counties endorsing the home-based service proposal and committing themselves to share resources and support in treatment planning for the families served. In order for a county to receive state money for a mental health home-based program, all child-serving systems had to agree beforehand to a process of ongoing collaboration.

In the ten years since the first home-based services were funded through allocations by the state legislature, alternative funding mechanisms have been identified that have allowed these programs to expand into a statewide network. Pennsylvania family-based in-home services are now funded through a combination of Medicaid, fee-for-service and managed care companies, private insurers, and state/county funds (available if there is no other coverage).

PREPARING AN AGENCY AND ITS COMMUNITY

Phase One

Mental health home-based services are currently offered in rural, urban, and suburban geographic areas. Programs are sponsored by public and private agencies and institutions. Whether a program is located in an agency, hospital, or private practice setting, there are common helpful strategies that can be utilized in the initial phase of program development:

- Create a mission statement clarifying what the *purpose* of the new program will be.
- Clearly identify the program's *goals*, including how the program will fit within the scope of existing programs in the community.
- Identify the *target population*.
- Outline the *services to be delivered* and the *method of delivery*.

Here is a sample mission statement by the Family Therapy Center of Williamsport, Pennsylvania, for family-based in-home services:

We believe that individuals and their families have within their own power the ability to adapt and to deal with life's inevitable stresses and difficulties. The mission with which we are charged is to cultivate those adaptive skills in order to empower individuals and families in their community.

We further believe that services which may be needed must be provided in a manner and setting which respects human dignity (Houser, 1995).

Below is a statement of program goals and objectives used in Williamsport's program. Note how it describes the relationship of family-based services to other mental health and community services:

The primary goal of family-based mental health services is to enable parents to care at home for their children who have severe emotional and/or behavioral disturbance and to reduce the need for child and adolescent out-of-home placements. Related objectives are to strengthen and maintain families through therapeutic intervention, family support services, coordination of services, improving coping skills, teaching family members to care for the child or adolescent and serving as an advocate for the child or adolescent. Family-based mental health services provide access to mental health treatment services for family members who may be unable or unwilling to participate in traditional outpatient programs. Finally, these services provide a transition to agencies and practitioners in the community who will provide services and support for the family, child, or adolescent after family-based mental health services are ended. (Houser, 1995)

The following statement provides a clear definition of the population targeted for family-based in-home programs:

Services are targeted to children and adolescents under 21 years of age having emotional and/or behavioral disturbance who are at risk of psychiatric hospitalization or out-of-home placement and their families. The child or adolescent is or can be registered with their local MH/MR Base Service Unit and has a *DSM-IV* diagnosis. A determination of eligibility and recommendations for treatment shall be made by a licensed physician or licensed psychologist prior to the initiation of services, and at least one adult member of the family shall agree to participate in the service. (Houser, 1995)

Finally, this program description highlights how services are provided and by whom:

Services are provided by a team consisting of a children's mental health professional (master's level) and a children's mental health worker (bachelor's level) or two children's mental health professionals. Additional staff persons possessing lesser qualifications may provide support services but not treatment. Each team may serve a maximum caseload of eight consumer families at a time, and shall have a minimum of two face-to-face consumer family contacts per week. Services shall be available on a 24-hour basis, 7 days a week; contacts shall be regularly scheduled and available as needed.

Although family-based mental health services are intended to be an intensive and comprehensive service, the child or adolescent who is identified as the consumer may have been involved in ongoing intensive case management services and psychiatric partial hospitalization services which may continue during the delivery of mental health in-home services.

There may also be a need for professional services not available from the treatment team, such as psychiatric clinic medication visits or inpatient services which cannot be provided by the treatment team. Providers shall have written agreements with other child-serving agencies and frequently used community contacts to ensure a cooperative effort in serving consumer families and to facilitate continuity of care. (Houser, 1995)

Phase Two

Once the program is clearly defined, the second phase of development involves communication, trust-building, and marketing within the host agency and community. Agencies that have not been involved with child/adolescent-focused family-centered practice or community outreach programs may view the "nontraditional" home-based services with suspicion or disregard. The mission and philosophy of the program must be congruent with that of the sponsoring agency in order to survive. A healthy organizational hierarchy will enable servers of the home-based program to function both autonomously and interdependently within their agency. Directors of home-based programs need to receive strong support from the agency director. Ensuring regular meetings with other program managers within the agency will clarify the nature of home-based work and the process of making referrals within the agency. Monthly case review meetings with multiple program managers can be a valuable opportunity to gain understanding about the unique issues each agency program faces when working with difficult clinical cases. In preparing the larger community, common concerns regarding placement prevention need to be addressed. Many potential referents will still be focused on out-of-home placement as the preferred solution to troubled families. An ongoing educational process should be initiated to enhance community awareness that residing with one's biological family is a basic emotional and social need for children. Another area requiring clarification is the tendency to equate in-home services with the child protection services. Consumers often need assurance that mental health home-based services do not place children in foster care.

Creating an advisory board, committee, or panel that meets at least quarterly can be a helpful mechanism in the initial phase of program development as well as throughout the program's duration. Board members should be selected based on their ability and willingness to support the program's mission and services. For example, one mental health home-based program selected a board that was comprised of representatives from all the main systems that would affect, or be affected by, the program. From the *mental health system*, they selected the director of the agency housing the mental health home-based program, the county mental health/ mental retardation administrator, the director of an inpatient psychiatric unit of a nearby hospital, and the director of a local partial hospitalization program. From the *education system*, they chose the superintendent (or designate) of the school system served by the program, the director of special education, and the director of pupil personnel. From the *juvenile justice system* came the presiding judge of the juvenile court; from the *drug and alcohol system*, the director of a local detoxification program; from the *child welfare system*, the director of the local children and youth agency; from the local *parent advocacy group*, a representative of the statewide parent advocacy network; from the *community*, the director of the local YMCA/YWCA and a priest from a Catholic church serving many Latino families in the area. This diverse group of board members was helpful in explaining and marketing the new program to the community, recruiting collaborative relationships with other community agencies whose resources might benefit the new program, and formulating policies regarding the referral process and release-of-information procedures.

Marketing a home-based services program to a community can be done through a variety of measures. A press release in local newspapers is an effective way to introduce the program. Publishing an informational brochure that can be distributed to consumers and potential referral sources is always helpful. A quarterly newsletter from advisory board members to key community readers can inform them of program updates as well as moments of positive collaboration with other agencies working together on a family's behalf. Last but certainly not least, there is no substitute for grassroots informational sessions conducted by the program director and a parent advocate hosting politicians, physicians, clergy, teachers, guidance counselors, child welfare supervisors, probation officers, community organizations, agencies, and parents.

DEVELOPING THE HOME-BASED PROGRAM

Program Components

Home-based services are often described as requiring a "whatever-it-takes" philosophy, reflecting the need for flexibility and creativity in designing services that meet the needs of families, not the convenience of professionals. Families should be viewed as partners in both the *design* and *delivery* of services. Effective mental health home-based services generally include four program components: family support services, therapeutic intervention, case management/service coordination, and emergency crisis intervention. These components are interrelated and flow from the treatment goals developed by the family.

Family support services include the provision of concrete services, respite care services, and funds for use in the therapeutic process. *Concrete services*—the provision of food, clothing, shelter, and other essentials—are obviously necessary because families cannot address therapeutic issues if their basic survival needs are not met. Existing community services are first explored to meet these needs. For example, Goodwill and the Salvation Army are excellent resources for obtaining inexpensive clothing, furniture, and toys. Some home-based programs have negotiated deductions with these organizations for specific furniture items (such as beds). Many churches provide food at no cost and/or food and clothing banks, which families can access. Program family support funds are available to supplement existing community resources.

Respite care services are seen as a necessary family support service, since parents and children sometimes need planned or unplanned (emergency-related) breaks from each other during the treatment process. For example, a planned respite service is offered when a treatment objective includes exposing a child to social experiences away from the family, helping parents pursue adult activities such as job training and educational experiences, or acknowledging parents for their efforts by treating them to overnight hotel accommodations. Respite methods for planned breaks include sitter services, day camps, overnight summer camps, after-school or Saturday activities, and recreational events.

When a crisis occurs in the family, every effort is made to utilize this intense period as an opportunity to promote family change and to engage the family's problem-solving abilities toward the goal of keeping the child at home. Families who can learn to resolve serious issues without anyone "leaving," even for a short period of time, fare better in the long run. For this reason, respite services must be offered judiciously. When a family views respite as the easy way out, the opportunity for growth is lost (M. Sowers, personal communication, 1997). However, there are times when an emergency necessitates the child's removal from the family for a night or several days. This type of unplanned respite should be used only after considerable negotiation with the family has proved ineffective. As a last resort, overnight respite will be given. In cases of abuse, the perpetrator is usually asked to leave the home. If the perpetrator refuses to leave and the child, children, or adult caretaker is at risk, respite will also be provided.

One program reports that 80% of families served have used both types of respite services (Archacki-Stone, 1991). Contractual arrangements with other child service systems, as well as supplemental funding, are often established to allow for the therapeutic provision of respite any time it is needed. Ensuring the availability of several types of respite is extremely helpful. Specialized foster care or emergency shelters, arranged in collaboration with the child welfare agency, can be used for short-term planned respite and for emergency respite in severe crisis situations, without requiring a court order and revoking parental custody of the child. Here a voluntary placement agreement is pursued and the child is placed in foster care for 30 days. During this period, the in-home team—family, child, and foster care "host" family—work on salient issues. Discussion of the respite is framed as a needed hiatus, so that families don't feel a sense of failure. Usually it takes less than 30 days to achieve the necessary stabilization.

In some instances program servers have recruited and trained community families to provide respite for client families. Often these "host home" families have continued supportive relationships with client families after in-home services are terminated. Other programs ask client families to designate individuals in their informal support system who could provide respite, and these individuals have been paid through the program's family support funds. Whatever the contractual arrangements for respite may be, strong collaboration and coordination are needed between respite providers and home-based staff.

The *therapeutic component* of mental health home-based services is critical and differentiates these services from mental health intensive case management services, which usually rely on traditional outpatient mental health services. As discussed in Chapter 2, family therapy, which may also include individual and couples treatment, is provided in the home setting or in other settings as suggested by the family. Family therapy is used to address the specific concerns of the child within the family support network. Primary therapeutic goals include strengthening and stabilizing the family unit by increasing the members' life management and coping skills, developing strategies for enhancing parenting skills, and promoting effective family communication. The guiding philosophy of the therapeutic component is to empower families by helping them to utilize their own strengths and resources to find alternative methods of solving problems other than out-of-home placement of the child. Therapeutic intervention also includes activities of case management (described below). When funds for family support services are part of the program's budget, as in the Pennsylvania mental health home-based program, the therapeutic process has additional flexibility. Creative applications of these funds include such activities as meeting with a child after school at a local fast food restaurant or offering parents their choice of reward, such as movie tickets for a night "off-duty." Other creative treatment plans have used family support service funds for karate lessons for nonassertive children; to purchase memberships in organizations such as Boy Scouts, Girl Scouts, or YMCA/YWCA; to build walls in homes that have no private space; and for transportation to self-help group meetings. Funds have also been used to create agency psychoeducational libraries for families, which provide resource materials such as books, videos, audiotapes, and games. Home-based programs have sponsored joint activities for families and staff, such as picnics and trips to amusement or state parks. Program staff have also developed and implemented events specifically for children receiving family-based services, such as a five-day overnight wilderness challenge. One program invited 45 family members to visit the Smithsonian in Washington, D.C., for the day. The families were free to wander wherever they wished; one family chose to spend the entire day at the Viet Nam memorial wall. The mother in the family had lost her father in the war and her children wanted to pencil trace their grandfather's name (M. Sowers, personal communication, 1997).

Open-ended parent groups also can be an important therapeutic intervention when transportation is not a problem. Led by parents, these groups provide an experience wherein participants can share information about parenting, community resources, and opportunities for parent advocacy. Once home-based services are terminated, these parent groups can provide interested parents with a continuing support network.

Case management and service coordination are viewed as important program components for two reasons. The case management service works closely with a family to develop links to those community resources that will best meet their particular needs, including medical care, welfare, education, job training, legal services, and follow-up therapeutic services. Case management is oriented toward empowering families to access services on their own. For example, families are given notebooks to record resource information and phone numbers they will need immediately or in the future. Service coordination attempts to integrate the family's treatment plan when it involves utilizing informal helpers and services from multiple agencies. A system-based treatment plan is formulated within the first 30 days to document the service responsibilities of each service system. While the in-home worker can serve in an advocacy role for the family, the primary focus of responsibility is on improving communication between the family and outside systems.

Crisis intervention makes it possible for families to receive help when they are the most distressed. Therefore, another critical program component is the availability of an on-call emergency service that operates 24 hours a day, 7 days a week, 365 days a year. Frequently, crises will occur during the first weeks of treatment, creating many opportunities for change as the family grapples with new ways of dealing with old problems. Most home-based programs use their own staff to provide this service; others contract with an outside mental health emergency service. When the crisis intervention service is operated by the program, a home-based worker is available through a beeper system, by telephone, or in person to ensure the safety of family members and to suggest methods of de-escalating the crisis. Therapists usually rotate on-call responsibilities on a weekly basis and cover all of the families participating in a program. Staff members are briefed on other workers' families during weekly group supervision scheduled on Fridays. Potential "hot spots" are discussed and interventions suggested to the person who will be on-call. Most crises can be handled over the telephone. However, if necessary, the on-call therapist may choose to meet with the family in person, call in other home-based personnel, or notify other services, such as the police, a probation officer, or the county's emergency mental health services. The family's regular home-based worker then meets with the family the following day to explore alternatives for prevention and management of future crises.

Staff Qualifications, Responsibilities, and Selection

Mental health home-based service programs need a full-time *program director* who has a graduate degree in the field of human services. Optimally, a minimum of three years of direct family therapy experience with children and adolescents and two years of mental health supervisory and administrative experience is required. Certification as an approved supervisor from the American Association of Marriage and Family Therapists is desirable. The responsibilities of the director include overall administration of the program, clinical supervision of the cases, and interfacing with referral sources. Administrative supervision involves reviewing each family's treatment plan, goals and objectives, and problems or concerns. Clinical supervision enhances staff skills in assessment and treatment intervention. Generally, a maximum of six clinical staff handling 24 active cases can be supervised by the program director. In the temporary absence of a staff home-based worker, the program director may also function as a case clinician.

Some home-based programs use two-person teams; others have used a non-team approach. The authors recommend a team approach consisting of either two mental health professionals or a child mental health professional and a mental health worker. Using a team approach with *all* cases may not be a viable option for some home-based programs because of funding limitations. However, these programs can still maintain a flexible staffing pattern for those families whose specific needs require, on occasion, the use of more than one home-based therapist.

A *child mental health professional* should have a graduate degree in a field of human services plus two years of clinical experience. A *child mental health worker* should have a bachelor's degree in a field of human services plus one year of experience in a child-related service system. To provide for the gradual expansion of a program, a qualified third person may be added to a team and participate in treatment for assigned families, until an additional person can be added, thereby creating a new team. Given comparable training and experience, the two team members function as co-therapists to the family. If one of the team has considerably more training and experience, he or she can be the lead therapist and assume overall responsibility for the treatment. Additional staff members who possess lesser qualifications may be designated to provide family support services but may not participate in treatment for assigned families, unless a member of the designated team is present to conduct the treatment session. It should be noted that the treatment team also includes the parent(s) or participating adult family member(s) of each family being served. The identified child or adolescent should be included in the team planning and review when appropriate in relation to his or her age and/or functioning level.

The job interview is used to identify applicants' specific qualities and levels of knowledge and skills. Program directors need to have empathy, humor, flexibility, strong leadership and interpersonal skills, and the ability to nurture others. The directorship requires a person with a solid clinical background with families and children/adolescents with emotional and behavioral disturbances, so that the necessary clinical skills can be taught to staff members through supervision.

Program directors as well as staff need to know how to set boundaries between their personal and professional lives. The nature of home-based service calls for high energy, commitment, and time involvement; without boundaries, therapists become as overwhelmed as the families they serve. Therapists who are tired of traditional mental health jobs and are looking for innovation and flexibility in the job setting are often reliable choices. Home-based family therapy differs markedly from the traditional agency-based outpatient family therapy setting characterized by order, control, and structure. Dedicated home-based therapists enjoy these differences. Being able to experience family life fully can be immensely satisfying:

from assisting the mother to cook dinner to alerting the mother to the sound of a sick child in the bathroom—it takes a special type of therapist who wants to become part of the intimacy of a family's life. Like the traditional social worker who goes beyond therapy to provide for a family's needs, the in-home therapist is one who can see that providing food for a family's dinner is part of the therapeutic goal of strengthening the family unit. At the same time, the therapist must assist the family to find solutions rather than enabling helplessness. (Linn, 1991, p. 16)

Potential staff members must be receptive to a systemic strengths-based orientation rather than adhering to an individualistic pathology-based perspective. An applicant who has had job experience working with children and parents together would be preferable to one who has worked with children in isolation from their parents (as is the practice in many residential and outpatient settings). Discerning receptivity to the central assumptions of an ecosystemic approach—that all families have strengths, that parents are essential partners in the therapeutic process, and that the professional never has all the answers—is a *sine qua non* of the selection process.

During the job interview applicants might be asked to discuss case scenarios designed to elicit their values and assumptions regarding individual and cultural differences in multiproblem families. In evaluating the applicants' discussions of the case material, the following issues are significant: Does the applicant rush to solve the problems described in the case scenarios, or is there a comfort level in seeking collaboration with the family? Does the applicant demonstrate warmth, flexibility, humor, intelligence, initiative, and creativity? Does the applicant appear to have a satisfying life outside the workplace, or does this job represent a life's mission? Does the applicant respond to feedback during the interview in a way that indicates an openness to learning? Does the applicant acknowledge a need for direction through a supervisory process, or does he or she overly emphasize a need for independence? (C. Ericson, personal communication, 1996; J. Houser, personal communication, 1996). Given the autonomy of conducting clinical off-site work, when checking references it is important to inquire about applicants' ethics, maturity, and judgment. Effective home-based treatment requires the therapist's ability to enact supervisory directives and employ individual personal judgment in an off-site setting—often, in tandem.

MAKING THE PROGRAM WORK

An effective home-based program should create a written manual of clinical policy and procedures comprised of the following information:

- a signature page for the agency director verifying an annual review
- intake, assessment, treatment planning, and termination policies and procedures
- a description of the services provided
- an explanation of how round-the-clock availability to children and families is maintained
- an explanation of how round-the-clock clinical support to program staff is maintained
- policies for providing continuity of care for children and their families discharged from the program
- procedures describing the participation of other agencies involved in the program's delivery of services
- a confidentiality policy regarding client records
- a description of staff supervision and training
- policies defining how risk management issues (i.e., safety, availability of staff and financial resources to adequately respond to difficult cases over time) will be handled
- procedures to address how the program will respond to complaints and grievances by consumers and family members regarding the quality of services
- procedures for appealing decisions made in response to complaints and grievances, including time frames for their review
- a quality assurance and utilization review plan (see p. 76–78)

Intake, Evaluation, and Screening of Referrals

Each developing mental health home-based program should specify the age range of the population served as well as criteria for admitting children and their families to the program. In Pennsylvania, for example, the age range served is birth to 21. While most programs establish a generic criterion for case selection as "at risk for out-of-home placement," more specific program criteria are often necessary. For example, one Pennsylvania program (Linn, 1991) delineated the following characteristics, some combination of which is exhibited by, or associated with, children "at risk" during the preceding three months:

- active suicidal, homicidal, or psychiatric symptoms
- severe acting-out behavior or the potential for violence
- severe impulsive behavior with no stabilization through medication
- presence of severe family stress, (i.e., divorce, mental illness, drug and alcohol abuse, domestic violence, physical illness, homelessness, unemployment)
- difficulty accessing services (i.e., mental health treatment, medical, food, shelter and community resources)
- high risk for abuse, molestation, and/or severe neglect
- several systems involved (i.e., special education, juvenile probation, Office of Children and Youth)
- history of running away or truancy
- legal involvement for juvenile crimes or misdemeanors
- behavior problems within the school setting of sufficient severity to warrant consideration of removal or exclusion from the school
- other children in the family identified as problematic based on their *DSM-IV* diagnoses

Several general questions are considered when screening referrals (see Table 3.1). A central guiding question is whether other less intense and intrusive services, such as outpatient treatment, should be considered first. If a family's level of functioning allows for immediate access to and benefit from outpatient services, referral

Table 3.1
HOME-BASED MENTAL HEALTH SERVICES
DIAGNOSTIC ADMISSION CRITERIA*

Home-based Mental Health Services (HBMHS)
(Must meet I/II)

I. & II. [Combined] Diagnostic Indicators
   [Axis I or Axis II; D&A on Axis I, and MR on Axis II do not stand
   alone] (Must meet A, B, C, & D)

A. Services must be recommended as the most clinically appropriate for
the child, by the prescriber, as informed by the treatment team as an
alternative to out-of-home placement or as a step down from inpatient
hospitalization or residential treatment, or as a result of little or no
progress in a less restrictive/intrusive service,

AND

B. Severe functional impairment is assessed in the child's presenting behavior. The intensity of service is determined on an individualized basis
according to the following parameters: severity of functional impairments,
risk of out-of-home placement, and risk of endangerment to self, others,
or property.

   1. There is serious <u>and/or</u> persistent impairment of developmental
      progression <u>and/or</u> psychosocial functioning due to a psychiatric
      disorder or serious emotional disturbance, requiring treatment to
      alleviate acute existing symptoms and/or behaviors; or to prevent
      relapse in the child for the prescribed period of time to allow the
      therapeutic process to hold its effectiveness with symptoms <u>and/</u>
      <u>or</u> behaviors that are in partial or complete remission;

                              and

   2. Treatment is determined by the treatment team to be necessary in
      the context of the family in order to effectively treat the child, and
      a. the family recognizes the child's risk out-of-home placement
         and the problem of maintaining their child at home without
         intensive therapeutic interventions in the context of the family;
         and/or
      b. the child is returning home and HBMHS is needed as a step
         down from an out-of-home placement;

                              and

   3. Presence of at least one (1) of the following:
      a. Suicidal/homicidal threatening behavior or intensive ideation

---

*Reprinted with permission from the Commonwealth of Pennsylvania

Table 3.1
continued

---

    b. Impulsivity and/or regression
    c. Psychophysiological condition (e.g., bulimia, anorexia nervosa)
    d. Psychomotor retardation or excitation
    e. Affect/function impairment (e.g., withdrawn, reclusive, labile, reactivty)
    f. Psychosocial functional impairment
    g. Thought impairment
    h. Cognitive impairment
and

4. There is an exacerbation of severely impaired judgment or functional capacity and capability, for the child's developmental level, such that interpersonal skills and/or self-maintenance in home/school/community is/are severely compromised;
and

5. Following referral, service must be recommended as the most clinically appropriate and least restrictive service available for the child, by the HBMHS treatment team. Parent(s)/guardian(s), and/or caretaker, as appropriate, case manager (when assigned) and the child must be involved in the planning process;
and

6. Significant psychosocial stressors are affecting the child and the family as a whole, increase the risk that the child's functioning will decrease for his/her developmental level;
and

7. Symptoms improve in response to comprehensive treatment at a higher level of care, but child needs HBMHS to sustain and reinforce stability while completing the transition back to home and community.
AND

C. Behavior is assessed to be manageable in the home setting, and degree of risk is assessed to be responsive to, and effectively reduced by, the implementation of the treatment plan, as a result of:
    1. the delivery of the therapy and casework services in the home, required to serve the child's specific treatment needs;
and

    2. there is documented commitment by the family to the treatment plan
and

Table 3.1
continued

---

3. if endangerment/destruction is a relevant feature of the presenting problem, both child or adolescent (age 14+) and family member develop a safety plan, which the family member signs.

AND

D. The severity and expression of the child's symptoms are such that:
1. continuation with a less intense level of care cannot offer either an expectation of improvement, or prevention of deterioration, as identified above;

and

2. on-site intervention in the home or community offers a more effective preventive to longer term consequences.

---

should be made to this less intrusive service. Home-based services should only be considered if less intrusive services cannot meet the family's needs. For example, outpatient services may not provide an adequate treatment response for crisis-prone, multiple-agency-involved families who have a child at risk of placement due to a severe emotional or behavioral disorder or a severe mental illness.

Given the high demand for home-based services and the limited numbers of families that can be served, referrals should be evaluated with regard to family factors that would inhibit maximum benefit of these intensive services. For example, requiring that a parent with a chronic substance abuse problem participate in a drug rehabilitation program before the family enters the home-based program may be a more powerful intervention than accessing the services immediately. Similarly, requiring parents with mental illness to establish a record of medication compliance before beginning in-home treatment may be critical. Clearly, a family's motivation and willingness to participate on a voluntary basis is crucial before accepting a referral. The family's agreement to allow communication with all other service providers is one way of assessing the level of motivation.

Some families agree readily enough in the beginning, but their subsequent actions reveal reluctance. Consequently, many home-based programs have an admissions policy specifying the first 30 days of service as an "evaluation" period, allowing the staff time to determine the appropriateness (or not) of their services. A case may be deemed inappropriate if, at the end of the 30 days, the family or involved agencies fail to meet basic necessary treatment goals, as contracted. For example, a family accepted into the mental health home-based program for an initial evaluation period agrees to be available for in-home therapy and the child welfare worker agrees to continue her role of monitoring the safety of the child and the family. However, when the in-home worker arrives at the home for scheduled visits, the family is never home. Furthermore, the child welfare worker does not return the in-home therapist's phone calls to discuss the situation and plan a collaborative intervention. In this instance, the family may not really want the service, and the mental health in-home worker does not have the authority to address the safety issues of the child.

Providing written guidelines for the referral process is essential to avoid misunderstandings. Referents should fill out a referral form, sign for the release of information, and indicate that they will support the referral by participating in a collaborative treatment process. Referral sources need to be aware that acceptance of referrals is not an automatic process. Case selection should always be a job function of the program director, who, as previously described, must be able to place demands upon the family and involved agencies, when necessary, prior to program acceptance (Linn, 1991). In addition, program directors determine the best fit between a particular family and home-based team. Knowing the travel time to families, as well as the skill level and caseload distribution of staff, allows program directors to make the best informed decisions regarding case assignment.

Case Assignment and Staff Scheduling

Each two-person team serves a maximum caseload of eight families at a time for a period of up to 32 consecutive weeks—less, if the child or adolescent has achieved the goals established by the treatment plan. Additional periods of service may be provided if the child continues to meet the eligibility criteria and an updated recommendation has been made by a physician or psychologist. Team members, either individually or together, should have face-to-face contacts with the child and other family members on a regularly scheduled basis, as well as at other times as clinically indicated. There should be a minimum of two hours of in-home contact per family per week, except during transition for discharge, during which time the amount of contact in person is expected to decrease and should be dictated by the discharge transition plan.

Home-based services are designed to be intensive, ranging from two to ten hours of contact per week. Generally, greater amounts of time are necessary in the initial treatment phase, with a gradual lessening of time in the late-middle and termination phases. Services must be delivered at times most convenient to the family, including evenings, early mornings, and weekends. In addition to the comprehensive assessment and treatment of the family, home-based therapists engage in case management, provision of family support services, collaborative treatment planning with other agencies, medical record-keeping, staff conferencing, training and supervision. An example of a typical weekly schedule, given a caseload of eight families per home-based team, appears in Table 3.2. While most family sessions occur in the home, sessions requiring immediate supervisory input for evaluation or planning purposes may take place at the agency. Marital sessions are often purposefully scheduled at the agency to reinforce the therapeutic message that couples need time and space away from children to work on marital issues. Thoughtful scheduling is extremely important so that overly responsible therapists don't overwork, and structure is provided so that job tasks are performed efficiently. For example, while one therapist is conducting an individual session in the home, the other team member can be at a nearby pay phone making necessary calls. It's been said that more progress notes are written at fast food restaurants than any other place, since home-based therapists often combine dinner-on-the-road with their paperwork tasks.

Safety Issues

Safety policies are derived from specific knowledge of communities and families served by home-based programs. For example, one program providing services to a location known for high drug sales mandated no in-home visits to that area after 2:00 p.m. on Fridays when welfare checks were received. Another program designated a public housing project as off-limits for in-home workers because there was only one route in and out of the project. If an area is considered extremely unsafe, families may be seen at a local school or other public setting such as a fast food restaurant or shopping mall. If staff do not know whether a neighborhood is safe, they can ask families to assess the area and let them know appropriate places to meet. Many agencies have purchased vans with car phones for their in-home program staff. If staff are expected to use their own cars, programs often provide cellular phones. Staff are also provided with telephone credit cards for regular or emergency use. "Universal precaution" buckets containing CPR masks, infectious waste bags, gloves, first aid kits, latex heavy gloves, and other items are stocked in staff cars.

Staff safety can also be threatened by substance-abusing clients or families evidencing domestic violence. Client safety issues occur when there is risk of homicide, suicide, or physical abuse. Policies are obviously needed that support staff training and supervision in how to prevent and respond to these risks.

Lastly, programs should purchase liability insurance that covers the transportation of clients in agency or staff vehicles, staff accidents on clients' properties, and clients' accidents on agency property.

Reporting and Billing Requirements

Reporting requirements for program funders include *client numbers* (the number of identified patients and families and the total family members served yearly by the program) and *placement rates* (the number of placement episodes and the number of days of placement occurring during treatment for each family served.)

In Pennsylvania, billing requirements for Medical Assistance and other third-party payors have been based on the number of 15-minute service units accrued by the individual home-based therapist as well as those accrued by the team. There is an expectation that 40% of service time will be individually generated and 60% will be team generated. Each program uses a prescribed rate-setting formula to determine the cost per unit. The formula considers the costs of administration, personnel, space, family support monies, training, and other budgetary items. For example, if the cost per

Table 3.2
TYPICAL WEEKLY TEAM HOME-BASED SERVICES SCHEDULE

Monday	Tuesday	Wednesday	Thursday	Friday
8:00 a.m.–10:00 a.m. Pick up parents, drive to a treatment meeting at school and return home	9:00 a.m.–10:00 a.m. Individual home session with mother (Family #4) (Staff #2) Phone calls (Staff #1)	7:30 a.m.–8:30 a.m. Pick up mother and grandmother and drive to psychiatric hospital (Family #7)		9:00 a.m.–11:00 a.m. Progress notes Family #2-Staff #2 Family #3-Staff #1 Family #4-Staff #2 Family #5-Staff #1 Family #8-Staff #2
10:00 a.m.–2:30 p.m. Non-working staff time	10:15 a.m.–11:30 a.m. Team supervision (office)	9:00 a.m.–10:00 a.m. Discharge meeting for identified patient (Family #7)		11:00 a.m.–12:30 p.m. Take father to Neighborhood Services agency for budgeting (Staff #2, Family #1) Phone calls (Staff #1, in office)
2:30 p.m.–3:30 p.m. Individual home session with identified patient (Family #1–Staff #1) Phone calls (Staff #2)	11:30 a.m.–12:00 p.m. Lunch (office)	10:00 a.m.–11:30 a.m. Family #7 session (held at hospital)	1:00 p.m.–2:00 p.m. In-office phone calls	12:30 p.m.–1:30 p.m. All staff lunch
3:30 p.m.–4:00 p.m. Pre-plan Family #1 session	12:00 p.m.–3:00 p.m. In-office evaluation of mother and identified patient (Family #5, Staff #1, #2 and supervisor)	11:30 a.m.–12:30 p.m. Lunch with Family #7	2:00 p.m.–3:00 p.m. Couple session (office) Family #8	1:30 p.m.–3:30 p.m. All teams group supervision

4:00 p.m.–5:15 p.m. Family #1 home session 5:15 p.m.–6:00 p.m. Travel to Family #2, Pre-plan session 6:00 p.m.–7:00 p.m. Family #2 home session 7:00 p.m.–8:15 p.m. Travel to Family #3 Pre-plan session Eat dinner Write progress notes Family #1–Staff #1 Family #2–Staff #2 8:15 p.m.–9:30 p.m. Family #3 home session	3:00 p.m.–3:30 p.m. Pre-plan session in car (Family #6) 3:30 p.m.–5:00 p.m. Family #6 home session (first treatment session)	12:30 p.m.–2:00 p.m. Drive family home and return to office 2:00 p.m.–3:30 p.m. Progress notes Family #3–Staff #1 Family #4–Staff #2 Family #5–Staff #1 Family #7–Staff #1 Intake report Family #6–Staff #2	3:00 p.m.–4:00 p.m. Couple session (office) (Family #2) 4:30 p.m.–5:30 p.m. Couple session (office) Family #3 5:30 p.m.–7:00 p.m. Ice skating and dinner (Family #4) 7:00 p.m.–7:30 p.m. Travel to Family #5 7:30 p.m.–9:30 p.m. Family #5 home session	3:30 p.m.–4:00 p.m. Respite Planning meeting (Family #5), team and supervisor 4:00 p.m.–5:00 p.m. mother (Family #5), supervisor, respite parent, team, collaborative session in office
9 hours	7 hours	8 hours	8 hours	8 hours

15-minute unit is determined to be $30, a one-hour session would be billed for $120. Approximately half of that amount is matched through the Pennsylvania Medicaid program for families on Medical Assistance. Direct collateral contact, direct client contact, telephone collateral or client contact, and travel time (to a *scheduled* session, even if the family does not keep the appointment) are all billable services in Pennsylvania's Medicaid home-based program.

For the first six to eight weeks of the service, the program usually bills three hours per week per client, which may reflect two hours of direct patient contacts, a half-hour of travel time, and a half-hour of collateral contacts by telephone or at interagency meetings. This contact time increases during crisis times and decreases near termination. One program reported that its staff spend an average of three hours daily traveling to off-site appointments. As the home-based service continues past eight weeks, therapeutic contact diminishes slightly. One project director estimated that after the eight-week point, his program tended to bill eight units or two hours per week until the last service month, when there was a drop to four units or one hour of service reflecting the termination/discharge phase of treatment (M. Sowers, personal communication, 1997).

Program directors sometimes compare teams on the number of face-to-face, phone, and meeting contacts to evaluate team's differing styles and/or abilities. Laptop computers for staff and customized software for the program director can greatly facilitate the record-keeping and billing processes. As staff members make progress notes, they can also assign billing and location codes, date, and the type and length of contact. Project directors can download this information weekly and generate an electronic billing record that reduces the need to hire a program billing clerk (Houser, 1996).

Quality Assurance and Utilization Review

In order to ensure continual quality assurance and improvement, providers of mental health home-based services need to develop policies and procedures for (1) clinical case reviews, (2) periodic staff supervision and conferences, (3) staff training requirements, (4) client/family satisfaction (Appendix A), (5) client outcomes (Appendix B), (6) intra/interagency collaboration (Appendix C), and (7) written documentation of utilization review. The utilization review process should occur at various intervals within the designated service time frame and address the following questions (Dunlap, 1997; J. Houser, personal communication, 1996):

- Do those consumers who need home-based services receive them?
- If consumers don't need the services, are they referred elsewhere?
- If consumers have received what they need from the services, are the cases closed?
- Are consumers benefiting from the service?

Pennsylvania's family-based mental health programs have developed indicators and standards of quality care that are rated along a continuum of compliance from substantial (meets all provisions) to minimal (fails to meet provisions). Monitoring is required for those aspects of care that uniquely define these mental health home-based services.

Service delivery standards

- Services are family-driven.
- Services are generally provided out of the office.
- The scheduling needs of families have been considered.
- Twenty-four-hour availability occurs at the time of crisis.
- The service is primarily team delivered.
- Casework services are provided.
- Family support services are provided.
- Family advocacy occurs in schools, agencies, etc.
- Ecosystemic structural therapy is conducted with families and extrafamilial systems and reflected in the comprehensive assessment and ongoing evaluation of the child and family's needs.
- Treatment services are individualized and varied.

Coordination of services

- The referral sources are satisfied with the level of communication between them and the program.
- Interagency letters of agreement are in place.

- Progress notes indicate at least monthly review of families' participation and progress with other involved agencies.

Treatment planning

- The plan reflects the CASSP principles.
- Treatment demonstrates measurable goals and objectives that reflect systemic change.
- The plan reflects continuity of the treatment process from month to month.
- Treatment expands family strengths and capabilities.
- Plans are reviewed every 30 days.
- The treatment plan provides for family evaluation.
- Documentation of collaboration among systems is included.

Discharge planning

- Clinical records document the family's involvement with discharge planning.
- A joint meeting of all involved systems reviews the family's experience one month after discharge.

Utilization review

- An intensive evaluation is conducted to determine possible causative factors, trends, or patterns.
- Suggestions for remedial action are provided in the following situations:
  - ✓ any instances of unusual increased usage of crisis services
  - ✓ suicide attempts or suicides
  - ✓ physical attacks upon staff
  - ✓ homicidal behaviors
  - ✓ unplanned placements
  - ✓ suspensions from a community center or school
  - ✓ need for an "endangered client" report in cases where the client is suicidal or homicidal, or when child abuse or client runaway behavior is reported (Dunlap, 1997)

Mental Health Home-Based Services and Managed Care

Nine of the fifteen large national managed care organizations responded to a Managed Care Industry Survey. They reported that, on average, 44% of their employer clients include in-home care in their benefits packages (Tuttle, 1996). Within the managed care health delivery system (both private and public sectors) in Pennsylvania, mental health home-based services are viewed as either an in-plan service benefit or an alternative service option to outpatient, day treatment, or inpatient services.

Home-based services are provided by the managed care plan's in-network providers who meet the plan's credentialing requirements. If a managed care plan does not have an in-network mental health home-based services provider, the employer client can request provision of services from an out-of-network provider. Credentialing requirements usually include: meeting the plan's standards for professional practice (i.e., education, training, experience and specialization requirements); possessing a current professional and state license; maintaining liability insurance; and acquiring reference checks and a signed ethics statement.

Providers of mental health home-based services receive referrals from physicians, hospitals, residential programs, schools, human service agencies, day care centers, other behavioral health service providers, the managed care plan case manager, or self-referred families. Once a child is identified as a member of a managed care plan, the provider follows that particular managed care plan's procedures for the authorization of services.

Mental health home-based services require prior authorization (i.e., precertification) from the managed care plan before service initiation. If there are emergencies, however, the provider initiates services immediately and applies subsequently for authorization. Services are authorized for a designated time period or number of service hours based on medical necessity criteria. Concurrent reviews are performed by the managed care plan, which authorizes the continuation of services, tapering of service hours, or discharge from services. The frequency of concurrent reviews is dependent upon the plan's utilization management policy and procedures. Managed care plans require thorough documentation. Requesting the service requires assessment reports, treatment plans with clearly articulated goals and interventions, and treatment notes that demonstrate progress or the reasons for lack of progress. In addition, successful communication with the managed care plan's utilization manager, who authorizes the services and conducts the concurrent reviews, is critical. The utilization manager will want documentation of specific, individualized, measurable, and observable outcome measures of the child's functioning within the family and other relevant social contexts.

The mental health home-based services provider markets services to managed care plans to secure contracts as an in-network provider. Marketing materials must clearly describe the service, including interventions and therapy modalities; description of the treatment population served including ages, disorders, and contextual issues for which this service is best suited; course of treatment; outcome measures; and cost for the team-delivered/individual-therapist-delivered services.

The mental health home-based services provider who has a contract with a managed care plan as an in-network provider receives the plan's provider manual describing policies and procedures to be followed, including utilization management criteria, forms, and reporting requirements. The provider's complaint and grievance procedures should be clearly described, as well as those appeal procedures for the managed care plan's members. A member handbook may be available upon request.

In October 1997, Pennsylvania's Office of Mental Health and Substance Abuse Services developed medical necessity criteria for use by public and private sector managed care plans in authorizing mental health home-based services (Commonwealth of Pennsylvania, 1997). These criteria include specified diagnostic indicators appearing in Table 3.1 that relate to the admission process and severity of symptoms. In addition, other criteria include: (1) support factors, such as availability of on-site clinical expertise appropriate to the severity of the child's or adolescent's behaviors, plus family and community commitment to the treatment process; (2) continued care requirements, such as reevaluation of the child by the treatment team every 30 days for the purpose of updating the child's progress and a reevaluation by a psychiatrist, psychologist, or physician at the end of the 32 weeks, demonstration of progress toward developing community linkages, and treatment plan documentation for the necessity for continuing in-home services; and (3) discharge criteria indicating any of the following: completion of up to 32 weeks of service, satisfactory attainment of treatment goals, ineffectiveness of service in attaining treatment goals, concerns that service dependency is interfering with the family or child's functioning, and the request of the parent or guardian or adolescent, 14 years or older, for reduction in service or termination of the service.

Creating a Collaborative, Competent Context

Making a mental health home-based program work obviously requires more than attention to administrative detail. The most important task is to create a supportive context wherein staff are empowered and encouraged to perform competently, creatively, and enthusiastically. Successful program directors are attentive to the parallel processes occurring between agency/program dynamics and community/family dynamics. Collaborative partnerships need to develop between (1) the hierarchical administrative levels within the agency/program, (2) the home-based program and the community resources, (3) the in-home worker and the family, and (4) the family and the community resources. These collaborative relationships empower the program director with the knowledge that the agency's home-based program is not the only resource available to the families served. Agency resources can help provide a "safety net" and "respite" when service demands on the home-based program become overwhelming. Similarly, having collaborative community partnerships creates the knowledge that we can all help each other to help these families in turmoil. In a collaborative program context, all staff members are a part of making programmatic decisions. The program director's willingness to listen to staff input and make ongoing changes is crucial to creating a shared sense of accountability for the program's success. Putting staff in charge of generating solutions to problems is analogous to what staff do with families. And, just as effective home-based family treatment recognizes that families sometimes need to be nurtured, to play rather than work, and to take a break when enough is enough, the same holds true for the staff. Successful program directors incorporate into the staff's weekly schedule a time to reflect and a time to be nurtured. Off-site staff retreats are held at least twice a year. Celebration rituals occur on a regular basis. As one program director said, "We *look* for things to celebrate about ourselves, our work—anything at all. We just celebrated the end of October!" (Archacki-Stone, 1991).

Now that we have seen how home-based services are organized on the agency level, let us look at the experience of the clinician in the field.

CHAPTER 4

Key Elements in Home-Based Practice

Connections are made slowly, sometimes they grow underground. . . .
Weave real connections . . . build real houses . . .
for every gardener knows that after the digging, after the planting,
after the long season of tending and growth, the harvest comes.

—Marge Piercy, 1982

REFERRALS TO mental health home-based services occur when (1) a youth's and/or family's behavior heightens the youth's risk of out-of-home placement, (2) less intensive services (such as traditional outpatient treatment) have been ineffective, and (3) the need for intensive intervention is apparent. When escalating crises occur in families being served by outpatient mental health services, schools, and the juvenile justice system, referrals to more intensive home-based services are made to avoid placement in foster care, a treatment center, or psychiatric inpatient facility. Other common reasons for referrals to home-based services include when a child is returning home from foster care or treatment in inpatient hospitalization services. Families with multiple agency involvement and complex problem areas that overlap these agencies may also be considered for referral.

ISSUES AND CONCERNS IN THE REFERRAL PROCESS

In communities with newly developed mental health home-based services, referrals are often made with the notion that these services represent the last resort in efforts to keep a family together. In some cases, the possibility of avoiding placement is minimal, and the real referral issue is finding a service system that will pay for placement. In other instances, this "last resort" message may, in fact, motivate families to change.

Referring agencies that have experienced ineffectual treatment in mental health outpatient and/or inpatient services may be skeptical about what this new treatment service can provide that hasn't already been tried. The referral source expects failure, and there is tremendous pressure on the home-based service to prove itself both to the referral source and to the family. Those referral sources who want to "dump" the family or child often abdicate any continuing responsibility for providing resources to the home-based service. In these situations families may feel cut off from previous helpers, even abandoned—all too similar to life experiences in their families of origin or in current familial or social interactions. Conversely, referral sources who have been overinvolved with the child and family may be reluctant to discontinue their prior therapeutic relationship and consequently interfere with the work of home-based clinicians.

It is preferable to meet with the referral source before accepting a referral and setting up any meetings with the family. Also, the family's agreement to sign release-of-information forms from the referring agency should be a requirement for referral to the home-based service. By having an exploratory meeting with the referral source, abdicating professionals can be given a clear message that immediate abandonment of the family will not be encouraged. Referral meetings can also be used to explore the feasibility of boundary setting and role clarification with overinvolved referents. Additionally, conflictual relationships between families and referring professionals can be assessed. *Isomorphism*, the tendency to replicate emotional process across subsystems, is all too common in family/agency relationships (Compher, 1989). Helping professionals must create a relational system with the family that is more functional than the family's own home environment if there is to be any possibility of achieving positive treatment outcomes. A healthy, collaborative treatment system will respond flexibly and quickly to family needs. Clear boundaries and hierarchical relationships will create clarity about exchange of information and leadership roles. Regularly scheduled informational meetings about the family, mutually agreed-upon goals, and open encouragement of consumers to take an active voice in treatment planning are also critical ingredients of healthy treatment systems.

Interagency Dynamics and Pitfalls

In gathering information from the referral source, it is important to obtain answers to the following questions:

- Why is the referral being made at this particular time?
- How is the problem viewed?
- What are the relationships between the referring person, his/her agency, and the family?
- What has been the frequency of contact?
- What past and current solutions to the problem have been initiated by the referral source?
- Which of these solutions were helpful?
- Which were ineffective, and why?
- What other formal or informal helpers have been, or are currently, involved with the family?

By meeting with the referring professional, the home-based therapist encourages a collaborative, collegial relationship wherein hidden agendas become clarified and mutual empathy engaged. For example, referrals are sometimes made to resolve a conflict regarding appropriate treatment between two agencies. If professionals from two different agencies disagree about a child or family, they may refer the family to a third agency to determine which agency has been working "correctly." Achieving successful resolution with a case where someone else has failed inevitably underscores the other agency's failure. In response, the agency that failed may sabotage the other's success by withdrawing resources or reclaiming the family as its own. The effective agency will bring all referring agency representatives together and establish direct communication and collaborative treatment planning efforts. Instead of any one agency feeling blamed for being a part of the problem, all agencies can be identified as having a significant role in creating future solutions.

Families involved with multiple agencies don't need heroes or

heroines with fantasies of rescuing people from the erroneous interventions of other professionals. However, other professionals' failures can be a source of learning, especially about the negative
impact of biases. Discovering what did and did not help the child
and family is crucial from both the family's and the professional's
point of view. Home-based therapists must keep in mind that they
are members of the professional system and not the family system.
Giving up the belief in one's central importance to the change
process and sense of patient ownership is essential to a collaborative
process. Effective home-based treatment requires therapists to assume a humble, neutral position as they advocate for incremental
changes for the child and family. When a conservative point of view
that supports the importance of working toward small changes is
assumed, anxiety is reduced in the family as well as in the therapist
(Jones, 1992).

It may be helpful initially to accept a family involved with multiple agencies into a period of "evaluation" rather than "treatment."
If the initial helping process is *not* framed as treatment, therapists
can more easily resist the pressure from other agencies and/or
families to immediately bring about major changes or "cures."
Therapists then have time to carefully assess the situation without
jumping in and creating unrealistic expectations. The idea that
forming a relationship is an assessment process makes sense in
all contexts. For example, when you first meet someone you are
attracted to, you don't say, "Let's get married," you say, "Let's
date."

Goals, Near and Far

In the referral stage it is extremely important to arrive at clear,
obtainable goals, so as to circumvent triangulation between the
referring agency, the home-based worker, and the family about
the treatment agenda. In the initial collaborative meeting with the
referral source, a possible menu of family goals can be developed
for use in the subsequent meeting involving the referral source, the
family and the home-based worker. The goals should be kept small
and lead toward a specific, desired outcome. These are sometimes
termed *proximal* (intermediate) and *distal* (outcome) goals. The
proximal goals are the steppingstones to a larger, distal goal.

An example: In the Roberts family, 12-year-old John has been hospitalized on two different occasions because of depression. Since these hospitalizations, John's school attendance has become a problem. At an initial meeting with referring school counselor, Doris, the home-based worker learns that Doris feels very frustrated that John is not attending school and thinks that he should attend a day treatment program. She has met with Mother and John on several occasions to no avail. The in-home therapist validates Doris's concern for and knowledge of the family, and emphasizes the patience they both need while helping the family. The two professionals then discuss the advantages and disadvantages of referral to a day treatment program versus John's continuing at his current school. Doris ultimately agrees that referral to a temporary day treatment program would only postpone the problem of John's achieving success in school attendance at his current school.

The therapist invites the school counselor to attend a family meeting with Mother and John so that they can all identify the initial proximal goals to be met before John attempts the major outcome goal of regular school attendance. Within the family meeting, the obstacles to school attendance are identified. In the process, the therapist discovers that the mother has difficulty getting John up in the morning in time to catch the school bus. Since the family lives in a rural area and the family car is used by the father, who goes to work very early, there is no alternative way for John to get to school if he misses the bus. Mother and John end up in tremendous hassles every day over this issue. Further exploration of obstacles reveals that John dreads going to school because his teacher treats him disdainfully in front of the other children. He has lost school time because of his psychiatric hospitalizations and he feels slow and inadequate in the classroom.

Brainstorming with the family about how to overcome these obstacles leads to the identification of the next set of proximal goals. One of these may be for John to get himself up in the morning by 7:00 A.M. and to dress and eat breakfast in time for the bus. A series of tasks that will facilitate this behavior (buy alarm clock, practice setting alarm, Mother busies herself in another part of the house, leaving the responsibility of getting up to John, etc.) is identified and rehearsed. A final proximal goal is developed by Mother, John, and the school counselor. The three will meet with

John's teacher to develop methods of increasing John's comfort in the classroom and to explore whether supplemental tutoring services are available.

Since child welfare and juvenile probation systems have more power in determining residential placement than the mental health system, it is important to ascertain the flexibility of these agencies' goals and their expectations of a family's accountability prior to meeting with the family. The legal mandates of these systems to protect children and communities can provide a powerful incentive for some families to make necessary changes. However, system representatives must be willing to invoke these mandates with families who continue high-risk behavior. If these systems do not use their power to provide consequences when high-risk family situations continue, mental health home-based programs may decline to accept the family for services.

In one case, 15-year-old Karen moved back and forth in a mediating role between her separated, feuding parents. The ongoing marital battle resulted in both parents' abdicating their provision of parental controls for Karen. Not surprisingly, Karen's acting-out behaviors escalated to truancy, drug usage, and living on the streets when she felt like it. A drug overdose led to a subsequent inpatient hospitalization. Because of the parents' history of neglect of Karen, a petition had been filed that allowed the child welfare worker to monitor Karen's situation and report to the court. The worker referred Karen and her parents to the mental health in-home program following Karen's hospitalization. Unbeknownst to the in-home therapist, after one month of in-home services, the child welfare worker wrote a report to the court indicating that Karen's circumstances had stabilized. The case was discharged from the court and closed by the child welfare agency. Without child welfare's mandate that placement would occur unless the parents worked to reduce Karen's high-risk behaviors, the in-home therapist was ineffective in helping the parents to pull together on Karen's behalf.

Because of such common circumstances, a provisional acceptance may occur wherein the home-based service specifies a period of time to work on small goals with the family in order to discuss the family's motivation for change. In exploring family reunification with the child welfare worker, for example, the circumstances under which the child will be returned to the home may be predicated on specific changes in the child's and parents' behavior, and/or on mastering new techniques in dealing with interpersonal conflict.

If out-of-home placement is being considered, it is essential to establish—and make it clear to the family—that placement will definitely occur if specific problems remain unresolved. If the case concerns a juvenile offender, for example, the probation officer can be asked to specify the conditions under which the youth will violate his/her probation. What are the consequences if the youth misses therapy sessions? Will there be follow-through if the youth breaks probationary limits? The in-home worker must have a realistic grasp of the time demands on other professionals in relation to their level of involvement with the family. While the home-based worker will have the primary relationship with the family, a collaborative agreement must be made with the child welfare worker or probation officer. For example, these two professionals may be asked not to take any action with the family without first discussing the situation with the home-based therapist.

GETTING STARTED

First Introductory Meeting

The concept of home-based services should be introduced to the family in a session that includes the referring individual(s) and the home-based supervisor and therapist(s). When possible, this session should be held at the referring or the home-based agency rather than in the family's home to distinguish the meeting from the home-based treatment itself. When the initial session is held in the family's home, members often feel intruded upon and forced to accept a suggested service. In the early stages of establishing a collaborative relationship between family and home-based therapist(s), it is extremely important that parents feel empowered to make the initial decision of accepting or declining this new relationship. Holding the initial meeting outside the home allows the family to meet the new in-home therapist(s), hear a description of what home-based service can offer, and freely decide whether to choose this new service. In rural settings, where there may be considerable geographic distance between the agency and a family's home, this introduction to home-based services may need to take place in the form of a conference call. If the family does not have a phone, the referral source and in-home worker can meet with the family in a geographic setting designated by the family. In high-crime urban areas, the parent(s) can select what they consider to be the "safest" setting (e.g., a local restaurant or the neighborhood school).

For this first introductory meeting, the home-based therapist should have clear goals with regard to both the referral source and the family. *Goals for the referral source* might include:

1. reinforcing the development of a trusting, collaborative relationship between the therapist and referring agency
2. clarifying the goals of the referral source in the presence of the family
3. observing and assessing the nature of the relationship between the referral source and the family
4. determining what resources the referral source can contribute to the new treatment plan with the family
5. obtaining necessary releases of information
6. developing appropriate feedback channels with the referral source regarding the home-based treatment

The home-based therapist's *goals for the family* include:

1. developing a collaborative, respectful, caring relationship with each family member
2. describing the goals and components of the in-home service: assessment, treatment planning, clinical treatment (individual, marital, or family therapy, medication, etc.), 24-hour crisis intervention, family support services (respite care, concrete assistance, wraparound services), case management and advocacy with other service systems
3. clarifying misconceptions and expectations regarding length of service, who is to attend sessions, location, frequency, and length of sessions, use of videotaping for supervision and training, etc.
4. specifying factors that will jeopardize services (e.g., physical

> violence or threats of violence to in-home therapists, sub-
> stance abuse before or during a session, etc.)
> 5. eliciting information from the family about in home diatrac
> tions that could occur during sessions and the family's ideas
> about reducing these distractions

Creating an agenda, structure, and collaborative process in the initial meeting with the referral source and family members establishes a foundation for agency/family collaboration and accountability throughout the treatment process. As one in-home worker has said, "Accountability is more than a one-way street. It is at least a four-way intersection. At each corner there is the family, the therapist(s), the supervisor, and the agencies or eco-systems involved with the family" (P. Buch, personal communication, 1995). It is better to define expectations and risk the family's refusal of home-based services at the outset than to embark on an ill-defined journey. The hallmark of a collaborative relationship is *reciprocal accountability*, without which treatment will not be successful.

Working in the Family's Home (Despite Distractions)

Once the parent(s) has chosen the service, the home-based worker calls to schedule the first clinical session. In families having two adult caretakers, it is critical that both caretakers have given consent. For example, in one introductory session a mother assured the professionals that her husband wanted the service despite his absence from the session. When the therapist arrived at the family's trailer in an isolated rural area, she was shocked to find the father sitting at the kitchen table examining a gun. Despite her anxiety, she asked the obvious question: "Mr. Jones, did you want me to come to your home and help you and your wife with John's school truancy?" Subsequently, it was revealed that Mother had told Father about the scheduled visit a mere 20 minutes prior to the therapist's arrival. Father was emphatic about not wanting an outsider in his home. The therapist left her professional card and politely exited the premises. Father called the next week requesting in-home services.

If the therapist schedules several sessions but no one is at home when he or she arrives, it is appropriate to discuss candidly by telephone whether the family really feels the need for the service at this time. In such instances the family can be reassured that they can call the therapist and/or intake office if they desire the service in the future. The therapist should also contact the referral source about the unkept appointments and discuss the appropriateness of closing the case at this time.

While most home-based therapists are initially quite distracted by working in the home environment, they are equally impressed by the rich and realistic portrayal of family life that informs their treatment. Distractions can be categorized as those happening outside the home or in the home. Common outdoor distractions that simply need to be ignored include traffic noises, animal sounds, and children playing. Minor indoor distractions include clocks ticking or chiming, instruments being played, unexpected social visits from friends, relatives, or solicitors, washing machines and vacuum cleaners, baby noises, and sounds from children playing. While household pets make interesting "family members," they are also sources of distraction. Among the pets encountered by in-home therapists have been dogs, cats, birds, gerbils, hermit crabs, and rats. If a therapist is afraid of dogs or allergic to cats, he or she must be open and honest in requesting to the family to shut Bowser or Kitty away in another part of the home before the therapist arrives.

Among the most discomforting indoor distractions are smoking, ringing telephones and doorbells, loud televisions, radios, or compact disc players, extreme thermal conditions, extreme space restrictions, household insect infestations (e.g., flies, fleas, spiders, wasps, roaches), bad odors, and filthy homes with abundant trash. While some of these distractions may have been identified and discussed in the introductory session with the family, the therapist should be prepared for some surprises when arriving at the family's home for the first time. Without some relationship with the family, immediate attempts by the therapist to eliminate the distractions would be rude.

Therapists should first notice and comment positively on any features in the home that demonstrate the family's pride, beliefs, or uniqueness (e.g., family pictures, paintings, decorations, pets, etc.) Thinking about what he or she would want an outsider to notice when first coming into his or her home is a good place for the therapist to start. As a relationship with the family is formed, the therapist can be straightforward about his or her need to reduce the distractions:

- "You know, I'm allergic to smoke. Do you think we could have time-outs during our sessions so that the smokers could take a smoke break outside?"
- "I've always been afraid of dogs. Would you mind keeping Gooch in the bedroom during our sessions?"
- "Do you think we could agree to keep the volume down on the television when we meet? It's hard for me to hear the important things you want to tell me."
- "Mrs. Wilson, where is the quietest area in your home that we could meet for family sessions and not be interrupted by the neighborhood kids? If you'd like to talk to me sometimes without your children listening in, we could sit in my car and talk."

Many home-based therapists are particularly distressed by lack of cleanliness. Nevertheless, if the family does not specify cleaning the house as a treatment goal, the therapist needs to grin and bear it. Dressing for comfort and not for style helps. It's important not to impose one's own values about cleanliness upon another. However, a very dirty or disheveled home may be a sign of the family's depression about its present situation. Home-based workers often find that, as the family's problems are addressed and resolved, the condition of the house improves as well.

Experienced in-home therapists learn how to transform distractions into moments of family competence. For instance, a home-based team was conducting an initial session with an inner-city family with a severely enuretic nine-year-old son. The boy described his embarrassment about family members' hearing him when he used the toilet in the small, public housing apartment. Suddenly, one of the team had to use the family's toilet. The undisguised noises from the bathroom caused everyone to spontaneously burst into laughter. The other team member quickly responded, "He's probably embarrassed about *his* problem, too!" and the boy said humorously, "Well, at least I'm not THAT loud!"

Another home-based therapist was meeting at a family's urban apartment when a neighbor burst in with a bleeding arm. The mother, who had been somewhat passive in her response to a out-of-control daughter during the session, jumped up and effectively administered first aid to the distraught neighbor. The therapist told the mother that she was a natural crisis worker and just the person to handle her daughter's crisis.

In a neighborhood known for its drug problems, a therapist's in-home visit focused on transforming a single mother's helplessness about the influence of drug dealers on her son's behavior. At the end of the session, when the mother opened her door for the therapist to leave, a drug dealer on the street yelled to him about having drugs for sale. Through the support of the worker, the mother was able to firmly tell the drug dealer to leave her family and home alone.

A rural couple raised piglets in their kitchen to supplement their meager income. The scheduled session's agenda that night was to discuss the son's explosive outbursts toward his mother. However, upon entering the home, the therapist first commented on how healthy the piglets looked—thereby recognizing the family's competence in one area and creating a climate of receptivity for increasing their competence in another: managing their child's behavior.

Another "true story": A female therapist was enthusiastically greeting the family's children when her long hair became tangled in sticky fly-catching paper that hung from the ceiling of the family's trailer. This unplanned state of affairs turned out to be a wonderful opportunity for the mother to become the "helper" to the therapist, as she painstakingly unwound the therapist's hair from the fly-paper! This incident heightened the sense of collaboration between the mother and the therapist.

Perhaps the most striking example of a home-based therapist's ability to transform distraction into competence occurred when a rural father exhibited his hunting talent by showing the therapist one of two rattlesnakes—five feet long with ten rattles—which he had mounted. Not only did the therapist verbally acknowledge the father's prowess as she held the mounted snake, but when he told her that the second snake was wrapped in cellophane in the freezer, she said smoothly, "You never know when that snake meat will come in handy!" Home-based work provides many opportunities for spontaneous, meaningful, and genuine recognition of a family's strengths and competencies.

Providing Structure in Sessions

The context of an agency's outpatient office implicitly defines the roles, rules, and boundaries of the therapeutic relationship within a structured environment. The home-based therapist cannot have the same expectations for order, control, and structure. What is gained, however, is additional flexibility and creativity in the treatment process, as well as the opportunity to establish a truly intimate relationship with family members (Linn, 1991). Indeed, the sense of intimacy created by the home environment sometimes creates boundary issues for therapists. The most frequent dilemma posed by therapists is how to serve a *therapeutic* rather than a *social* function in someone's home. Many a therapist begins his or her home-based experience by displaying either a polite social attitude or an overly informal stance rather than initiating the therapeutic process.

Maintaining professional boundaries while in the home begins with defining for families what the process of treatment entails, the ground rules for sessions, and what the home-based therapist's and family's roles will be. Following is one worker's overview, given in a first visit to a family's home:

Families sometimes have other people come into their lives who tell them how to live. It shouldn't be that way. It should be up to you and your wife, as parents of Ron. That's why I will just be meeting with the four of you. Will Eric [older son] be coming tonight? If not, that's okay, but I would like him to come to future sessions because I'm sure he has good ideas to share.

What we will deal with in the therapy are the problems you want solved. I cannot solve your problems; only you can do that. What I can do is communicate with you and you with me. I can make suggestions when I have ideas to contribute. I don't have the power to take your kids out of the home or make you do anything. What I will try to understand is what you want to do to solve your problems, when you desire that to happen, and what I can do to help you in that process. In our therapy sessions, it is important that you say what you think or feel. We need to establish a policy of honesty with one another. If you're not honest with each other and with me, the therapy won't work. If you want something from me, tell me. Tell me what you expect of me and I'll tell you what I expect of you. I won't tell you that I have all the answers, because I don't. We'll develop the agenda for our sessions together, when we'll meet, and who should be present. During sessions each family member will have a chance to speak about what is concerning him or her. It's not helpful to say hurtful things about someone else; what is helpful is to speak about yourself. For example, "I feel bad when Ron doesn't listen to me," instead of "Ron is so disobedient, he never listens to anything I say." Tonight, I'd like to get to know each of you and what's special to you. After that, I'd like to know what concerns each of you have about your family life and what you'd like to change.

After the guidelines and mutual roles within the therapeutic process have been clearly articulated, the assessment process begins. It is recommended that therapists come into each in-home session with a prepared and *specific* agenda focusing on the content and process goals that need to be accomplished. Establishing a structure for each in-home family contact and adhering to it creates crisp and focused sessions despite the informality of the home setting.

ASSESSMENT AND TREATMENT PLANNING

Whenever possible, the goal of family assessment and treatment planning is to utilize existing resources in the child, family, and community to ensure that the troubled youth remains with the family (or is reunited with the family) and attends school in the family's community. It is acknowledged that maintaining the youth in the home is not the only criteria for treatment success. Planned placement of the child or another family member may be essential to reach the appropriate long-term goals of the family. The ecosystemic structural family therapy model described in this book uses assessment to develop an understanding of the biopsychosocial context wherein the strengths and difficulties of the youth are manifested. While the identified concerns of a particular child or adolescent become the point of entry into the family unit, the focus of assessment and treatment planning involves all family members and their extended social networks. Specific issues of families and agencies are addressed and approaches to promote positive changes are identified. For example, a mother may want to alter the school counselor's perception that the mother does not care whether or not her son attends school. Mother may want the home-based therapist to arrange a meeting that includes the school counselor, mother, her truant son, and the mother's uncle, who has expressed willingness to transport the boy to school daily.

Treatment planning incorporates short-term, concrete, practical, action-oriented solutions that meet the child and family's needs, while simultaneously helping to shift a particular pattern of behavior, attitude, or perception among individual family members and/ or in the extended network. The main components of treatment in home-based services include:

- assessment and clinical intervention
- case management, including liaison, advocacy, collaboration, and sometimes intervention with other service agencies and natural support systems of the family (e.g., extended family, neighborhood and community service resources)
- emergency crisis intervention
- respite services (e.g., temporary child-care services or short-term respite placement)
- family support funds (used for emergency food and housing problems as well as unique needs identified during the treatment process)

Conducting the Assessment Interviews

All family members living in the home and significant extended family members invited by the parent(s) are asked to attend the initial family assessment interviews. Also, individual sessions are often held with each parent and the child identified as needing help. A description of home-based services is provided to family members who did not attend the introductory session and written permission is obtained for videotaping the clinical sessions for those in-home services using camcorders (see Appendix D for a sample consent form). If a family expresses reservations or concerns about videotaping, the therapist should readily agree that the family should not permit it at this time. It is suggested that the family may want to reconsider this opportunity in the future, when the family and therapist know each other better. It is explained that, through videotaping sessions, more consultative help can be given to the family via the agency supervisor. If the home-based program staff are participating in clinical training, families are informed that the videotapes might also be shared within a regional training group composed of other therapists and consultants, who are also able to provide helpful ideas to the family's therapist.

In the beginning phase of assessment, the therapist focuses on developing rapport and overcoming resistance with each family member, as well as on demonstrating a collaborative, strengths-based clinical approach. Therapists must keep in mind that how family members are treated and spoken to is ultimately more important than the services they will receive. First, however, therapists must deal with their own feelings of being overwhelmed by the litany of problems many families and/or agencies present to them. Having the genuine belief that the family is the source of *solutions* for change, rather than merely being the source of the problems, is critical to engendering hope in therapists and, subsequently, in clients.

It is important for the therapist, the family, and the identified patient to feel at ease with each other in this new encounter. The therapist asks the family members to identify strengths, resources, goals, and aspirations in themselves, other family members, the family as a whole, and the extended family. This initial focus on positives rather than problems or deficits has the effect of reminding family members of the strengths they possess individually and collectively and begins to instill hope and confidence that problems can be overcome by working together. While some therapists have family members complete and discuss a strengths-based assessment checklist, such as the one developed by Elko (1997) (see Appendix E), others prefer to have a more informal dialogue with family members about the positive aspects of their family life and their desires to make it even better.

Children and adolescents are asked: "What activities do you most enjoy? Why? What would you like to be able to do this year [next year, or when you grow up]?"

Parents are asked: "What do you do that makes you feel good or relaxed? What other activities would you like to do this year [next year, or five years from now]? Tell me something you especially like about each of your children. What good things would you like to happen for your child, yourself, and your family right now or in the future?"

Families are asked: "When are the times and situations you enjoy yourselves as a family? What are other activities that you would want to do as a family?"

The therapist also converses with the family members about their cultural strengths, beliefs, rituals, and other unique aspects of the family's life. The therapist acknowledges that all families have difficulties at one time or another but that families also share positive moments. As the family describes a positive camping experience, Richard's Nintendo expertise, or Joan's conscientious caretaking of the family pet, the therapist verbally confirms and underscores these nonproblematic areas. Confirming strengths creates a feeling of normalcy, enhances self-esteem, and strengthens the therapeutic relationship with each individual and the family as a unit. Confirmation of each individual's strengths has added power when it occurs in the presence of other family members. It should be emphasized that confirmation of strengths is not confined to the beginning phase of treatment but is an ongoing process throughout the therapy. The therapist conveys an attitude that he or she understands the family and its members and is working with them and for them. Without a caring, collaborative relationship based on mutual respect and accountability, assessment and therapy cannot proceed effectively.

Some families require several sessions devoted exclusively to this process of developing mutual trust and a collaborative relationship with the therapist. In one instance, at an initial visit with an isolated rural family, the therapist was met by the mother at the end of a long driveway leading to the family's home. Rolling down her car window, the therapist exchanged pleasantries about the weather with the mother. After several minutes the mother said good-bye and walked back to her home. The therapist made two more visits, each conversation with the mother occurring further up the driveway toward the house. Finally, at the third visit the mother invited the therapist into her home to meet her son and husband. In forming a relationship with this family, it was important to have the mother control access to her family until she felt safe with the therapist—despite the one-hour round-trip travel time per visit!

Clarification of Areas of Concern

The second phase of the assessment process addresses the specific concerns that each family member has about the presenting situation, leading to identification of treatment goals, objectives, and desired outcomes. Here the issues that necessitated in-home services are contextualized by the therapist in relation to the family's current and past stresses and familial and extrafamilial relationships. Assessment includes understanding the identified child's strengths, symptoms, and behaviors within the family, peer group, school, and community.

In conducting this phase of assessment, the therapist asks each family member about areas of change that would make family life better for him or her and what he or she would be willing to do to support such a change. Family members are also asked to identify specific indicators of these positive changes. While family members usually focus on changes they want to see in the child or adolescent who is at risk of placement, this type of open, general inquiry about family life and relationships allows for additional information to emerge that may be germane to the presenting concern. An example:

THERAPIST   Mrs. Jones, what changes would you like to see in the family that would make a difference for you?

MRS. JONES   I'd like John [identified patient] to listen to me when I tell him to do something.

THERAPIST   What could you do that would make it easier for John to listen to you? How would you recognize that he was listening to you? If he did listen to you, what could you do to let him know how pleased you were?

* * *

THERAPIST   [*turning to John*] John, as the oldest boy in the family, what changes do you want to occur?

JOHN   I'd like my Mom to stop treating me like a four-year-old.

THERAPIST   John, what could you do so that your mother would treat you like a teenager? What would be the ways you would know if your mother treated you like a teenager? If your mom treated you like a teenager, what could you do to show her your appreciation?

* * *

THERAPIST   [*turning to the other sibling*] Susan, what changes would
you like to see in the family that would make a difference
to you?

SUSAN   Every time Dad drinks, Mom and John argue—which gives
me a headache. If Dad wouldn't drink, maybe the fighting
would stop.

While the initial questions to Mother and John focused on the
complementarity between these two family members, the question
to Susan expanded the problem definition to include father as a
third member in a problematic family pattern.

Continuing inquiry into the specific concerns existing among
family members should examine the onset and duration of these
concerns, as well as the content and process sequences in the family
relationships at the time the problem(s) occur(s). Ways of uncover-
ing these sequences include questions regarding *who* says *what* to
whom when, and *who* does *what* with *whom when*. For example,
the therapist might inquire: "Mrs. Jones, when do you and John
argue? What is Mr. Jones doing or saying at these times? What is
Susan doing or saying?" The therapist should also inquire about
the content and process sequences in family relationships when
problems are *not* occurring. For example, the therapist might ask:
"Mrs. Jones, when you and John are *not* arguing—when you are
getting along well—what are you saying or doing? What is John
saying or doing? What is Mr. Jones saying or doing? What is Susan
saying or doing?"

Mapping the Family's Structure

While asking family members about their relationships, the therapist also observes the family's preferred patterns of relating:
hierarchical characteristics, boundary functioning, and emotional
connections. The therapist assesses the relationship between the
youth's presenting concerns and the organization of family relationships along the dimensions of power, proximity/distance, and
affective expression. Specific questions to be answered in the assessment include:

Hierarchy and power

- Who is in charge of what in the family?
- Who has to ask permission of whom and about what?
- Who supports or undermines this executive hierarchy?
- What is the parenting philosophy and the range of parenting skills?
- What are the rules of the house and the consequences if rules are disobeyed?

Boundary functioning

- Who is close to, or in conflict with, whom and around what issues or situations?
- What is the nature of the relationships between the family and extrafamilial resources?
- What cultural beliefs are operating in the family?
- Is the family organized as a nuclear or extended system?

Affective relationships

- To what degree are family members emotionally connected to, or disengaged from, each other? Is the degree of emotional connection appropriate to each individual's developmental needs?

As the therapist observes repetitive behavioral sequences among family members, three structural maps emerge (Figure 4.1) depicting the family's unique patterns of organization with regard to (1) *hierarchy and power* (inversions and cross-generational coalitions), (2) *boundary functioning* (alliances, coalitions, and conflicts); and, (3) *affective relationships* (emotional closeness and distance). In a family with a symptomatic child, one or more of these patterns inevitably will be nonadaptive. Therefore, while the therapist will follow the content of the family by responding to the family's own treatment objectives, he/she will also intervene to alter family patterns and support effective family solutions to the presenting situation.

Figure 4.1
STRUCTURAL MAPS OF THE "G." FAMILY

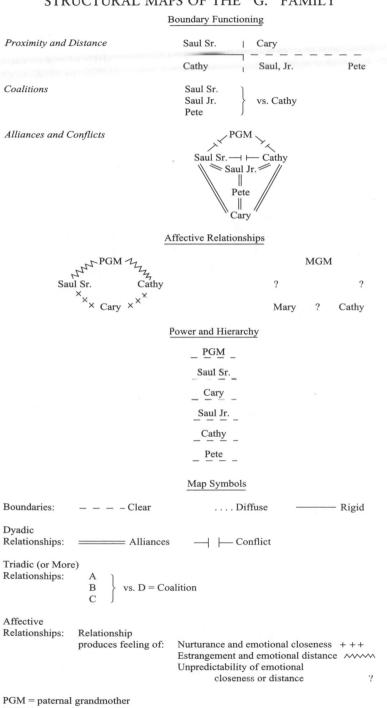

Boundary Functioning

Proximity and Distance

Saul Sr. | Cary

Cathy | Saul, Jr.   Pete

Coalitions

Saul Sr.
Saul Jr. } vs. Cathy
Pete

Alliances and Conflicts

Affective Relationships

MGM

Saul Sr.   Cathy   ?   ?

Cary   Mary   ?   Cathy

Power and Hierarchy

PGM

Saul Sr.

Cary

Saul Jr.

Cathy

Pete

Map Symbols

Boundaries: – – – – Clear   . . . . Diffuse   ——— Rigid

Dyadic
Relationships: ═══════ Alliances   —| |— Conflict

Triadic (or More)
Relationships: A
           B } vs. D = Coalition
           C

Affective
Relationships: Relationship
               produces feeling of: Nurturance and emotional closeness   + + +
                                Estrangement and emotional distance ⌇⌇⌇⌇
                                Unpredictability of emotional
                                     closeness or distance   ?

PGM = paternal grandmother
MGM = maternal grandmother

Creating Eco-Maps

After ascertaining the family's functioning, the therapist explores the family's interactions with social services, support services, and other extrafamilial supports or stressors, creating "eco-maps" of these extrafamilial relationships (Figures 4.2 and 4.3). Critical assessment questions include: What kinds of resources does this family have available to it during troubled times? How has the family managed to use these resources to make difficult situations better? What does the family report about their relationships with formal service helpers, such as school personnel, child welfare workers, physicians, other mental health helpers, probation officers, etc.? What supports or stressors does the family have related to jobs, finances, legal or political issues, safety, housing, day care, advocacy, information and referral, education and training, support groups, community programs, in-home and out-of-home respite, transportation, health, tangible goods, recreation or ethnicity? What other supports do family members rely on (neighbors, friends, work or school peers, extended family, community or spiritual leaders)?

Eco-maps can be developed that highlight the positive, negative, and/or neutral relationships between family members and extrafamilial resources. Seeing their social network diagrammed in black and white can help many families identify sources of support that could be strengthened and sources of stress in need of attention.

Additionally, the therapist should explore the family's past attempts to resolve problems with the help of outside systems and determine which interventions and services were effective, which ones had no effect, and which tended to aggravate or escalate the problematic situation. Questions focused on the present flush out stress created by current problem(s), environmental conditions, economic pressures, etc. Examples of these questions could include: How do you feel about applying for medical assistance so that your daughter's hospitalization is reimbursed? How has being evicted from your apartment affected you as a parent? Do you feel your child welfare caseworker has been helpful to you during this difficult time? Future-oriented questions underscore the therapist's belief in the family's problem-solving capacities and in members' wisdom regarding their own best solutions. Sample questions in-

Figure 4.2
SOCIAL SERVICES ECO-MAP OF THE "G." FAMILY

Eco-map symbols: + = positive relationship with agency or agency
worker
   − = negative relationship with agency or agency
worker
   ± = ambivalent relationship with agency or agency
worker
   * = possible service to explore

Child Welfare
− Saul Sr. investigated by child
  protection worker (1986)

Education
+ Cathy (10th grade, public school)
− Saul Jr. (8th grade, public school)
+ Pete (special school)

Juvenile Justice
  No involvement

Medical
+ Pete (Children's Hospital)

Developmental Disabilities
+ Cary and Pete (special educa
  tional services for Pete)

Drug and Alcohol
  No involvement or referral
* Saul Sr.'s bingeing overnights
  and weekends (1993)
* Cathy began excessive drinking
  (1993)

Mental Health

Outpatient Services
      + Cathy sees a therapist at the NT Agency (1996)
Crisis Services
      + Cathy's suicide attempt was evaluated by a crisis worker at
        PGH for referral to inpatient services (September, 1997)
Inpatient Services
      + Mary was hospitalized at RU (1993)
        Cathy was hospitalized at HC (September, 1997)
      + Cathy's relationship to therapist
      − Saul Sr.'s relationship to therapist
Mental Health In-home Services
      + Following discharge from inpatient, family was referred for
        in-home services (October, 1997)

Figure 4.3
SUPPORT SERVICES ECO-MAP OF THE "G." FAMILY

Ethnic Supports
Family is German;
no involvement with
ethnic organizations

Politics
No involvement

Religion
Family members are Lutheran;
no church involvement

Job
–Saul Sr. has been laid off from
  office management (1993)
–Cary works a 13–16 hour day
  both as a secretary and a
  waitress

Housing
Saul Sr. owns the attractive
three-bedroom home housing
the family

$ Support
–Saul Sr. remains on welfare in
  order to pay for Cathy's
  hospitalization and mental
  health services
–Cary's salary supports the
  family

Neighborhood
Family has just moved to a new
middle-class neighborhood
–Saul Sr. feels estranged from
  neighbors because of his
  unemployment

Legal
No involvement

Transportation
Both Saul Sr. and Cary own cars

Recreation
+Saul Jr. belongs to a wrestling
  club
–Cary and Saul Sr. rarely engage
  in social activity outside the
  home
–There have been no "family
  activities" for the past year

Friends
+Cathy has many good friends
–Cathy's boyfriend has a temper
  and damaged a neighbor's
  fence
+Saul Sr. has several male
  friends
–Cary has no time to see her
  friends
+Saul Jr. has good friends
+Pete has friends in his
  specialized school placement
  and in the neighborhood

clude: How do you as a family envision the future? How can I best work with you in the coming weeks? Which of the in-home services offered by our program would best meet your needs? What other services would be helpful?

These eco-maps help the therapist to generate systemic hypotheses about the meaning of symptomatic behaviors within the family, significant clinical themes, relationship patterns that need to be changed or supported, and directions for treatment.

Genograms

As an assessment tool the genogram serves as an efficient way to gain an overview of family relationships at a particular point in time. Resembling a family tree, a genogram records some of the important "whats" of family life: births, deaths, cohabitations, marriages, separations, divorces, medical and emotional illnesses, and other significant events (Figure 4.4). The genogram also provides the "whens"—the dates of these significant events. The "whos" identified by a genogram refer to all biological, legally sanctioned, and cohabitational relationships across generations (Carter & McGoldrick, 1988). Generally, a three-generational genogram is sufficient for in-home assessment. The "whys" of individual and family living, however, are more clearly revealed in the structural map of daily family life interactions, whereby affective concerns, boundary problems, reverse hierarchies, and other relational patterns become evident.

Family Timelines

Although dates of some major family events are included in the standard genogram format, it does not depict the *sequences* of events or patterns. Using only the genogram, there is no way to answer the question "Why *now*?" in relation to the onset of problems or the family's decision to enter treatment. A chronological sequencing of critical life events and problems that have had an impact on the individuals in a three-generational family allows the therapist to form hypotheses about the "coincidental" timing and interrelationships of life events and clinical problems (Figure 4.5). The critical life events that are important for in-home assessment

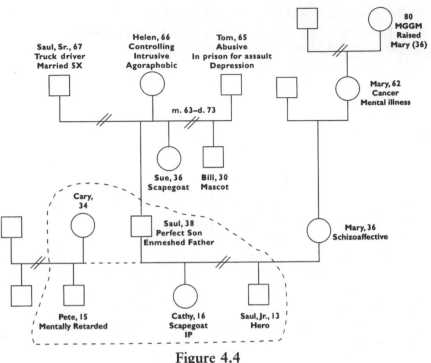

Figure 4.4
"G." FAMILY GENOGRAM

include: births, adoptions, cohabitations, marriages, separations, divorces, deaths, medical or emotional traumas; changes in family finances, residences (home and out-of-home placements), schools, jobs; emergence of symptoms, decisions to seek outside help or terminate helpers, starting or stopping psychotropic medications, hospitalizations, and so on. All of these events on the family's timeline become part of the stories told to the therapist.

According to DiNicola (1997), "Cultural family therapy is an interweaving of stories (family predicaments expressed in the narrative of family life) and tools (clinical methods of working with and making sense of these stories in cultural context). By interweaving stories and tools, cultural family therapy is aimed at understanding *and* change" (p. 5). When cultural sources of stress and/or developmental transitions occur at the same time, the problems in families may be compounded.

Figure 4.5
THE "G." FAMILY TIMELINE

9/59	Saul (father) born.	
8/61	Mary (mother) born.	
1962	Saul's father (Saul, Sr.) walks out on family.	
1969	Saul's mother (Helen) remarries Tom while he is in prison.	
	Saul witnesses mom being strangled by stepfather and discovers Tom bleeding after a subsequent suicide attempt.	
1977	Saul leaves home.	
3/8/81	Saul and Mary marry.	
10/81	Cathy born.	
1981	Saul started working with the "tugs" 7 days a week.	
9/84	Saulie (Saul, Jr.) born.	IP-3 yrs.
1986	Saul "fondles" Cathy; reported to child welfare.	IP-5 yrs.
1987 1990	Saul and Mary separate and reconcile four times.	IP-6–9 yrs.
	Children baby-sat by a succession of teenagers; mom working three jobs.	
1991	Mary starts showing signs of mental health problems.	IP-10 yrs.
	Children baby-sat by aunt.	
1993	Saul and Mary separate for the last time and divorce.	IP-12 yrs.
	Mary hospitalized for mental health problems.	
	Children move in with MGF and mother.	
	Children move with mother and MGF to a nearby state.	
	Saul lost job on "tugs."	
	Children go live with Saul.	
	Saul receives training in office management.	
	Saul laid off from management job.	
	Cathy starts "drinking like crazy."	
	Saul "bingeing" overnights and weekends.	
	Cathy takes over the mother role in the family.	
	Saul reads Cathy's diary and jokes about it with Saulie in front of Cathy	

continued

Figure 4.5
continued

1995	Cathy moves in with MGM after fist fight with Dad.	IP-14 yrs.
	Cathy has her first sexual experience.	
	Cathy begs Dad to return home.	
1996	Cathy returns to live with Dad.	IP-15 yrs.
	Cathy begins seeing an outpatient therapist. Saul begins a relationship with Cary who moves into the home with her 15-year-old son.	
9/97	Cathy is hospitalized after an altercation with father that left her feeling abandoned and suicidal; she overdosed and was referred to inpatient services by the crisis unit.	
10/97	Home-based services begin, following a smooth transfer meeting with the family and inpatient therapist.	

For example, a 17-year-old teenager from a Jewish family, whose parents were Holocaust survivors, was suddenly hospitalized in a medical setting due to severe bone pain. Despite orthopedic surgery, the pain continued and no organic cause could be determined. Initially, the surgeon considered referring the youth to an inpatient psychiatric unit, but the family's doctor interceded and recommended home-based services. The pain prevented the teenager from attending school or accessing outpatient services. The boy's story revealed that during the past year he had begun exploring sexual intimacy with a new girlfriend with a Christian background, in spite of his mother's and maternal grandmother's anguish. Both women had been excessively involved with every aspect of the boy's life since birth and reported feeling that the boy had betrayed them. The therapist's clinical hypothesis, gleaned both from the family's stories and his observations of the family's interactions, was that the bone pain symbolize the boy's psychic struggle to separate from his family and their values (expressed in his selection of a Christian girlfriend) and yet remain loyal to his family's legacy of suffering.

By examining the ages of family members relative to significant life events, the therapist can gain an appreciation of the concomitant developmental impact on individual family members and the family as a whole. Additionally, changes in the family's structure due to life events are revealed through the timeline, as are probability patterns suggesting how changes in family structure may influence future events. Spouses in second or third marriages, for example, can reasonably anticipate additional stress around family graduations or weddings, when former spouses and their new partners and children may expect to play a significant role in the gathering. Critical to hypothesis-testing is noting the correlations between the timing of external and/or internal stressful events, changes in family structure, and the evolution of clinical symptoms.

Using the Tools

Developing both the genogram and the timeline in a family session can serve the dual function of assessing the family's current functioning and making a therapeutic intervention. These methods of assessment are introduced to the family as ways of better understanding their experiences. Gathering information for the genogram is presented as a family activity involving all members. Spreading chart-sized paper on the kitchen or dining-room table and asking family members to help put together a "family tree" can create a feeling of family unity. Most children and adolescents, and sometimes even spouses or cohabiting partners, have never heard the family history. While the genogram is being drawn, the other team member (if there is one) or the oldest child is given a legal pad and asked to create a chronological timeline of dates given on the genogram. After the genogram is completed, the therapist completes the chronology of critical life events by having family members tell their life stories, beginning with the parents' births and continuing to the present. Children can be engaged in this process by having them identify family events that hold particular significance for them, such as the time they adopted a puppy or traveled to the seashore together.

How much sensitive information to elicit for the genogram and timeline can only be determined by observing the reactions of the adult caregivers. If a caregiver appears uncomfortable, confused, or reluctant about providing information, the therapist should not push for more detail but express appreciation for whatever information has been provided. As treatment with the family continues, additional information will no doubt emerge and can then be added. Using these assessment methods to engender a more informed and compassionate relationship with the family is more important than gathering of specific facts. The attitude of the in-home therapist should be one of authentic, personal, sympathetic interest in the family's story, not that of a dispassionate interviewer.

Families sometimes see for themselves the interrelationships between life-cycle events and the onset of problems. This awareness often serves to normalize the family's experiences. Understanding the cyclic patterns of their symptoms or problems can help families realize what they *can* do to change the present or future and thereby break the cycle. For therapists, tracking the cyclic pattern helps them stay focused on the important themes that need to be kept in the treatment foreground. This is particularly the case in crisis-prone families, where compelling emergencies routinely threaten to distract the therapist from the relevant clinical task. Once the family is familiar with the structure for organizing significant information, a similar timeline inventory can be used to track and celebrate the family's progress in meeting stated goals and objectives within a given time frame (Stanton, 1992).

Reframing

The ultimate goal of assessment is to elicit a feeling of hope that problematic behavior can be diminished or, ideally, eradicated. Families usually come to treatment focused on the problematic behavior of one family member (e.g., aggressive David, underachieving Mark, depressed Susan). Sometimes families perceive their years of accumulated experiences with a troubled child as a series of repetitive failures—a perception that tends to narrow their flexibility in implementing alternative responses to the child. Part of the assessment process is discovering alternative ways family members can respond to the presenting situation. This is not to minimize the very real challenges parents face when dealing with children with severe emotional disturbances or neurological impairments. Accepting and validating the family's reality is, in fact, paramount to the therapeutic process. The child's symptoms, which are the reason the family is seeking help, need to be directly acknowledged.

When family members are provided with alternative ways of thinking and behaving, new solutions become possible. Family therapy interventions can include *reframing* and *enactments*. Reframing expands the family's cognitive frame of reference, and enactment interventions direct the child and parent on how to interact differently with each other (Minuchin & Fishman, 1981).

The first step in creating a solvable problem definition is to either *depersonalize* the problem or *restate* it in terms of familial or extrafamilial transactions that are resources for change. For example, the therapist shifts the definition of the problem from the troubled child—"aggressive David"—to either describing an interactional process—"David becomes aggressive when his mother withdraws from him"—or depersonalizing the problem so that *David* is not the problem—"David's aggression is heightened when his medication dosage is not sufficient"—or both—"David becomes aggressive when his mother withdraws from him *and* the medication dosage is not sufficient." Here the presenting concern regarding David's aggression is not ignored, but its meaning is reframed for the family as having its own legitimacy within a given set of circumstances. It then becomes solvable by changing those circumstances.

Using reframing, the therapist gives emphasis to information that is not normally emphasized by family members (Jones, 1986). Reframing means "to change the conceptual and/or emotional setting or viewpoint about which a situation is experienced and to place it in another frame which fits the facts of the same concrete situation equally well or even better, and thereby changes its entire meaning" (Watzlawick, Weakland, & Fisch, 1974, p. 95). Sometimes the symptomatic behavior expresses in metaphor the relationships in the family or the concerns of the symptomatic person. Reframing addresses questions regarding *who* is being helped or protected by the person with the presenting problem and *what* that person is being protected from. There are instances when symptomatic behavior provides interpersonal gains for both the troubled child and the family.

While reframing expands a family's conceptual perception of the problem, the therapist's creation of new patterns of interaction between family members, termed *enactments* (Minuchin & Fishman, 1981), focuses on the family's immediate relationship experiences. Enactments enable family members to experience directly their ongoing interpersonal processes with one another. Enactments can be used to diagnose as well as to alter family patterns. When enactment is used for assessment purposes, the therapist is decentralized, so that he or she can be "in a position to observe the family members' verbal and nonverbal ways of signaling to each other and monitoring the range of tolerable transactions" (Minuchin & Fishman, 1981, p. 79). The therapist's observation of enactments can help to confirm or disconfirm his or her hypothoses about problematic transactional patterns in the family. Here the therapist recreates the pushes and pulls of the family dance that relate to the presenting problem.

For example, a father tells the therapist that he and his 10-year-old son do not communicate. Mother says that communication with her son is not a problem. The therapist invites the father to talk to his son about their communication difficulties as the therapist and mother observe. As father and son attempt to talk to each other, the therapist observes what *each* family member—father, son, and mother—does to help or hinder the communication process between father and son. In this example, the therapist observes that the son is slow to respond to his father because he continually looks to his mother for cues that may indicate her approval or disapproval.

Following such assessment, the therapist can also use enactments as interventions to help family members create and experience more positive, productive ways of interacting. These new interpersonal experiences can be used both to expand the family members' view of the problem and to widen their repertoire of flexible responses and solutions. There is a variety of ways a therapist may choose "to elicit the enactment via a frame that invites and motivates the family" to try something different. It is the family [however] that effects and presides over this search for alternatives (Simon, 1995, p. 19). The therapist in the above case example uses a frame of challenge through humor to invite the mother and son to change their behaviors. He says, "Mother, your son seems to be using you as his 'seeing-eye dog.' Do you think he is old enough to use his own eyes to figure out how to talk to Dad?" Here the therapist is assuming that the family has the competency to change an outdated structure (i.e., son can only "know" father through mother's eyes) and create a new one (i.e., a 10-year-old boy can establish his own relationship with father).

Often reframing and enactment are used together, as in the next case example. Returning home from working a night shift, Ms. Jones appeared physically exhausted and totally unresponsive to her four-year-old, whose unsuccessful attempts to engage her mother eventually escalated into a full-blown tantrum. This was a typical pattern in their daily routine. The therapist reframed the child's attention-seeking efforts as her "immature" way of trying to get Mother's mind off her problems at work. An enactment was suggested wherein mother and child would cuddle on the couch and watch television together, allowing them *both* to relax.

Creating solvable problem definitions helps the therapist begin to identify who in the immediate family, extended family, or an outside system might be most effective as a resource and suggests an outline of the stages in which treatment will proceed. Treatment usually begins with those family members living in the home and, when clinically appropriate, expands to include family members living outside the home as well as helpers from both natural and formal support systems.

This process can be seen in the following case example (this is the same family depicted in Figures 4.1–4.4). The problem that prompted the "G" family's referral to home-based services was 16-year-old Cathy's continuing to share suicidal thoughts with her father, Saul, Sr., and his partner, Cary, despite a recent three-week inpatient hospitalization. During the initial home visit, the therapist elicited Cathy's story about the changes that had occurred in the family since Cathy was six years old. From age six to nine her parents separated and reconciled four times. They finally separated when she was 12. Following the separation, mother's depression led to a psychiatric hospitalization and Cathy lived briefly with her maternal grandmother. Subsequently, Cathy and her younger brother, Saul, Jr., began to live with father and Cathy took over her mother's role in the family. At 14 years, Cathy and her father began having conflicts and Cathy again moved in with her maternal grandmother. Six months later Cathy returned to father's household and their relationship stabilized until father's partner, Cary, began living in the home. An argument with father precipitated the suicide attempt that resulted in Cathy's hospitalization.

As Cathy shared her story, the therapist observed the family's interactional patterns. Saul, Jr., and Pete, Cary's son, sat on chairs by the couch, where Cathy sat next to Cary. Father sat on the opposite side of the room. Cary appeared to be supportive and held Cathy's hand while she talked. Cathy, however, kept looking over at her father, as if seeking reassurance. Father kept his gaze on the floor and seemed not to know what to do or say.

The therapist's hypothesis was that Cathy felt displaced by Cary in her relationship to father and did not know how to bridge the gap between them. To create a solvable problem definition, the therapist first reframed Cathy's "suicidal thinking" as "deep longing for reconnection with father." Increasing the intensity of her own affect, the therapist then directed an enactment wherein father was seated next to Cathy, given her hand to hold, and told that he must convince Cathy how important she was to him— that she must live because he could not exist in a world without her.

As father attempted to reach out to his daughter, the therapist encouraged him and gently challenged Cathy to trust her father's love for her. While father and Cathy reconnected, the therapist observed Cary's, Pete's, and Saul, Jr.'s reactions. All appeared to support the emerging change in the father-daughter relationship.

Now that a solvable problem had been defined with the family, the therapist proceeded to develop a tentative outline of initial treatment goals. These would include: first, putting father in charge of developing a no-harm contract between Cathy and the adults (father, Cary, and therapist); second, continuing the proximity between father and Cathy until the two could communicate appropriately as father and teenage daughter; and third, increasing connectedness between Cathy, Cary, Saul, Jr., and Pete, so that Cathy would feel that she had a place in the family.

CROSS-SYSTEMS COLLABORATION
AND TREATMENT PLANNING

Building a Knowledge Base

Many families served by mental health home-based services are involved with multiple service systems. Before beginning the process of cross-systems collaboration and treatment planning, the in-home therapist needs to have knowledge about the dynamics of these systems and clarity regarding his or her role in relation to them. The major systems encountered in home-based work are education, child welfare, juvenile justice, mental retardation, and other mental health or drug and alcohol services, such as inpatient psychiatric facilities, day treatment programs, and residential treatment facilities. All of these systems have more power when it comes to decision-making regarding the identified patient than the home-based therapist: Child welfare can remove children from their families; juvenile justice can remove youth from their families and community; schools can suspend or expel youth from their educational communities; psychiatric hospitals, residential treatment centers, and day treatment programs can exclude home-based therapists and families from their treatment decisions and processes (Schwartzman, 1985). The only way for the in-home therapist to gain power is to form a collaborative relationship with helpers from these institutions or programs and elicit an agreement to work *together* on the family's behalf.

Being knowledgable about each institution's culture will facilitate this relationship-building. It is important for the home-based therapist to understand the differing concerns and predictable responses to problematic youth by the different service systems. Education, juvenile justice, child welfare, and nonfamily-centered psychiatric or substance abuse inpatient units, day treatment programs, and residential facilities are primarily concerned with individual children and youth, not with their families. *How* the youth is functioning is the focal concern of mental health, education, and drug and alcohol systems. *What* the youth has done to the family or community is the concern of juvenile justice. What the parent(s) has done to the youth is the concern of child welfare (Dore, 1991a).

The predictable responses of educators to children with severe problems is to evaluate and refer them to a more appropriate educational placement within or away from the school, or to refer them to mental health, child welfare, or juvenile justice services. Traditionally, the mental health and drug and alcohol systems treat youngsters in outpatient, day treatment, inpatient, or residential facilities. Before the advent of family preservation programs, child welfare's typical response was to place a child in foster care or residential placement. Similarly, the juvenile justice system generally removes youth from their families and communities through incarceration or mandates community treatment via the mental health and child welfare systems (Dore, 1991a). Rather than being critical of systems that don't address the needs of both family and child or don't advocate keeping families together, home-based workers need to appreciate that other helpers are equally concerned about accomplishing their clients' goals and often have resources that can be effectively used in collaborative treatment planning.

Conflicts and Triangulations

Ideally, all families should be served by healthy service delivery systems. Like a well-functioning family, a healthy service system would have explicit role definitions and clear boundaries around these roles. Communication would be direct, clear, and regular in occurrence. Flexibility and timely, adaptive responses to change would be apparent. Compassionate leadership would guide decision-making—not hierarchical power plays. Regrettably, the child service systems frequently replicate both functional and dysfunctional patterns in their interactions with each other and with the children and families they serve. Often inadequate communication among providers promotes redundancy of services and/or poor coordination and discontinuity in care. "Burned-out" providers may convey unresponsiveness or disorganization in service delivery to clients who already feel overstressed and disenfranchised. Divergent goals (family togetherness versus child rescue and placement) create varying degrees of triangulation among helpers, who in turn direct or support the client toward differing, often conflicting, goals. The triangulation of service helpers not only effectively reduces the possibilities for change but, in effect, supports the family's original nonadaptive patterns (Compher, 1989).

It is a well-established axiom in family systems practice that when a family's relationship to an agency is stressful and therefore unstable, another agency may be triangulated in to diffuse the conflict (Carl & Jurkovic, 1983). Home-based therapists should be aware of the common triangles that form. A typical triangle involving the education system, mental health, and the family occurs in the following way: A child has problems with learning, peers, or teachers but is well behaved at home. Both parents and therapist blame the school for the child's difficulties, while school personnel define the problem as the parents' ineffectiveness with the child and the therapist's ineffective treatment of the parents.

Child welfare and mental health agencies and families who are mandated for treatment form another common triangular pattern. A typical scenario: The child welfare worker is considering placing a child to protect him from mother's explosive outbursts; she views mother as an angry, uncaring parent. The mental health therapist views mother as a caring parent who is uncertain about how to handle her hyperactive child and whose depression triggers her volatile behaviors. The child welfare worker feels the therapist is too "soft," and the therapist feels the worker is too "hard." The mother experiences varying degrees of triangulation by the two professionals because of their divergent views.

Another type of triangulation occurs when, for example, a juvenile justice agency cautions a probation officer to keep tabs on an out-of-control delinquent with ineffective parents, the mental health therapist works to empower parental authority, and the youth doesn't know whom to listen to—the probation officer or the parents.

The home-based therapist needs to recognize when he or she has been "inducted" into unwittingly participating in one of these common triangles. The quickest way out of the dilemma is to add a fourth person. The therapist's supervisor or the program's consultant can be this fourth person, providing a neutral perspective regarding the therapist's position in relation to the family and other service systems. An example: A home-based trainee presented a case to her trainer involving an intellectually challenged single mother with a three-year-old developmentally disabled child. The more the child welfare worker insisted that the mother was incapable of providing for her child's needs, the more the therapist advocated on behalf of the mother. During frequent home visits, the therapist had observed many instances of effective parenting. In contrast, during the child welfare worker's home visits, the mother appeared ill at ease and, consequently, ineffective with her child. The trainer suggested that the child welfare worker and therapist form a collaborative alliance and jointly make a decision that would be in the best interests of the child. Based on a mutual agreement, they made several home visits together to assess the mother's capabilities. Once the mother saw that the two professionals were united in their concern for her child, she was able to be open about how she saw her child's needs and to ask their advice about obtaining special resources for her child. The child welfare worker was impressed by the mother's keen awareness of her child's needs, and the therapist learned more about the complexities confronting the mother in raising a developmentally disabled child.

MULTISYSTEM TREATMENT PLANNING MEETINGS

Preparing Families and Professionals

When families are receiving services from two or more agencies, service providers must collaborate in treatment planning to guarantee that services are complementary. By teaming with other professionals and natural helpers available to the family, the home-based therapist can ensure that services are coordinated, resources pooled, and creative treatment plans developed that best serve the unique needs of a given child and family. Pre-planning with the family and other meeting attendees is crucial to the effectiveness of the multisystem meeting. The home-based therapist's assessment and treatment planning with the family will result in a plan that requires resources and responsiveness from other helpers. The purpose of the multisystem meeting is to produce service decisions and plans of action.

Participating as equal partners with agency professionals in such a meeting may be difficult for some families. In preparing caregivers, it is often helpful to have them articulate clearly what they want for themselves and their child as well as the rationale for their requests (Jones, 1992). When developmentally and functionally appropriate, the identified patient should also be coached to advocate for his or her needs. Role-play can then be used, in which the caregivers and identified patient practice their "parts" in the anticipated meeting.

The home-based therapist also needs to establish a relationship with the other agencies' helpers, particularly since the therapist may function as a family advocate as well as a mediator between the family and the professional systems represented at the meeting. In advocating on behalf of the family, the therapist can make small requests of the other professionals prior to the meeting. For example, to help ease a timid mother, the therapist might ask a male professional to speak softly and let the mother know he wants to hear her opinion at the time of the meeting. In the case of a noncustodial parent who has frequently been left out of school meetings concerning his or her child's behavior, the therapist might ask the principal to personally greet the parent and emphasize how grateful the school is for the parent's willingness to participate in finding solutions to the child's difficulties.

In situations where there has been a history of defensive posturing in the relationships between the caregivers and certain professionals, the home-based therapist has the dual role of family advocate and systems mediator. Before bringing the family and professionals together, the therapist must engage in relationship-building and coaching with both groups to reduce the level of defensiveness.

For example, overwhelmed parents with two young children with hemophilia encountered resistance from the children's hospital hematology staff, whose negative history with the parents led them to believe that the parents would bully home care staff and not comply with their suggestions. The parents' request for medical home care was denied by the hospital, despite the importance of this service in reducing the stress of frequent emergency visits to the hospital. Every encounter between parents and hospital staff resulted in stalemate and defensiveness on both parts. In preparing for the treatment planning meeting, the home-based therapist carefully coached the parents to acknowledge at the meeting how their feelings of stress caused them to become defensive. They were also encouraged to share with the hospital staff how much they needed and appreciated the staff's expertise. They practiced specifically explaining how the medical home care would reduce their stress level. The mother developed techniques to cue her husband to short-circuit his defensive outbursts of anger. In addition, the therapist met with the physician and nurses to help them understand the parents' concern for their children and how many difficult issues the family was dealing with, including the grandmother's cancer. The physician and nurses were asked if they would greet the parents with a smile at the beginning of the meeting and allow the parents to speak first. The coaching of both the medical staff and the parents resulted in a successful meeting and the family received the needed home care.

Guidelines for Conducting Multisystem
Service Planning Meetings

While the above example describes a treatment planning meeting between three systems (family, mental health home-based therapist, and medical professionals), many families receiving in-home services have a large number of helpers. For example, attendees at one multisystem meeting numbered 20! In such complex cases, it is advisable to utilize meeting guidelines (Meehan, 1994) that emphasize who should participate, what agenda and ground rules should be followed, and what questions should be addressed in the written service plan.

Pre-meeting relationship-building should occur with all participants. If attendees feel they have an ally who understands them and they know what to expect, the anxiety about participating in a multisystem meeting is reduced. Before holding a scheduled planning meeting, the participating family should sign a release of information form so that all pertinent information is available (see Appendix F). Additionally, attendance of providers needs to be confirmed and replacements obtained if key information-givers or decision-makers cannot attend.

Preferably, the scheduled meeting should last no longer than 90 minutes; the time may be adjusted based on the number of representatives from different systems. During the first 45 minutes, the following agenda is suggested: First, the home-based therapist asks participants to introduce themselves, explains the confidentiality statement, and obtains participants' signatures (see Appendix G). A statement is then given that supports all treatment team members in their efforts to successfully accomplish the dual purpose of the meeting: (1) to encourage the parent(s) and child to tell their story, describe their needs, share their vision of the future, and elicit the opinions of other helpers; and (2) to collaborate on the development of a service plan that will implement the family's goals. Ground rules are established regarding both the amount of time allotted to speakers and participants' questions and expected process rules, such as directing questions only to the most recent speaker, no interruptions, and keeping the focus on current issues rather than the family's lengthy history. A flip chart is used to list areas discussed during the meeting, such as goals, strengths, child and family issues, services currently received, future services to be delivered, and expected time frames.

The second part of the agenda during the first half of the meeting is to conduct a thorough discussion among all attendees of the strengths and resources of the child and family within their unique cultural context, as well as the strengths and resources of the family's community. Community resources include the natural resources available to the family, such as church, educational and recreational opportunities, civic activities and organizations, as well as interagency resources and relationships.

The third part of the agenda during the first half of the meeting focuses on a discussion of the current issues of the child and family. Meehan (1994) suggests using the term *issues* rather than *problems* or *difficulties* to underscore the strengths-based orientation as well as to respect the sensitivity of children, if present. It is important to include a discussion of the child's needs and goals using nonpathologizing language from recent psychiatric and/or psychological evaluations. If a child had a severe learning disability, for example, the psychologist would highlight the specific ways the child learned most effectively rather than flatly stating, "Howard has a severe learning disability." The primary speakers during this part of the meeting are those most knowledgeable about the child—usually the child's caregiver(s), the child, the home-based therapist, a teacher, and, if present, the psychiatrist or psychologist. Since these issues are the focal point in developing the service plan, it is important to have group consensus on them.

The goal of the second half of the planning meeting is to develop a written service plan that addresses the agreed-upon issues regarding the child's specific needs and proposes goals, objectives, and tasks to be accomplished in a specific time frame. After reviewing the services currently being delivered, group discussion focuses on service delivery gaps. The child and caregiver(s) are given the opportunity to suggest treatment approaches, solutions, and services they perceive to be needed. The resulting service plan should bridge any existing gaps in services and promote delivery of these services within the least restrictive setting, usually the child's home, school, or local community center. Table 4.1 presents a sample written plan, again applied to the "G." family.

EFFECTIVE TREATMENT PLANS

A comprehensive strengths-based assessment of the needs, concerns and desired outcomes for the child, family, and community is meaningless unless it leads to a well-developed treatment plan. Hodas (1995) has described the most common pitfalls in crafting treatment plans. Problems of language usage involve: confusion in maintaining a strengths-based language, using technical or "culturally incompetent" language rather than a family's language, and lacking clarity in describing and differentiating goals, objectives, and interventions. Problems of process include: neglecting to involve parent(s) and child in describing their needs and strengths so that the treatment plan is personalized and failing to clearly define the roles of family, mental health professionals, and other resource persons in treatment implementation. Funding sources may refuse to authorize or re-authorize home-based services because of inadequately prepared treatment plans. Therefore, it is essential that home-based staff possess effective skills in writing individualized treatment plans that clearly identify the family's stated needs and strengths, treatment goals, objectives, and interventions.

Table 4.1
MULTISYSTEM TREATMENT FOR THE "G." FAMILY

What services are needed?	1. Mental health home-based services • Family therapy: Mr. G., Ms. Cary S., Cathy, Saul, Jr., Pete • Family recreation (outside home): Mr. G., Ms. Cary S., Cathy, Saul, Jr., Pete • Crisis intervention: Family 2. Self-help groups • Alcoholics Anonymous: Mr. G. • Al-Anon: Ms. Cary S. • Al-Ateen: Cathy, Saul, Jr. 3. Job counseling: Mr. G. 4. School counseling: Saul, Jr. 5. Medication monitoring: Cathy
What services will be provided?	All of the above
Who will implement the service?	Home-based team
When and where will the services be delivered?	1. Family's home: 10/11/97–6/1/98 2. Community: 11/1/97–3/1/98 3. Child welfare agency: 11/1/97–3/1/98 4. Junior high school: 10/15/97–6/1/98 5. Psychiatrist's office: 10/2/97–Indefinite (Cathy and psychiatrist's decision)
Who is responsible for case management to ensure that agreed-upon services are delivered in a timely manner?	Home-based team
What are the child's specific responsibilities as an active agent of change?	Cathy will: • Make a genuine commitment to life • Engage in more private time with her father • Learn to talk about her feelings of anger and sadness • Plan and implement family activities that give her feelings of pleasure and connectedness to family members

continued

Table 4.1

continued

	• Participate in family therapy, family recreation, Al-Ateen, medication monitoring
What are the caregiver(s)'s responsibilities as an active agent of change?	Mr. G. will: • Monitor Cathy's safety at home • Spend private time with Cathy • Communicate with Cathy about her feelings of sadness and anger • Provide transportation for Cathy to appointments • Participate in family and couple therapy, family recreation, job counseling, and Alcoholics Anonymous Ms. Cary S. will: • Support Mr. G.'s efforts with Cathy • Provide transportation for Cathy to the video store weekly • Participate in family and couple therapy, family recreation, and Al-Anon
Who is responsible for overseeing whether progress occurs in achieving specified outcomes as a result of services being delivered?	Supervisor of the home-based team
What will be the lines of professional communication and supervision, and the role of the multisystem team (including the family) in the ongoing case management and monitoring process?	The home-based supervisor will meet biweekly with the team. The home-based team will: • meet weekly (as needed) with the family • communicate weekly with the child welfare worker and school counselor • communicate bimonthly with the psychiatrist The multisystem team will meet monthly.
When will the next multisystemic planning meeting be scheduled?	11/15/97

Identifying Goals and Objectives: A Case Example

At the outset of the comprehensive assessment of Cathy in the "G." family, her family clearly expressed their primary concern: "Cathy is at risk for returning to the inpatient unit due to her continuing talk about suicide to us." A major family strength was each member's commitment to address this concern. Treatment goals were then developed based on Cathy's and her family's stated needs and strengths. A treatment goal is a brief clinical statement of positive resolution regarding an individual's identified need or problem; it specifies an anticipated change in the person's functioning that will result from treatment. In this case, one essential treatment goal was identified.

Goal: Cathy will make a genuine commitment to life. Notice that the goal is stated in terms that indicate a positive outcome by demonstrating a new behavior, not simply a reduction in the frequency of a negative behavior. Note also the personal use of the patient's name, which emphasizes what *she* will accomplish as an outcome of treatment. Finally, the identification of only one goal is important, for it provides clarity with regard to expected outcome and conveys a realistic appreciation of the need to take "one step at a time." Also, treatment goals (unlike treatment objectives) do not require specification of target dates.

What individualizes any treatment plan, however, are the treatment objectives. Goldman (1990) defines a treatment objective as "the concrete representation of a clinical goal; the observable and measurable manifestations(s) of a treatment goal or the individual steps in the course of pursuing and achieving such goals" (p. 5). A clearly written treatment objective will allow the reader to imagine Cathy doing or saying something *specific*. Continuing with the above example, the following treatment objectives were developed in collaboration with the "G." family:

Objective 1: Cathy will sign a contract with her father (Mr. G.), Ms. Cary S. (her father's partner), and the home-based therapist (Ms. Jones) agreeing not to kill or harm herself.

Strengths: Cathy is motivated to change her outlook. Mr. G. is able to verbalize how strongly he wants Cathy to be safe and not harm herself. Ms. Cary S. genuinely cares about Cathy's well-being.

Treatment Interventions: Ms. Jones will conduct a family meeting wherein Mr. G. and Ms. Cary S. (as the responsible adults in the family) will draft a contract, which Cathy will sign. The contract will be witnessed by Ms. Jones, Mr. G., and Ms. Cary S. Ms. Jones will carefully assess the degree of suicidal risk and ascertain whether a psychiatric evaluation is indicated. She will also assess the commitment of the family to supervise Cathy and to call the in-home crisis service should any concerns arise.

Date Initiated: 10/1/97. Date Achieved: 10/1/97.

Objective 2: Mr. G. and Cathy will engage in more private time with each other.

Strengths: Mr. G. loves Cathy and is motivated to enhance her well-being. He is able to listen. Cathy wants to spend private time with her father because she feels there is too much emotional distance between them.

Treatment Interventions: Mr. G. will sit quietly with Cathy for 15 minutes four times daily. Ms. Jones will discuss what this experience was like for the two of them in a weekly treatment session. She will emphasize the importance of Cathy receiving appropriate attention from her father as an adolescent daughter, as well as confirm all instances of positive relationship-building between the father and daughter.

Date Initiated: 10/1/97. Date Achieved: 10/1/97, 10/8/97.

Objective 3: Cathy will learn to talk about her feelings of anger and sadness.

Strengths: Cathy has good verbal skills and demonstrates insight about what troubles her. Mr. G. has the ability to acknowledge Cathy's feelings.

Treatment Interventions: Cathy will verbalize at least one feeling of anger or sadness during each of the four 15-minute daily sessions with her father. Ms. Jones will facilitate a discussion between Mr. G. and Cathy about this intervention in a weekly treatment session. Within this discussion, Ms. Jones will affirm any attempts on Cathy's part to verbalize angry or sad feelings to her father and validate any of Mr. G.'s efforts to understand what Cathy has communicated to him.

Date Initiated: 10/1/97. Date Achieved: 10/30/97.

Objective 4: Cathy will plan and implement family activities that give her feelings of pleasure and connectedness to family members.

Strengths: Each family member has expressed commitment to being part of a plan to help Cathy.

Treatment Interventions: Ms. Cary S. will drive Cathy to the video store weekly so that Cathy can select a comedy video that family members (Mr. G., Ms. Cary S., Pete [Ms. Cary S.'s son], and Saul, Jr. [Cathy's brother]) will watch together. Cathy will describe her experience of the family activity experience to Ms. Jones in a weekly family therapy session with all family members present. In the session Ms. Jones will support Cathy's efforts to express herself, highlight all instances of positive support given by family members to Cathy and to each other, and validate all successes by the family in achieving a pleasurable activity.

Date Initiated: 10/14/97. Date Achieved: 10/16/97, 10/23/97, 10/30/97, 11/6/97.

These four individualized treatment objectives represent a beginning series of steps intended to lead to the attainment of the desired goal. Since the objectives and interventions are based on the family's strengths, they are attainable. The objectives are based upon observable behaviors that can be reported and measured within a specific time frame. *Assignments* and *tasks* are considered treatment interventions; they are the means to the end of realizing the treatment objectives. A well-constructed treatment *objective* always includes a reference to an anticipated change in the concerned individual's behavior. An *intervention* states how or what treatments the home-based therapist (or other helpers) will utilize to facilitate this change in behavior (Goldman, 1990). The *role responsibilities* (i.e., who will do what) of family members and the therapist should be clearly stated. Changes in the family's original pattern of relationships are likely to occur because family members have been partners in developing and endorsing the treatment plan. Indeed, each participant signs and dates the treatment plan. Legally, for children under the age of 14, parents must sign the plan; there is a legal obligation for children age 14 or older to sign the document themselves.

The case example described above focused on an initial primary goal for the "G." family. As any treatment plan proceeds, however, new goals and objectives are added. For example, in this case, not only did Saul and Cathy want to change the pattern of distance between them, but Saul also wanted to be in charge of the family rather than having his mother make family decisions. In addition, Saul and Cary wanted to have a relationship that was separate from their relationships with the children. All family members wanted to learn how to resolve conflict without scapegoating another family member.

Whatever new goals emerge during the course of treatment, Cathy's and her family's progress toward attaining each and every treatment objective are logged in the progress notes that are ongoing and cumulative—day to day, week to week, or month to month—depending on the intensity and duration of the home-based services. If progress has occurred, the effective interventions should be clearly stated. Similarly, the reasons for lack of progress need to be cited. Before each progress note, the letter of the goal and the number(s) of the objective(s) should be indicated to help monitor the treatment over time.

We have described the key elements of ecosystemic home-based practice needed by therapists. Now let us look at how clinicians use this knowledge to confront clinical challenges presented by families with children at risk.

CHAPTER 5

Clinical Challenges

Take time to listen
You can't help before you learn . . .
Listen to their story . . .
Yes, respect gives people courage
And respect shows that you care
And it all begins with listening
To the family sitting there

—Gordon R. Hodas, 1996b

EVEN THE MOST CHAOTIC FAMILIES are doing their best to make it. Underlying feelings of hopelessness, exhaustion, despair, guilt, and anger is the desire to stay together. In-home therapy requires the therapist to participate in the family's struggles and to help create experiences of negotiation, compromise, joy, and hope. Becoming a player in each family's drama exposes the therapist to the tragedies, traumas, successes, and day-to-day processes of "making it."

CORE CLINICAL COMPETENCIES OF HOME-BASED THERAPY

The treatment of families "off-site" rather than in an agency setting creates a unique therapeutic system, and requires refinement and expansion of therapeutic skills. Helping families co-create competence when confronted by internal and external chaos poses specific challenges to all family therapists.

Responding to these clinical challenges requires the therapist to master core clinical competences of home-based therapy, such as:

1. maintaining a systemic perspective
2. maintaining professional boundaries within a collaborative relationship
3. being effective on someone else's turf
4. making the most of crises
5. encouraging positive change and competence
6. assessing with complexity yet focusing treatment with simplicity

Maintaining a Systemic Perspective

The process of in-home therapy often requires sessions with "parts" of the family or the family and community rather than with the "whole" (i.e., entire family or community system session). *Maintaining a systemic perspective* encourages the therapist to continually ask the questions: Where am I in relation to each individual in the system at this point in time? For example, an individual session might be held with the mother at home in the morning while the children are at school. The husband and wife may be seen for a marital session at the home-based agency. A meeting with the teenager and his or her friends could occur at the local basketball court. Grandmother and therapist might schedule a session at school with the school counselor. Clinical competency in this complex context requires the therapist to maintain awareness of the "whole" while working with the "parts," always bearing in mind that what happens with one "part" will reverberate throughout the entire system. Being "unaware" can render the therapist vulnerable to triangulation. If a well-developed systemically focused treatment plan is followed, each session will have a specific focus that relates to the overall goals. Reactions by other family members or community helpers to what occurs in a "part" treatment session may be foreseen by the therapist or can provide feedback on how to alter future session objectives.

Maintaining Professional Boundaries within a Collaborative Relationship

Home-based therapists struggle continually with the challenge of *maintaining professional boundaries within a collaborative rela-*

tionship. Adhering to the following axiom may prove helpful in clearly delineating the expectations within a collaborative relationship:

The family is in charge of itself; the therapist is in charge of the therapy. Assuming responsibility for the therapy does not mean that the therapist takes responsibility for the family's problems. Each family makes choices about how family members will live their lives. The therapist can present alternative choices for family members to consider.

This process can occur only within a therapeutic context that is built on integrity and accountability. When the family members implore, "Help us, fix us, change us," the therapist's collaborative response is, "How? What can I do? How can I help? Tell me what's wrong? What do you need? How can I respond to you? Although you feel badly, there are still other alternatives to try. If you'd like, we could try these new experiences together." When family members experience mutual trust, support, and confidence that they can be responsible for themselves, they are empowered to cope more effectively and, perhaps, even to "outgrow" problems.

Being Effective on Someone Else's Turf

Many home-based therapists are concerned that the familiarity of interacting with family members in their home will decrease the impact of professional interventions. In fact, the opposite is true when the therapist understands *that being effective on someone else's turf* involves the clinical skill of working in proximity while guarding against induction into the family's dysfunctional patterns. Effective family assessment and treatment are based on knowing family members from the inside—their pain, concerns, strengths, language, etc. Conducting therapy in the family's natural habitat suggests the possibility that family members can become truly "known"—in sharp contrast to the outpatient setting, characterized by the therapist's frequent question, "Is this the way Johnny behaves at home?"

What is also true, however, is that familiarity with family members breeds induction into their dynamics. Working in such proximity, the home-based therapist will rapidly and unwittingly begin accommodating to the emotions, transactional structures, and communication rules of the family. For example, as the mother begins to feel hopeless about her daughter's behavior, the therapist begins to feel hopeless about the mother's behavior with her daughter. Or, as the therapist notices that father and son are "ganging up" against the daughter and decides to support her to see what will happen when the son leaves the room, the therapist unwittingly lapses into criticizing the girl along with father. Despite the best intentions, *any* therapist can be lured into the family pattern. One of the advantages of home-based *teams* is that one team member can be designated as the primary therapist who actively conducts the sessions, while the second team member functions as an observer to the process and signals his or her partner when induction occurs. After sessions, when the team discusses the primary therapist's experiences of induction, valuable assessment information can be obtained about how a family member might feel about the fixed family role assigned to him or her.

Making the Most of Crises

Out-of-control behaviors coupled with feelings of helplessness characterize a high percentage of the families served by mental health home-based programs. *Making the most of these "crises,"* which often represent a call for outside helpers to reinstate control in the family (Kagan & Schlosberg, 1989), is a recurring challenge. First, therapists need to assess whether the family is experiencing an "emergency" or a "crisis," so that the appropriate action can be taken (Itzkowitz, 1995). An *emergency situation* with a family is assessed as one requiring *the therapist to take responsibility for action*. For example, if a parent cannot function because of severe depression, there are no expectations that he or she should make a cogent decision regarding an adolescent's need for inpatient hospitalization. Here the therapist needs to take responsibility for this decision and subsequent required actions.

In contrast, a *crisis* is "a crucial or decisive point" in a sequence of events that is viewed as an opportunity for change and growth (*The American Heritage Dictionary*). Here the therapist needs to refrain from taking over and allow *the family to take responsibility* for the required decisions and course of action. In the face of a "crisis," however, many families become paralyzed and expect the therapist to solve the problem for them. They have lived with events others would consider "crucial or decisive" for so long that they do not expect their decisions or actions will make a difference. The family, with support of the therapist, can use a crisis as a catalyst to mobilize change, remembering that the goal is not only to manage symptoms but also to transform the system. Even when faced with an adolescent's potential for suicide, the family and therapist can step back from the crisis and explore why this is happening. Together they can examine the choices of hospitalization or 24-hour parental monitoring. Just the process of helping a family explore the event and reach a decision can begin to transform the system.

Encouraging Positive Change and Competence

Home-based therapy is not a means of managing a myriad of support services for a family in hopes that members will thereby change. In the strengths-based approach, the family itself is seen as possessing the best resources for change. The home-based therapist views himself or herself as a change agent working in collaboration with the family to generate alternatives. Working in proximity with the family, the therapist exhibits an attitude of respectful curiosity, caring, and a firm belief in the family's resilience and ability to change. Repeatedly, the therapist asks, How come? Why are family members limiting themselves to repetitive interpersonal patterns that do not meet individual needs? What new patterns can evolve to address what is missing in family relationships? (Colapinto, 1983).

The therapist provides the fuel that drives the therapeutic process. Challenging the family's status quo through creating new interpersonal experiences of emotional closeness and distance, being listened to and listening to another, allowing conflict to be expressed and resolved, encouraging a parent to take charge of an out-of-control child—all are ways of promoting individual and interpersonal competence. Additionally, the parent(s) and therapist can mutually decide how and when the unique resources of home-based services can best serve the therapeutic process. Do Mrs. Williams and her teenage daughter need a "time-out" through the use of respite services to experience individual space? Does Mr.

Beck think that a YMCA membership paid for by family support monies will facilitate opportunities for father-son recreational activities, given the lack of safety in the neighborhood and the father's unemployment? If Mrs. Young, as an unemployed single parent, has the opportunity to receive job training, will it be helpful to use family support monies to provide daily transportation and assistance to day-camp personnel for her son?

Assessing with Complexity Yet
Focusing Treatment with Simplicity

Before addressing a child or adolescent's clinical problems, such as depression, aggression, and attention or impulse disorders, the therapist will need to identify each family's developmental, structural, and cultural variations, as well as the developmental strengths each family member brings to the resolution of problems. Eight key assessment questions guide the home-based therapist in the task of organizing complex data into hypotheses that create focused treatment directions:

1. What is the developmental time frame of the child/adolescent/family?
2. Is the family system organized in a manner that ensures that the varying developmental needs of family members are met? (For example, do parental expectations match the child's or adolescent's abilities?) If needs are not being met, do new patterns need to be developed?
3. Does the child/adolescent/adult have the developmental capability to respond to internal or external emotional challenges?
4. What current and/or historical stressors correlate with symptom development?
5. What needs and dilemmas in the family are expressed by the clinical symptoms?
6. How do these symptoms impair the child's functioning across social contexts, including the home, school, peer group, and community?
7. What strengths and resources will family members, thera-

pists, natural helpers, and other professionals bring to this collaborative therapeutic process?

8. What are the cultural traditions, values, and belief systems that provide meaning for the clinical symptoms?

ASSESSMENT OF PARENTING STYLES

Assessing both the family's general style of functioning (efficacy of hierarchy, patterns of proximity/distance) and the specific parenting styles is central to creating treatment interventions for all clinical problems. When evaluating the parental subsystem, there are two essential areas of inquiry. One area relates to the type of response a caretaker receives for his or her parenting efforts. Parents tend to do best when they are validated and not undermined by another adult caretaker or an aversive environment (e.g., neighborhood violence). Receiving a positive response from a child also enhances parental functioning. The second area examines the parent's efforts to enhance a child's strengths and respond appropriately to a child's vulnerabilities. Does a parent demonstrate sensitivity to the child's specific developmental needs in organizing daily routines, establishing clear and age-appropriate rules and consequences, creating pleasurable experiences, and providing emotional support?

Taffel (1991) has described optimal parenting styles for children at different developmental stages. From birth to eight years children need "parent-protectors" who can provide stability, safety, love, acceptance, and forgiveness. Preteens may test the ability of parents to maintain a necessary "chum and cop" posture, in which reassurance is balanced by firm expectations and negotiation, by knowing when to hold the line. Between 13 and 16 years, adolescents still need parental connection in addition to a realistic but not excessively reactive response to their (often exasperating) struggle for independence. Whether a parent's style is overly responsive or too distant, the most common parenting problem is having inappropriate developmental expectations for a child, which results in unrealistic consequences. For example, a 60-year-old grandmother became the parent of a forgetful five-year-old boy when his cocaine-addicted mother abandoned him. After one incident when the boy couldn't find his new sneakers, the frustrated grandmother would not allow him to play with his friends for three weeks.

Enmeshed families often produce parent-child relationships characterized by excessive responsivity. The underlying affect triggering the intensity of the reaction is a fear of abandonment and an inappropriate identification with the child ("he [or she] thinks and feels just like me"). Rather than asking about and responding to the child's unique emotions and needs, the enmeshed parent will rely on "mind reading"—somehow knowing, without inquiry, what the child needs and wants.

Heightened parental reactivity toward a child's daily routine may take the form of scheduling too many daily activities for the child that must be completed on a tight time schedule. While the child is involved with the activity, the parent may be intrusive in his or her attempts to monitor the process (Jones, 1997). The excessive closeness between parent and child may prevent the application of consistent discipline, as the parent vacillates between a reactive, critical stance and being overly solicitous. In the area of emotional expression, the parent may react with narcissistic fear to the child's anger and react by personalizing the child's negative behavior: "You know that I was hurt by what you did. How could you hurt me?" Another inappropriate response would be to punish the child by withdrawing affection. In families having more than one caretaker, triangulations among children and caretakers are common. The overinvolved parent may avoid conflicts over limit-setting by triangulating the other adult: "Your father doesn't understand how much you like to read at bedtime, and he says you have to go to bed by 9:00 P.M."

In contrast, the parent-child relationship in disengaged families is characterized by a lack of responsiveness, distance, and an absence of nurturing interactions. These families may appear to be chaotic, lacking any form of parental direction, or as isolated empty shells, too overburdened and depressed to create even chaos. Though these families are not comfortable with closeness, they also fear abandonment. Disengagement between parent and child results in minimal communication about what a parent feels is desirable or undesirable about the child's behavior; conversely, the child does not communicate his or her needs. When conversations do occur, they are often parental monologues—not dialogues between parent and child. Generally parent and child abort a conversation so that salient issues are never addressed in depth. Consequently, the child feels that the parent does not want to listen to or understand his or her point of view and often gives an "I don't know" response to questions (Faber & Mazlish, 1987). The subsequent parental response is either a sharp "Do this or else" or a nagging lecture. While anger and conflict may be expressed, the communication is abrupt, resulting in little, if any, conflict resolution. Often the disengaged parent will retreat from setting limits to avoid creating even more distance in the parent-child relationship.

Therapists (particularly those who have never raised children themselves) need to realize that parenting is not just a set of principles that one absorbs and then applies daily and rationally. Parenting occurs within an emotional and social context wherein parents are reacting to a child at the same time they are reacting to many other internal and external processes. Both parent and child bring their idiosyncratic characteristics and emotional needs to the interaction. Consequently, a parent may have a better "fit" with one of her children than another. No parent functions well or poorly all of the time. Parental competence *half* the time is laudable, given the demands all parents encounter daily. For parents needing to improve their parenting skills, even an incremental change is hard-won, even remarkable (Jones, 1991).

Parents receiving home-based services have generally suffered numerous life traumas and often experience therapeutic suggestions about their parenting as criticisms. A strengths-based treatment approach always highlights the "constructive intent" that underlies any behavior, negative or not. Jones (1991) presents several examples illustrating how the therapist can reframe parental behavior by emphasizing its constructive intent:

1. A parent who constantly criticizes a child is likely to care too much and have overly high standards.
2. A parent who laughs at and teases a child may be trying *not* to criticize.
3. A parent who scapegoats a child may be trying *not* to hit the child.
4. When a parent scolds or spanks a child who has sustained

a physical injury due to impulsivity, the real intent of the parent's behavior may be to express fear that the child could have been very seriously injured.

5. An angry parent may be expressing underlying feelings of hurt and betrayal.

A trusty "parallel process" axiom for home-based therapists is a paraphrasing of the New Testament teaching: "Do unto others as you would have them do unto *others*." For example, if you want a parent to have a more respectful relationship with his or her child, always be very respectful in your relationship with that parent. Sometimes a parent needs to be supported before he or she can support a child. Once a supportive relationship with the parent has been established, the therapist can remain watchful for spontaneous parent-child interactions in the home and teach parenting skills in the context of the moment (Jones, 1991). The therapist selects one sequence of the observed parent-child interaction and validates *any* instance where the parent demonstrates successful parenting. Then, the therapist introduces a new parenting idea or skill, building on the observed success. This is truly a collaborative process because the therapist is, in fact, "teaching" the parent based on what the parent has just accomplished. For example, a therapist observed that mother spontaneously hugged her four-year old when he looked sad. "How caring you are," the therapist said to the mother. "Now encourage your son to use words or gestures to tell you why he feels sad."

Understanding parenting styles, developmental needs, affective relationships, family patterns, and cultural norms, in combination with knowledge about specific problematic behaviors, allows the clinician to create focused treatment interventions. While synthesizing this assessment information is a complex task, the end result is a simple but on target intervention. As mentioned previously, many of these interventions involve enactments that require the therapist to create a new type of interaction between family members (Minuchin & Fishman, 1981). Enactments often take the form of asking the parent and child to talk to each other or to engage in some activity in a new way. As the parent and child interact, the therapist may offer helpful suggestions or behaviorally facilitate the emergence of desired new behaviors in the relationship. When the therapist leaves the home, tasks may be assigned that encourage the continuation of the new behaviors experienced during the enactment, as discussed in the following case example.

"Chaos" aptly described the first two in-home visits made by the team to a small trailer, housing father, mother, teenage daughter, four-year-old son, and nine-year-old Dan, who was inattentive and hyperactive. In the crowded living area, father lay on the couch listening to country music, exhausted after two consecutive work shifts. Equally fatigued, mother had given up any attempts to quell the loud, aggressive fights between Dan and his brother. After experiencing the defeated mood of the parents, the team devised an enactment to elicit humor in the family and energize mother to resume her disciplinary functions with the two boys. The team* wrote a scenario entitled "Wild, Wild West," giving each family member a role to play. Father was allowed to be "the laziest man in town" and do nothing but lie on the couch and listen to country-western music. Mother was to be the "sheriff" of the town, whose job was to impose law and order, including sending offenders to jail. Dan was assigned the role of "Deputy Dan," whose duty was to help the sheriff by having everyone obey the rule to "speak softly" in the town of Whisperville. The teenage daughter was to be "the prettiest girl" in town, who is captured by her four year old brother in the role of "the villain." After assigning the roles, the team encouraged and supported family members while they acted out their parts. Within the "as if" role of "Sheriff," mother enthusiastically "laid down the law" and put Dan or his brother in "jail" (i.e., time-outs) when either boy became too aggressive. At the end of the hilarious session, mother was given the task of continuing to be a successful sheriff whose job would be to jail offenders throughout the next week.

Whether proximity or distance characterizes the desired new pattern, or whether other family members are included or excluded from the enactment, depends on what needs to change in the family's typical way of relating to one another. For example, if a

---

*Sue Richards and Chris Telfer were therapists in this case.

parent and child have been too "glued" together, they may need a "solvent." Here the therapist develops an enactment that emphasizes the unique individuality or separateness of parent and child, such as directing a conversation between the parents and child. During the enactment, the parent would be encouraged not to speak for the child but, rather, to allow the child to have his or her own voice. Likewise, the child would be encouraged to share his or her own feelings and ideas and not depend on the parent for an "answer." Tasks can then be assigned that encourage separate activities for the parent and child, such as having the parent invite an adult friend over for coffee while the child invites a peer to play.

In families with two caretakers, parental splits may occur when an enmeshed parent repeatedly takes the child's side. Here an enactment between the two adults could be developed to encourage them to function more like a "team," thereby increasing distance between the too-close parent and child. After-session tasks can then be suggested so that the parents continue to set aside defined periods of time together to reach agreement on parenting issues.

For instance, in a two-parent family struggling with an out-of-control nine-year-old, the home-based therapist observed that mother and son continually aligned to discount father's disciplinary suggestions. Directing his comments to both parents, the therapist said, "Kevin is getting mixed messages from the two of you. He doesn't know what to do when mother says, 'You don't need to listen to your father,' while father says, 'Listen to me.' Unless you both decide to work as a team and give Kevin one clear message, he will continue to be out of control. What do you want to do? Talk to each other about whether you can work as a team on Kevin's behalf." Within the enactment, the parents began to talk to each other and eventually agreed to function as a team. The therapist then continued the enactment until the parents identified one out-of-control behavior Kevin needed to change in the coming week and what consequences would occur if he complied or did not comply. The after-session task given to the parents was that they spend 15 minutes together every night reviewing Kevin's behavioral progress and evaluating their effectiveness as a united team to help him achieve the expected goal.

In the disengaged family, where emotional and/or physical distance between parent and child is the norm, the enactment will bridge some of the chasm. For example, parent and child may be encouraged to spend private time together in a pleasurable activity, such as playing games or cooking. If the parent's pattern of distancing is related to an absence of support, an enactment can be created between the parent and the other caretaker or the therapist, in which the efforts of the distancing parent are acknowledged and warmly reinforced.

COMMON CLINICAL PROBLEMS

Families served by mental health home-based services present with complex needs, and the children, adolescents, and adults in these families may exhibit multiple disorders. An effective home-based therapist requires an in-depth biopsychosocial clinical knowledge base to provide comprehensive assessment, development of appropriate clinical hypotheses, and a focused treatment plan. The most frequent problematic child or adolescent behaviors manifested in the family, school, or community that necessitate referral to mental health home-based services include: depressed/suicidal; oppositional/aggressive/out-of-control/violent; and hyperactive/impulsive.

Many family histories also contain evidence of sexual or physical abuse; substance abuse; martial discord leading to separation, divorce, cohabitation, or remarriage; parents with mental illness; or family members with special needs. The "multiproblem" nature of these in-home referrals, together with their multiple agency involvement, is often overwhelming to the therapist. The greatest clinical challenge is to create, in essence, a wide-angle therapeutic lens that allows the therapist to conduct a comprehensive assessment and, at the same time, a focusing mechanism to zoom in on the key elements requiring change within the defined treatment period. The following section provides information about the common behaviors evident in home-based referrals and emphasizes the use of in-home services to circumvent out-of-home placements and to promote reunification following such placements. These illustrative cases show how home-based therapists used both a wide-angle lens and a zoom mechanism as they work to change family process through planned interventions.

DEPRESSED/SUICIDAL CHILDREN AND ADOLESCENTS

Diagnostic Description

The most common mood disorder found in home-based referrals is major depressive disorder. According to the *DSM-IV* (American Psychiatric Association, 1994), this disorder is characterized by single or recurrent episodes of major depression separated by at least a two-month period when there is either complete or partial resolution of symptoms. Adolescent and adult females are twice as likely to evidence this disorder as adolescent and adult males. Before puberty, boys and girls are equally affected. A severe psychosocial stressor, such as death of a loved one or divorce, will often trigger episodes of major depressive disorder. School performance, interpersonal relationships, and other important areas are negatively affected by depressive disorders.

Common signs of depression (occurring for at least two weeks) include:

- depressed mood and/or markedly diminished interest in things that previously seemed important

and four or more of the following symptoms:

- sleep, appetite, or weight changes
- physical complaints, loss of energy, or hyperactivity that involves risk-taking
- difficulty concentrating or making decisions
- feelings of worthlessness and/or inappropriate excessive guilt
- preoccupation with fatalistic or morbid thoughts, recurrent suicidal ideation without a specific plan, a suicide attempt, or a specific plan for committing suicide

Children who are depressed may not look sad. Some children show acting-out behaviors and irritable mood; others become strikingly withdrawn and quiet. Acting-out behavior is, in fact, highly correlated with suicide.

A significant number of referrals are made to home-based programs following the hospitalization of a child or, more often, an adolescent who has considered, planned, or attempted suicide. However, even if an in-home patient has had *no* presentation of suicidal behavior, assessment should always include an evaluation of *past* suicidal attempts, lethality, whether anyone was notified, how help was sought, previous acts of self-destructive impulsivity, ability to clearly state the reasons for suicidality, as well as possible *current* thoughts or plans for suicide. The adolescent may view suicide as a solution to both private and familial difficulties. Any threat of suicide must always be taken seriously. *Risk factors that correlate with adolescent suicidality include* (Carlson & Cantwell, 1982; Cohen-Sandler, Bermal, & King, 1982; Hodas & Sargent, 1983; Itzkowitz, 1992; Landau-Stanton & Stanton, 1985):

- marked impulsivity
- psychotic hallucinations involving self-destructive behavior
- substance abuse
- feelings of hopelessness, despair, shame, humiliation, and isolation
- social withdrawal
- poor self-esteem
- family or peer conflicts
- family history of suicide (especially siblings)
- exposure to peer suicide

When suicidal behavior is present, a psychiatric assessment should be scheduled to explore whether or not hospitalization is necessary. *Areas of assessment* with the adolescent include exploring his or her ability to form a strong therapeutic alliance, sign a no-suicide pact and promise the family that this pact can be trusted, identify alternative ways of expressing feelings, and describe some worthwhile behavioral attributes. Hospitalization may not be necessary in families who are working with therapists. However, the therapist must trust that the family can demonstrate the ability to recognize their child's distress, to strongly express caring and love in combination with the firm conviction that suicidal behavior is totally unacceptable, and to provide a 24-hour suicide watch to monitor the adolescent's safety. The family's history of impulsivity, violence, and other suicide attempts or completions must obviously be examined. Assessment should also include an evaluation of the available resources within the family's social network and the mental health resources available to the home-based therapist (i.e., emergency backup, hospitalization, legal assistance for involuntary commitment, if necessary). *Indicators for psychiatric hospitalization include* (Hodas & Sargent, 1983; Itzkowitz, 1992; Landau-Stanton & Stanton, 1985):

- continued suicidal ideation
- high lethality of attempt or repeated attempts with no cry for help
- expressing a wish to die at the time of the attempt (even though this is denied later)
- profound emotional or functional problems coupled with depleted coping resources
- psychotic, severely impulsive, or violent behavior
- highly stressed families (or therapists) who deny the seriousness of the suicide attempt
- disorganized, multiproblem families who cannot provide the necessary support or monitoring needed for the disturbed adolescent
- families with histories of completed suicides

The immediate therapeutic goal with adolescents who have evidenced suicidality is a common sense one: Keep the adolescent safe. The family's intensive monitoring process over several months intensifies the essential struggle of adolescence. As parental control increases, the adolescent's feelings of dependency also increase, but feelings of abandonment decrease. The adolescent must then prove he or she can behave responsibly, independently, and *safely*. If this critical developmental task is accomplished, the parents can gradually decrease their vigilance and control, while maintaining appropriate, nurturing connectedness (Itzkowitz, 1992; Landau-Stanton & Stanton, 1985). Shared responsibility between parent(s) and adolescent is encouraged for working through issues of impulsivity and other problematic behaviors (such as substance abuse, running away, and difficulty appropriately expressing feelings of loss and pain) (Landau-Stanton & Stanton, 1985; Richman, 1979).

Case Vignette: "Judy"*

"Judy" is a 15 year old Caucasian female referred to home based services following inpatient hospitalization and a nine-month placement by child welfare authorities in a group home. Presenting problems include conflicts with peers, truancy, and self-mutilation (cutting her arms). Judy currently lives with her 52-year-old father, a single parent who works in a factory.

Historical and current stressors. When Judy was seven years old, her 39-year-old mother died of a heart attack due to poor management of childhood diabetes. Three years later, Judy was placed in special education classes. At the age of 12, Judy began running away from home and being truant from school. A year later, when Judy and a girlfriend stole money from her father and his car, he reported the incident to the police. The girls were charged with theft, criminal conspiracy, and unauthorized use of an auto, and both girls were placed on probation. Two months later the school became concerned about Judy's depression and suicidal ideation and a referral for inpatient hospitalization was made. Three months following discharge, Judy was readmitted to the inpatient program. Then, against medical advice, Judy and her father decided that she would leave the hospital after one month. Four months later her father agreed to a nine-month placement for Judy in a group home. While Judy was at the group home, her 19-year-old brother left to go to an out-of-state college. Two months later, Judy returned home. Within four months, Judy's current symptoms of truancy, peer conflicts, and self-mutilation began.

Strengths of family members. Mr. S. is conscientious in his efforts to provide living essentials such as shelter and food, and is generous in providing the material things he thinks a teenage daughter needs (e.g., clothes, stereo). He wants to be a responsible parent and prefers that Judy live at home. Judy is physically attractive, honest, and trusting. She has a good sense of humor and wants to communicate who she is as a person with adults and her friends.

Observed family interaction in the home. The first home visit follows a brief, in-office session that oriented Mr. S. and his daughter to the home-based program. During the home visit, the male

---

*Pat Buch and Rick Haley were the therapists in this case.

and female team (Rick and Pat) sit on one side of the dining-room table with Mr. S. and Judy seated together on the opposite side. As Mr. S. tells his story, the team experience father's feelings of depression, isolation, and stress as a male single parent. Mr. S.'s perception that men can't provide nurturance has immobilized him when faced with his daughter's needs. Pat listens for an element in the father's story that she can use to reframe and alter the father's perception. Following is an excerpt from this portion of the session.

FATHER   I come out of work feeling pretty good, but by the time I'm home, I don't feel like doing much at all. As a result of being very tired, I was never pushed into any community or school activities, which I think would have helped.

RICK   After your wife died, there was a big gap.

FATHER   Oh, yes. I filled part of it with the cooking and supplying the clothes, buying food, taking off work to take Judy to the doctor.

RICK   As far as the "gap"—What's missing?

FATHER   The supervision, the love and devotion, the love and tenderness that Judy needs so that she can discuss her problems. If it's a minor problem, I don't want to hear about it. If she's having a fight on the street—what can I do about it?

RICK   I understand you want Judy to be responsible. When you ask what you can do—you could just possibly listen to what she says.

FATHER   I work a 12-hour shift and don't get home till 8:00 p.m. I'm dead tired. I don't want to hear nothing from nobody. I'm in bed within a half hour after I get home. I agree that I haven't been listening. My hope was that she would adjust. School's been the biggest problem. If she doesn't abide by their rules, they make waves.

RICK   When we met at the office the other day, you said you wanted to use therapy to do things differently. Those are some things you identified to work on.

FATHER   As far as trying to get more out of me—you won't get much. And every year that goes by, you'll get less.

RICK   [*To Judy*] How do you feel about that?

JUDY   I don't know.

FATHER   By *more*—the individual attention I should be giving you.

JUDY   I don't know, because every year that goes by, the less I'm here.

FATHER   What she really needs is a lot of tender loving care. What I provide is very crude.

PAT   You sound very caring.

FATHER   I care about my kid.

PAT   You can feel and hear it.

JUDY   I know he cares.

PAT   Yes, you can hear that. I can feel how much you care about Judy and how difficult it's been for you since your wife died—how hard it is to be a mother, father, brother, worker, supervisor—all the different hats you wear. Your caring for Judy is a real strength you have. Let's start there.

As the session continues, the team becomes concerned about Mr. S.'s minimization of his daughter's acts of self-mutilation. Recognizing that perhaps the father's distancing from his daughter's self-destructiveness is related to the same feelings of helplessness he experienced when his wife died, the team looks for the opportunity to create an enactment that will allow him to feel that he *can* positively influence Judy's behavior. As the following excerpt demonstrates, as the team focuses on activating the father's concern for his daughter's pain, Judy counters by strongly protecting her father from seeing the expressions of her pain, that is, the marks of self-mutilation. The team perseveres in their enactment, attempting to alter Judy's perception that her father needs protection, and ultimately uses Judy's protectiveness of her father as a way to elicit her agreement that she will take responsiblity for not harming herself.

RICK   [*to father*] Are you aware when Judy is depressed?

FATHER   Yes. I get depressed, too. Don't you get depressed?

RICK   Yes, but I don't get suicidal.

JUDY   I'm not suicidal.

FATHER   Okay, I take that back. She's got marks on her arm—that's what scares the *school*. I don't know what she does it with—a knife or what. She's got marks on her arm. [*To Judy*] Do you have them now?

JUDY   From last week . . .

RICK   Can we see them?

JUDY   Dad, do you have to look at this? I don't want you to see because then you're going to be, like—"you can never have a knife again." [*Judy is protecting her father by appearing to be concerned about the possible removal of knives.*]

FATHER   I want to see them. I can't stop you from having knives. You're here by yourself a lot of the time.

JUDY   Do I have to show you? I don't mind showing people who don't know me.

FATHER   I can imagine what they look like.

JUDY   You don't . . . [*sighing heavily*].

PAT   It might be important for Dad.

FATHER   I won't look if you want to show them. I'll leave the room. [*He stands up to leave the room.*] Are they on your arm? [*He then leaves the room.*]

JUDY   [*She stands, rolls up her sleeve, and leans toward Pat and Rick.*] There are the marks. The purple ones are scars. [*She rolls down her sleeve and sits.*]

RICK   Why don't you want your dad to see?

JUDY   I don't want him to see.

PAT   Will it hurt him if he sees them?

JUDY   Yeah. I guess that's why I don't want him to see. [*Father reenters the room and sits down.*]

PAT   You really want to protect your dad.

RICK   [*To father*] What do you think of Judy trying to protect you like that—as far as not showing you the marks?

FATHER   Is that protecting me? I know they are there even without looking. [*To Judy*] Maybe you've got a bunch of them. If you take a knife and make one mark on your arm—that's all it takes.

RICK   [*To Judy*] Why don't you show your dad?

JUDY   I'm not going to show him because I don't want him to know. He'll think his daughter is a total wacko.

RICK   Maybe he'll think . . . *my daughter is in pain.*

JUDY   [*To father*] These marks look like burns.

RICK   [*To father*] Are you curious?

FATHER   I'd like to see them.

JUDY   [*She turns to father, rolls up her sleeve, and shows him the marks.*] Like that—the purple ones are scars.

FATHER   You take the knife and run it up your arm like that, or with a sharp knife?

JUDY It doesn't have to be sharp. I could do it with just about anything.

FATHER She does it during periods of deep despair. I'm not aware when it's a deep depression because she's got the stereo blaring away. [*He sighs deeply and Judy leaves the room— again, as a way of protecting her father.*]

RICK What you're saying is important. Ask Judy to come back. She needs to hear this from you. [*Father calls to Judy, who returns to the room.*]

RICK [*To father*] You view Judy's marking her arm as a problem. Do you think a goal could be that Judy agrees to talk to you about her problems instead of marking her arm?

JUDY I get depressed at night, and I am NOT going to wake him up. I don't want to bother him with my problems!

PAT Since you don't really want your dad to know how much you hurt because you can't bear to hurt him, I have another idea. One way of not bothering and hurting him is for you to agree *not* to mark your arm every day and to show him your arm so he knows you are safe.

JUDY I could do that.

FATHER [*To Judy*] I want you to show me in the morning before I go to work. If anything was on your mind during the night, I want you to tell me what upset you. If you do mark your arm, I will insist that you come to work with me where I can watch you.

Hypotheses. After integrating the assessment data, the home-based team develops hypotheses about the needs and dilemmas in the family expressed by Judy's clinical symptoms. The following hypotheses form the basis for focused treatment interventions and directions:

1. Judy's previous truancy and runaway behavior may have represented her attempt to escape feelings of depression that she felt would overburden her sole biological parent. Feeling worthless, the truancy and running away might also have been a way of making an impact on the environment, thereby gaining some feeling of self-esteem through independent actions.

2. The reported cash and car theft might have been a message

that she was missing the emotional support of her mother and wanted to bring this to her father's attention.

3. The current self-mutilation may be Judy's way of saying: "I will handle my pain alone without burdening Dad."

Treatment interventions. The enactment conducted in this initial session allows the team to see the rigid complementarity between Judy and her father: Father's hesitancy in response to, or withdrawal from, Judy's pain activates her protectiveness of him, which takes the form of *her* withdrawing—which, in turn, maintains her father's distancing behavior. The team redefines the problem of self-mutilation as Judy's reluctance to cause her father pain by revealing her pain to him.

By continuing the enactment past the point when father and daughter would generally distance from each other, the team "turns up the heat." Not only is the seriousness of Judy's self-mutilation brought into the open for the first time, but a new pattern emerges: Father demonstrates that he can, in fact, respond to his daughter's pain. The missing ingredient—active nurturance from father to daughter—has been added. The team recognizes the fragility of this new pattern and plans daily sessions to nurture and support the father's beginning steps toward meeting Judy's emotional needs. At the same time, they will walk a fine line between supporting the father's efforts to participate in his daughter's emotional life and helping him (in conjunction with Judy) to decide whether psychiatric consultation is required—a decision he had previously abdicated to professionals. Eventually, the father will need support from the team to find ways of increasing his and Judy's network of social support. However, the most immediate goal is to ensure Judy's safety and her father's participation in helping to bring that about on a daily basis.

OPPOSITIONAL CHILDREN AND ADOLESCENTS

Diagnostic Description

According to the *DSM-IV*, the behavior of children with oppositional defiant disorder is characterized by recurring negativistic, defiant, disobedient, or hostile behavior toward authority figures that persists for at least six months. Frequently the child exhibits at least four of the following behaviors: loses temper, argues with adults, deliberately annoys other people, blames others for his or her own mistakes or misbehavior, becomes easily annoyed by others, is angry and resentful, or spiteful and vindictive. These behaviors create problems in social, school, and (later) job settings. Hostility is expressed verbally and not via the physical aggression seen in youth with conduct disorders. Attention-deficit/hyperactivity disorder, learning disorders, and communication disorders are common in children with oppositional defiant disorder. In a significant number of cases, oppositional defiant disorder is a developmental antecedent to conduct disorder.

This disorder has become the most common child-focused referral to mental health centers (Horne & Sayger, 1990). Defiant symptoms tend to increase with age, usually appearing for the first time before age eight years and not later than early adolescence (*DSV-IV*, 1994). While the family environment plays a significant role in the way symptoms manifest themselves, individual temperament and cognitive features are other predisposing factors. For example, according to the *DSV-IV*, oppositional behavior is frequently found in boys whose preschool histories include temperamental characteristics such as excessive reactivity and difficulty being soothed or overactivity, impulsivity, and inattention. School-aged children may evidence low self-esteem, unstable moods, low frustration tolerance, and early substance usage. The key element of oppositionalism is that it always occurs within an interpersonal context, that is, "you can't be oppositional by yourself—the problem occurs in relationships" (Mones, 1998, p. 148).

Jones (1997) posits that the meaning of oppositional defiant behaviors is best understood within a biological-developmental-systems model. By first understanding the unique biological-developmental characteristics of a child, parents and school personnel can more appropriately support the child's inherent needs. Defiant children demonstrate significant variability in the way they cope with their individual sensitivities and tendencies to become overwhelmed by environmental stimuli (Greenspan, 1997; Greenspan & Salmon, 1995). Jones (1997) has classified the coping styles of oppositional defiant children into three categories: "over-regu-lated," "under-regulated," and "angry." In the first category, children try to control their environment by becoming internally "over-regulated." Initial reactions are generally negative, and self-definition involves what they won't do rather than what they will do. These children are stubborn, intense, and highly persistent. They tend to become inflexible and rigid and to handle transitions badly. They are perfectionistic, compulsive, and stuck in all-or-none thinking. Their oppositionalism reflects an inability to deal with ambiguity. When anxious or afraid, they try to overcontrol the world and become very finicky about what they will or will not eat, wear, or do. They are bright, but concrete, overfocusing on insignificant details. They avoid complexity by restricting senso-rimotor, affective and social input. Parents will create defiance in the "over-regulated" child by intrusively imposing a parental agenda that overstimulates, overwhelms, over-organizes, over-in-structs, and overreacts to the child.

In contrast, "under-regulated" defiant children may become im-pulsive or excessively active in response to complex environmental demands. Highly demanding and easily frustrated, they are quick to anger. They don't always seem to listen, have difficulty staying focused, and appear disorganized. Difficulties with auditory and/or spatial processing, verbal expressive skills, and planning are common. They are bright but not reflective. Their have difficulty learning from their mistakes so that ordinary consequences are not effective. Parents or school personnel often err by interpreting the child's high activity level as "willful." Parents often over-instruct, over-focus on deficits, and inadequately monitor the child. When inappropriate expectations for good language skills and organiza-tional abilities are placed on the child, oppositional behavior oc-curs. In the face of inevitable failure and parental disappointment, the child feels victimized and gives up (Jones, 1997).

The "angry" defiant child does not show evidence of the biologi-cal sensitivity inherent in "over-regulated" and "under-regulated" defiant children. These children are well-organized and flexible in their efforts to meet environmental demands. Underlying the child's expressed anger is a feeling of having been wounded within a family context that is not meeting his or her needs. Often a lack of trust, problems of attachment, ineffective use of parental power, or insensitivity to the child's emotions exist in the parental-child relationship (Jones, 1997). Here oppositionalism can be viewed as "a dance of adaptation between child and parents" wherein the child controls the degree of proximity (connectedness) and distance (individuation) within the relationship. "Defiant behavior both pushes parents away (makes them angry) *and* keeps them involved (managing the child)" (Mones, 1998, pp. 148–149). The resulting escalating cycle of coercive behavior has been described by Barkley (1997) and other learning theorists (Horne & Sayger, 1990; Webster-Stratton & Herbert, 1994).

Barkley (1997) emphasizes that many of the behaviors associated with oppositional defiant disorder can be subsumed under the general rubric of "noncompliance." Parents complain that the child totally refuses to comply with explicit directives or the child only partially complies to adult commands within a reasonable time period. Also, the child invariably violates expected rules about behavior in the home, and sometimes in the school or community. A cycle of parent-child interaction develops and maintains the child's noncompliant behavior. Within this cycle, the child's lack of compliance to the parent's initial and subsequent commands leads to repetitive parental commands, escalating parental frustration, increased negative emotional and/or coercive behaviors from both the parent and child, and eventual parental coercion or abdication. Neither too much coercion nor too little guidance is desirable for the child's optimal growth. When the child is able to successively avoid or delay the command given by the parent (i.e., negative reinforcement) and continue what he or she wants to do (i.e., positive reinforcement), the noncompliance will continue in the future with the parents, other adults, or children. Over time, parents may overlook the child's problem behaviors, avoid praising the child's positive behaviors, or even shun potentially pleasant activities with the noncompliant child because of previous negative encounters. Barkley (1997) believes that family relationships are critical to shaping the child's behavior. Specifically, parents needs to become more effective in reinforcing the child's compliant behaviors while simultaneously using methods to extinguish oppositional behaviors.

Case Vignette: "Lydia"*

"Lydia," an African-American seven-year-old girl, was referred for home-based services because of a year-long history of frequent outbursts of temper and argumentativeness with her teacher and peers; dramatic fabrications at school about her mother indulging her with material gifts; verbal abuse and vindictiveness targeted at her one-year-old sibling, Maurice; and negativistic and opposi- tional behavior with her mother. Feeling totally overwhelmed and concerned about her own high blood pressure, Mrs. H., a 27- year-old single parent, called Child Welfare Services requesting placement for Lydia and was subsequently referred for home-based services.

Historical and current stressors. As a child, Mrs. H. had to parent her own siblings. She was physically abused by her siblings and sexually abused by a family member. Currently, there are economic stressors. Mrs. H.'s Public Assistance allotment is insuffi- cient, and her boyfriend spends his paycheck on crack cocaine during his binges.

Strengths of family members. Mrs. H. is articulate, cooperative, and friendly. She welcomes the relationship with the in-home thera- pist, since the severe psychiatric symptoms and substance abuse issues in her family of origin limit her access to extended familial support. Lydia is curious, friendly, does well academically at school, and excels at skateboarding in the neighborhood. Maurice is playful and doing well developmentally. Mrs. H's partner can be nurturing, playful, and insightful regarding Lydia's problems.

Observed family interaction in the home. Mrs. H., appearing tired and depressed, sits on the couch holding Maurice. Lydia sits on the opposite side of the room, continually spewing angry criticisms of her baby brother: "You're stupid and fat . . . You make me sick . . . I'm going to punch you!" After five minutes of Lydia's tirade, Mrs. H. retaliates in a "tit-for-tat" manner: "Enough of your mouth! I'm going to punch you, too." Lydia then argues in a similar fashion to her mother: "You—and who else? You just sit there and do nothing all day but feed that fat boy's face." This style of relating continues for another 15 minutes. Lydia then

---

*Cory Jex was the therapist in this case.

begins jumping up and down on a chair and Mrs. H. reprimands and criticizes her, saying, "Stop that! Come here right now! You're always messing with something!" Lydia sticks her tongue out at mother and yells, "I can't hear you! I can't hear you!" Mrs. H. puts Maurice on the floor and comes towards Lydia saying, "Now you're going to get it!" Lydia leaps off the couch, runs to the bedroom, locks the door, and says defiantly, "You've got to get me first!" Lydia begins kicking the door forcibly. Mrs. H. pounds on the door yelling, "You come out of there or else!" Maurice begins to cry in the living room. With frustrated resignation, Mrs. H. yells, "You're so bad, girl—don't you ever dare come out of that room!" Mrs. H. returns to the living room, picks up Maurice, and says to the therapist, "I told you how impossible she is—now you've seen it yourself. I can't take this anymore."

Hypotheses. After integrating the assessment data, the in-home therapist views Lydia's defiant behavior as primarily stemming from problems of distance and power imbalance in the mother-child relationship rather than from an inherent biological sensitivity. The specific hypotheses generated that lead to focused treatment interventions include:

1. Lydia's defiance and refusal to accept her teacher's authority may be a replication of her relationship with her mother. She appears to view her mother as a peer and not as an authority figure capable of providing structure and nurturance.
2. Mrs. H.'s self-perception is that of an abused woman with limited ability to respond to Lydia's seven-year-old needs. She is unrealistic in her expectation that Lydia is "grown enough" not to need the reassurance that Maurice receives.
3. Lydia has some anxiety about being separated from her mother because she is worried about her mother's health.
4. Lydia's fabrications may express her wish to be nurtured by her mother.
5. Lydia's oppositional behaviors connect her to mother; negative connection is better than no connection.

Treatment interventions. The treatment interventions focused on creating a closer, more positive relationship between mother and daughter and shifting the mother's position to a more authoritative one whereby she could implement more effective disciplinary methods. First, the therapist acknowledged that mother deserved a break wherein she could rekindle her energy before addressing Lydia's problems. Mother was treated to a new hairdo and lunch at a nice restaurant with the therapist. During the car ride, mother and therapist sang along to an audiotape of a song that highlighted the message, "you've got to accentuate the positive, eliminate the negative. . . . " Using the song theme, the therapist created a task wherein mother wrote down positive statements about anything Lydia had done that week and put the messages into a box labeled by mother, "I love Lydia." The therapist had also designed a box for mother labeled, "Mother is loveable." Both the therapist and Lydia put messages in the box about any positive behaviors mother had demonstrated that week.

During the in-home visits, the therapist created play and nurturing enactments for mother and Lydia. For example, while the therapist occupied Maurice, mother and Lydia played the following game. Lydia closed her eyes and drew a message from the box. Keeping her eyes closed, she tried to guess what her mother might have written. Then she read the message aloud. When it was mother's turn in the game, she also attempted to guess and then read a message from the box. Following this activity, the therapist gave mother and Lydia a brownie mix and encouraged the two of them to enjoy cooking brownies together. These enactments were designed to encourage enjoyable proximity and closeness between the mother and daughter.

After establishing a more positive affiliation between them, the therapist assisted the mother in assuring her daughter that she would not be placed out of the home and encouraged Lydia to share the reasons for her feelings of alienation, defensiveness, and anger. Lydia's defiance and oppositional behavior toward her mother were also depersonalized and reframed as a problem of distance that has developed since the arrival of the mother's partner and the birth of Maurice.

An individual session with the mother that explored her concerns and offered alternative disciplinary methods was particularly helpful. During sessions with both, the mother learned to recognize when she felt that Lydia was "pushing her buttons" and why; together, mother and daughter created incentives to encourage

Lydia's compliance. The next step was to create enactments between mother and daughter that reinforced the mother's position of authority and clarified for Lydia the expected rules for communication (i.e., how anger could be properly expressed), desirable behaviors, and consequences. For example, at the beginning of each home visit, the therapist coached mother on her new parenting skills. During the visit, mother reminded Lydia of behaviors that were not acceptable (e.g., jumping on the furniture, yelling, using disrespectful words) and consequences for these behaviors (e.g., five minutes on a time-out chair). If Lydia broke the rules, mother would say calmly, "I know you're feeling frustrated, but I still have a limit. On the count of three, you will sit in the chair for five minutes." Mother also praised Lydia for any positive behaviors. If Lydia seemed to be upset but did not break the rules, mother sat next to her, held her hand, told her she loved her, and then asked Lydia to share what she was feeling. After empathizing with Lydia's feeling, mother helped her to think through a plan that would make her feel better.

Individual sessions with Lydia were also designed using puppet play to help her learn how to assess social situations more accurately, to think before she acts, and to generate appropriate responses to problematic situations (Barkley, 1997; I. Walbridge, personal communication, 1997).

AGGRESSIVE/OUT-OF-CONTROL/VIOLENT
CHILDREN AND ADOLESCENTS

Diagnostic Description

According to the *DSM-IV*, aggressive behavior can be diagnosed as an adjustment disorder if it appears to be an excessive response occurring within three months after the onset of one or more identifiable psychosocial stressors (but not bereavement) and lasts no longer than six months after the cessation of a stressor. Psychosocial stressors can include: problems with the child's family (e.g., health problems, parental separation, divorce or marriage, abuse, parental overprotection or inadequate discipline), within school (e.g., academic problems, conflict with teachers or classmates), or within the peer group (e.g., loss of friends, discord with peers).

Subsequently, functioning decreases at school, in social relationships or at home. Adjustment disorders are associated with an increased risk of suicide attempts and suicide.

The next level of disruptive behavior is oppositional defiant disorder, which has been described in the case of Lydia. The most extreme out-of-control behavior by children or adolescents carries a diagnosis of conduct disorder. Behavioral disruptions that violate the basic rights of others or major age-appropriate societal norms or rules characterize this disorder. The ability of these children to empathize with others is limited. Even as young children they are not oriented to search for cues that will help them understand another person. The majority of youth who evidence conduct disorders exhibited oppositional defiant behaviors at an earlier age. When they felt misunderstood and victimized, they began to empathize less with people, leading to a downward spiral in the development of empathic skills. The behaviors that violate the rights of others fall into four main groupings:

- aggressive conduct that causes or threatens physical harm to other people or animals
- nonaggressive conduct that results in property loss or damage
- deceitfulness or theft
- serious violations of rules (truancy, runaway)

This diagnosis requires that three (or more) of these behaviors are present during a one-year period, with at least one behavior present in the past six months. These youth function poorly in social, school, and job contexts. Conduct disorder may coexist with learning disorders, anxiety disorders, mood disorders, and substance-related disorders.

Most home-based therapists express anxiety about treating children or adolescents who evidence aggressive, out-of-control, or violent behaviors. Reviewing the family's timeline often clarifies the correlation between family events and the emergence of aggressive behavior. For example, Cicchetti and Nurcombe (1993) have noted that aggressive symptoms in children or adolescents often appear following a significant cut-off from someone who has been emotionally important to them. Family patterns become more vulnerable when the continuity and stability of family life is threatened or disrupted. Aggressive symptoms, which can never be viewed as isolated acts occurring out of context, may emerge in response to caretakers who have unrealistic expectations or are emotionally disengaged, neglectful, and/or abusive in their parenting styles. Sometimes these caretakers are clinically depressed and do not share their uncertainties or fears with the child. In response, children invent their own explanations for a parent's behavior. The child's act of aggression may be a way to bring a depressed parent to life and/or to seek the truth beneath spoken fictions. The following case example illustrates the therapist's ongoing process of hypothesis-testing until an appropriate diagnostic understanding of the child's aggressive behaviors was attained.

Case Vignette: "Gary" *

"Gary," a nine-year-old African-American boy, was referred for home-based services upon discharge from an inpatient program following a suicide attempt. Prior to the hospitalization Gary had been diagnosed with an expressive language disorder resulting in a special school placement. His vocabulary was limited and he had difficulty articulating sentences with developmentally appropriate length or complexity. These difficulties interfered with his school performance, and, not surprisingly, he displayed a nasty attitude, fought with other children, and had no respect for authority. At home he would have violent temper tantrums and "jump" on his caretaker, Ms. P. Gary would alternate between states of withdrawal (refusing to talk) and aggression. Ms. P. would also withdraw and make furtive phone calls to the next-door neighbor. Gary appeared upset by the phone calls and wanted to know what Ms. P. had said to the neighbor. Ms. P. would indicate that it had nothing to do with Gary but that it was her own personal worry. Shortly after another series of these phone calls, Gary announced to Ms. P. that "someone" needed a hospital. When she ignored him, Gary put his head in the oven and turned on the gas. Ms. P. quickly took him to a hospital psychiatric inpatient unit. During the few days on the unit, Gary did not appear to be significantly depressed but told the psychiatrist that Ms. P. should see a doctor.

---

*Sarah Gardner was the therapist and C. Wayne Jones was the supervisor in this case.

Ms. P. was angry with the inpatient psychiatrist for not including her in Gary's treatment.

Historical and current stressors. Gary's biological mother was an IV drug-user who overdosed when he was two years old. An unrelated man raised him for one year, during which time Gary was severely emotionally abused. One time, Gary left the kitchen door open and his dog ran into the street and was hit and killed by a car. Gary was punished by being locked in a closet and then taunted by the male caretaker, who dressed up like a ghost and came into the closet to scare him. He also made Gary sleep with the dead dog. When Gary was three years old, Ms. P., who was also unrelated to Gary, became his caretaker. He subsequently referred to her as his "mother." The circumstances surrounding this "informal adoption" were never clarified. Ms. P. and Gary have been living together for the past six years. There are no other family members in their lives. The one social relationship they have is with Mr. S., a 50-year-old African-American man who is a widower and lives next door. Mr. S. has been a good friend to both Ms. P. and Gary.

Strengths of family members. Ms. P. has a deep commitment to promoting Gary's well-being. She is interested in seeking professional advice from those who are respectful of her knowledge as a parent. Gary cares deeply for Ms. P. He expresses his feelings well through drawings.

Observed family interaction in the home. During the initial session, Ms. P. complained about Gary's smearing feces on the bathroom walls and neglecting his homework. At first, Gary tried to respond with some assertiveness in the form of anger. After a while, however, Ms. P. shut Gary down by shaming him: "You went upstairs and messed all over the damn place and wiped it all over everything just to get back at me. That's why I have so many headaches." In response Gary slumped in his chair and pulled his jacket over his head. (The therapist noticed that Gary's expressive language skills were, indeed, limited. She also observed that his coping skills tended to be concretized and regressive, as seen in his withdrawal and smearing feces.) The mother's frustration, anger, and possible exhaustion suggested that she experienced Gary's behavior as a personal affront. Her immediate coping response was to withhold her affection for him.

After listening to Ms. P's concerns, the therapist empathized with her, saying, "Despite the previous professional help, things don't seem to be working. That must be frustrating for you. But you still have some hope. You say that Gary is 'golden' inside and that's what keeps you going. What I'm asking from you is some patience. I don't want to throw a plan together that won't be good. There's a lot I will need to know before I can be helpful."

Hypothesis. The school evaluation had indicated the presence of a learning disorder in the area of expressive language skills. Based on her observations of Gary's developmental limitations and Ms. P.'s descriptions of their struggles around homework, the therapist's initial hypothesis was that Ms. P.'s expectations might not match the boy's abilities. Perhaps that's why she was angry and critical of Gary, who, in turn responded with withdrawal or aggression.

Initial treatment interventions. When a therapist is not clear about the diagnostic formulation, it is best to continue gathering information. Parents who have been through difficult times with a child do not appreciate professionals who rush to form a judgment and reduce a complex situation to something simplistic.

Observed family interaction in the home. During the next home visit, Ms. P. offered her own hypothesis about Gary's misbehavior, saying that he was "twisted" (meaning "hurt") because of his early history of abuse. When Ms. P. said, "I think things were so painful for him that he blanks it out," Gary put his head on his mother's lap. Ms. P. continued: "He was an abused child. The things that happened to him shouldn't happen to anyone. He was very badly treated, and when I got him, he didn't know the difference between real pain and just a little scratch. Once he cut his leg and the blood went flying. I panicked, but he didn't even cry." Gary piped in, saying, "I cry now."

Hypothesis. The mother's observations are not uncommon; severely abused children will often use withdrawal and numbing as defenses. Developmentally, children have to learn to say "no" before they can say "yes." Before a child can cry, he or she has to feel safe. It was clear that, despite some of the tension identified in the first home visit, Ms. P.'s parenting had included many nurturing experiences or Gary would not have felt safe enough to cry. Thus the therapist discarded the first hypothesis that Gary's aggression was related primarily to emotional distance in the relationship with Ms. P.

While Ms. P. was clearly hypothesizing a connection between Gary's *past* history of abuse six years ago and his current symptoms, the therapist searched for clues in the *present* relationship between the mother and boy. Why had the boy made a suicide attempt? Perhaps Gary's behavior was expressing unspoken fears about what *might* happen to him and his mother in the future.

Treatment interventions. The therapist redefined the problem and assigned a task for Ms. P. to complete before the next session: "It seems like Gary is searching for answers to some important questions. I don't know what they are, but I think that until he finds some answers, he's not going to be able to settle down in his behavior and do what he's supposed to do—be a child, go to school, play, and respond appropriately to you. Find out three things that Gary feels inside."

Observed family interaction in the home. At the third home visit, the mother told the therapist that while Gary had not shared any feelings, he had told her that he liked to draw. This became the critical vehicle for communication between Gary, Ms. P., and the therapist. Gary was asked to draw a picture of three fears and the ways he could feel safe (Figure 5.1). His fears were: "Freddy" (the evil movie character, Freddy Krueger), the darkness, and a dog. What made him feel safe was: his mother, and he and his mother watching television. When the therapist validated how safe his mother made him feel, Gary snuggled up to her on the couch. The therapist commented: "You take care of your mother and she protects you—that's why you feel so close to each other." Gary then drew other pictures of "Freddy" and his mother and wrote the following words on the pictures: "He [Freddy] kill me when I sleep and dream. He kill you [his mother] when you sleep and you dream. I am scared that will happen. The bad me and the good me fight. He shot Freddy. He is scary."

The therapist interpreted to Gary the split inside of him that served to redefine his aggressive behavior: "This is the good one coming out. There is one that *behaves* badly—that's the one who is scared. Acting badly is a way of saying, 'I'm scared.'" Ms. P. agreed, saying, "That's his way of fighting back." The therapist responded: "He tricks you into thinking he's bad. When he acts

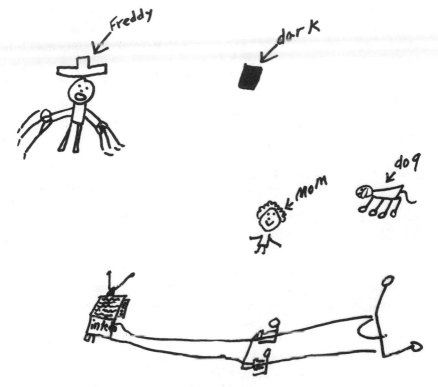

Figure 5.1
GARY'S DRAWING OF HIS FEARS AND SOURCES OF SAFETY

up, he pushes you away. I think he's acting out a fear. If he comes too close to you, what will happen if you're not around one day?"

The therapist continued to expand Ms. P.'s understanding of the problem: "I noticed you are the only adult he drew in his picture. It's significant. Lots of kids have several adults they can count on. I don't blame him for being scared. You are the only adult he can count on." Ms. P. began to cry, saying, "That's the truth. I'm the only one." The therapist inquired, "Do you think that could be scary for him?" In response, Ms. P. drew a picture of herself and Gary lying dead in caskets (Figure 5.2). The therapist said to Gary, "Is this what your mom is so afraid of? You two have the same fears. You need each other and are both afraid." The mother responded, "What will happen to him if something

Figure 5.2
MS. P.'S DRAWING OF HERSELF AND GARY
LYING DEAD IN CASKETS

happens to me? I have so many ailments. I'm afraid that all the progress he's made will disappear and another person might destroy him." Gary put his head on her lap and hid his eyes.

Meeting with the therapist alone, Ms. P. shared her fear that she might have a terminal illness because of her headaches. Ten years earlier, she had had cancer but currently refused to see a doctor. When she became excessively worried, she would call the next-door neighbor to share her troubles. The phone calls were always made with secrecy so that Gary would not hear her conversations.

Hypotheses. After the home visits, the therapist is now able to accurately integrate the assessment information and develop hypotheses about the meaning of Gary's symptoms. These include:

1. Ms. P. has not allowed herself to see Gary's fears because of her own. Before Gary came into her life, she lived on the streets as an alcoholic. Adopting Gary gave her life meaning. Her mission has been to live long enough to give him the skills to survive without her. She does not want Gary to worry about her and thinks that she is successfully protecting him from her fears. She feels she can hide her fear from Gary, but she senses something is wrong. Without any explanation from his mother, Gary can only assume the worst. He firmly believes that not only is he a "bad"

child but that his "badness" is the cause of this mother's headaches and fears.

2. Feeling helpless and frightened of possible abandonment, Gary withdraws and experiences depression.

3. At other times, Gary aggressively acts out the anger he feels, having no alternative way either to understand the unspoken issue of mother's health or to express his fears and anxiety.

Treatment interventions. From the fourth through the tenth home visit, the therapist:

- convinced Ms. P. to go with her to a doctor for a physical examination, which fortuitously revealed that her health was not a concern;
- coached Ms. P. to talk to Gary directly and honestly about what her fears had been and to reassure him that she was in good health; and
- held a session with Ms. P., Gary, and Mr. S., their close male friend, in which he made a commitment to Gary that he would adopt him if anything ever happened to Ms. P.

Follow-up. One year after the home-services had ended, Gary no longer required special educational services and was mainstreamed into a regular classroom. His aggressive symptoms had ceased.

Another systemic/structural hypothesis regarding aggressive or violent behavior emphasizes the role that multiple rigid triangulations play in the family. When a family system is organized into rigid triangles, such that one person is always the outsider, that individual may respond by displaying aggressive behavior. The following case demonstrates that optimal therapy will not occur when the therapists become unwittingly inducted in a rigid family triangle.

Case Vignette: "Mary"*

"Mary," a 14-year-old Caucasian female, exhibited severe acting-out and aggressive behaviors. During these outbursts she would

---

*The names of the therapists in this case have been changed.

scream, throw objects, and physically attack family members, which resulted in an inpatient hospitalization. Mary was able to control her behavior in the hospital, but at home, she would become enraged whenever her mother, Ms. L., attempted to discipline her. At various times, Mary threatened to overdose on Tylenol, iron pills, and to drink dish detergent. These suicidal threats made Ms. L. feel extremely guilty, in response to which she would back down from holding Mary to firm limits. Mary's behavior was often the source of conflict between Ms. L. and her partner, Mr. T., which resulted in violent altercations. When Ms. L. was too lenient with limit setting, Mr. T. became too strict.

Historical and current stressors. Mary's parents divorced when she was eight years old. Three years later Ms. L. began to date Mr. T. Seven months later, Mary moved to her father's house because she did not like Mr. T. After living with her father for two months, she returned home because he expected her to take care of *him* and, Mary admitted, she also missed her mother. Mary continued to talk to her father frequently on the phone and would see him on weekends. During the period that Mary lived with her father, Mr. T. and Ms. L. began living together. One year later Mary was hospitalized for her aggressive behavior.

Strengths of family members. Mary is very kind to other children and animals. She has the ability to behave and learn appropriately in school; her good friends enjoy being with her. Ms. L. values the importance of keeping her family together. She is cooperative, caring, giving, and able to focus on positive factors. Mr. T. is a good financial provider for the family and has continued to stay in the relationship with Ms. L. throughout Mary's repeated crises. Dawn, Mary's 12-year-old sister, obeys the family's rules, has a good relationship with Mr. T., does well at school, and has many friends.

Observed family interaction in the home. Prior to this home visit, Diane and Dave, the home-based team members, had met with Mary, Dawn, Ms. L., and Mr. T. for three family sessions. Attempts to structure sessions were ineffective because of Mary's escalating aggressive behaviors. The team's interventions in previous sessions were aimed at Ms. L. and Mr. T. and focused on creating firm expectations about Mary's behavior.

At the present session Mr. T. and Ms. L. sit on each side of the kitchen table. Diane sits next to Mr. T. and Dave sits next to Ms. L. Dawn sits at one end of the table (between her mother and Mr. T.) quietly doing her homework, and Mary sits at the opposite end of the table. The following transcription of a four-minute interaction videotaped in the session illustrates how the system rallies to maintain Mary's escalating, out-of control behavior:

MOTHER	[*To Mary*] If you were back at the hospital, how would you act?
MARY	Where's my hair band?
MOTHER	That's a nice, respectful tone of voice.
MARY	Spare me, Mom. I'm a little pissed off. WHERE'S MY HAIR BAND?
MR. T.	[*To mother*] Ignore her.
MOTHER	[*To Mary*] I told you where the hair band is—in the bathroom. You don't have to scream at me. [*Mary leaves the kitchen to go to the bathroom.*]
MARY	[*To mother*] Where in the bathroom?
MOTHER	On the sink.
MARY	NO, IT'S NOT!
MR. T.	Don't yell at your mother!
MARY	TOM [Mr. T.], WHY DON'T YOU LAY OFF?
MOTHER	Mary, if you don't sit down . . .
MARY	You said you'd drive me if I sat down and talked to you guys.
MOTHER	You're not talking, you're screaming. If you're not going to sit down and talk, you'll get nothing.
MARY	Why should I talk! NO ONE LISTENS TO ME!
MOTHER	If you talked, we'd listen.
MARY	I talked before, you didn't listen.
DIANE	[*Reading from treatment plan*] "When in conflict family members will not use name-calling or screaming as a means of communicating with each other."
MR. T.	You couldn't have said that at a better time. [*Diane laughs, in agreement with Mr. T.*]
DAVE	Mary isn't getting what she wants.
MR. T.	Exactly. It's just going to continue.
MOTHER	I don't know why this happened. Everything was okay.
MR. T.	You know why it happened: because . . .
MARY	WHY DON'T YOU SHUT UP, TOM—FUCKING ASS-HOLE!
MR. T.	She don't get what she wants.

DIANE   It would have happened sooner or later. [*The mother, her male partner*, and *the therapists are allied together at this point.*]

MARY   The doctor told me he don't think you have any right to have Tom live in this house whenever he treats me like that! The DOCTOR said that you put him in front of your own kids! The DOCTOR said that! You don't believe me? Call him! HE told me that! [*The adults begin to talk together about Mary.*]

MR. T. Nothing went wrong when she got everything she wanted. When she didn't get what she wanted, she threw a fit. [*To mother*] Last night you told her to be home. She gave you a hard time over the phone. [*Mary tries to explain but is cut off by Mr. T.*]

MOTHER I *did* tell her there would be a consequence if she didn't come home.

DIANE   I complimented you for having been strong.

MR. T. Exactly—cause you weren't taking any of her shit.

MARY   FUCK YOU, TOM! YOU'RE NOT MY FUCKING FA-THER!

MR. T. She's going to get with the program or go back in the hospital! I can sign her in and I will! [*The adults begin to talk about Mary as if she's not in the room. Mary stomps over to the phone and calls her father. When she gets her father's answering machine, she leaves this message: "Dad, this is Mary. Tom is hurting me. Call me."*]

Hypotheses. In conflicted families the content and process of their interactions are rarely congruent; in this family there is too much reactive *process* between family members and no attention to *what* family members are really saying. Integrating the videotaped observations of the family's interactions with other assessment data enables the supervisor and team members to form hypotheses about the meaning of Mary's aggressive behaviors. These hypotheses include:

1. Mary feels cut off from the nurturance she needs from her mother and father; Mr. T.'s entrance into the family has created distance in a previously close mother-daughter relationship, to which Mary has responded with aggressive behavior.

2. Mary's out-of control behavior stems from her being triangulated in four ways: between her mother and Mr. T.; between her mother and father; between Mr. T. and her father; and between the inpatient doctor and Mr. T.
3. Mary's statement, "no one listens to me," reflects her being on the outside of a triangle composed of herself, Mr. T., and her mother, as well as the triangles composed of the home-based team members, Mr. T., her mother, and herself.
4. Mary's mention of her doctor and her father in the current session reflects her need to have a supportive ally who will listen to her.
5. Mary is developmentally stuck at the age of eight when her parents' divorce occurred, and her mother continues to infantilize her.
6. Mary feels emotionally responsible for her father.

The unifying theme beneath these hypotheses is that Mary makes effective use of her 14-year-old capabilities and becomes out-of-control when she feels abandoned and without an ally in the home.

Treatment interventions. After intensive supervision in relation to this family's situation, the team implemented the following interventions. One of the team members (Diane) was designated to work with Mary individually and develop an alliance with her so that Mary had someone in sessions who would help others (especially her mother) listen to her. Mary's anger was reframed as sadness over her parents' divorce and her feelings that her mother loved Mr. T. more than her. Individual sessions with Mary focused on individuation issues and the need to consider feedback from her peers rather than relying solely on her parents' perceptions. In these individual sessions with Mary as well as the family sessions, the therapists encouraged and underscored Mary's age-appropriate competencies as a student, baby-sitter, and pet owner.

The home-based team also worked on *interactive process interventions* (enactments between family members that supported individual boundary functioning) and *content interventions* exploring the sadness that *all* family members felt, which had been denied in their singular focus on Mary's anger.

The most frequent interactive process interventions used by the team to support individual boundary functioning took the form of creating explicit session rules about *who* members would communicate with and *how* they would do that. For example, only one person would speak at a time. The person being spoken to had to restate what the speaker had communicated. If the speaker was misunderstood, he or she would attempt to clarify the intent of the communication. One team member (Diane) monitored the communications between Mary and mother and between Mary and Mr. T. The other team member (Dave) monitored communication between mother and Mr. T. If a family member interrupted a conversation, he or she was reminded by one of the therapists that a session rule had been broken. These types of interventions slowed down the high degree of reactivity between family members.

The content interventions underscored *what* content could be discussed in sessions, The team explicitly told the family that for several sessions individuals could only talk about the sadness each member had experienced during the formation of this cohabitating family. Within these sessions, Mary's out-of-control behaviors were gradually redefined by the therapists as her attempts to seek reassurance that her mother loved her and as requesting help from her mother in learning more appropriate ways of getting needs met. In subsequent sessions, as Mr. T. and the 12-year-old sister, Dawn, listened, Diane facilitated numerous conversations between mother and Mary. The focus on the mother-child dyad highlighted the love and emotional bond between them. Diane supported mother's efforts to negotiate expected rules with Mary and consequences if rules were broken. Mother told Mary that she would be Mary's sole disciplinarian in the home. Mother also emphasized that Mary had a right to express anger or disagreement about limits and that she respected her daughter's right to have her own opinions. Mother was also willing to help coach Mary in identifying ways for her to get what she wanted while obeying family rules.

Conjoint sessions conducted with Ms. L. and Mr. T. helped them to negotiate conflict without triangulating Mary. Individual sessions were scheduled with Mary's father, with the goal of encouraging him to support his ex-wife's parenting. Dyadic sessions held with the father and Mary had the goal of reinforcing the father's support of his daughter and his willingness to function as the adult in his relationship with his daughter.

Systemic/structural hypotheses are often based on the core assumption that behaviors are communications about relationships. When a parent abdicates responsibility for an aggressive youth's behavior, the parent's passivity may be viewed as implicitly supporting the violent behavior. In the following case vignette, the youth's assaultive behavior may represent the voice of the inactive stepfather.

Case Vignette: "Mike"*

"Mike" is a 15-year-old Caucasian boy who lives in an extremely isolated rural home with his mother (Ms. W.), a recovering alcoholic, 10-year-old stepbrother (Roger), and stepfather (Mr. C.). Mike was referred by Child Welfare Services when an unidentified person reported him for threatening to kill his stepbrother. The family had had no previous contact with agencies or institutions and was very suspicious of outsiders. It took the home-based team several weeks before the family would allow them into their home, and the family was quite cautious about providing background information.

One evening the female home-based team responded to an emergency page from the stepfather, who stated, "Get him out! He tried to kill my wife!" When the team arrived, the mother's arm was in a sling. Upon inquiry, they discovered that Mike had assaulted his mother and sprained her arm. When the team asked what had happened, Mr. C. described the events in a detached manner, as if recounting a television story. Mike had become agitated, wrapped an iron chain around his arm, and said to the stepfather: "Now I want to see the fucking bitch say anything to me now." Mother had a birch switch in her hand to show her son that she wasn't afraid of him. Mike ripped the birch switch out of her hand and shoved her down on the couch. As they wrestled over possession of the birch switch, Mike got on top of his mother and pressed his arm against her throat. Mr. C. reported, "I tried my damnedest to stay out of it! There's been so much damn shit between Mike and me. I didn't want Mike mad at me. Roger

---

*Joan Cashion and Hope Graves were the therapists in this case.

knows what's going on." The team takes the story that Mr. C. tells and punctuates it differently, creating intensity and a different reality: "This was an act of violence." They then emphasize parts of the story that were absent in Mr. C.'s account.

HOPE   You just watched? What did you feel? What did you want to do?

MR. C.   Wilma [Ms. W.] wouldn't let me hit him. She was on the couch turning more and more purple.

HOPE   Was she unable to fight back? Where were her arms?

MR. C.   One was pinned in back of her and the other was around Mike's back.

HOPE   Ms. W. wasn't doing anything?

MR. C.   No. I wanted to cold cock him right there. I went over and started to reach down, but Wilma jumped up, pushed Mike off, and said to me, "Don't hit him!" If I knew then what I know now, I'd have called the state police. He's out of hand.

           [*As Mr. C. tells the story, the mother sits quietly, adding nothing, appearing very distant from her husband—as if he were a TV reporter. Mike and Roger are standing on the other side of the room, watching. There's a striking sense of isolation in the family.*]

MOTHER   I told him to behave. He said he'd do what he wanted. I took the birch stick. He called me "a fucking bitch" and pushed me down on the couch. I wanted to see how far this little boy would go. He was hurting me, but I just wanted to see what was in him. I wanted to see how far he would go. If he'd gone all the way, then I'd know he was in trouble. He made noises like an animal. I was think-ing—let's see if he could do it. This boy has to learn limits somehow. I thought if I let him go as far as he'd go, maybe he'd learn something.

HOPE   Why are you protecting Mike? What lesson do you think he learned last night? [*Hope gently but relentlessly helps the mother to see her actions in a different light.*]

MOTHER   That he could push me around.

HOPE   Can you correct him by yourself? Who do you need to help you?

MOTHER   Chris [Mr. C.].

HOPE   Mr. C. is very concerned that you could have been seriously injured. Close your eyes and relive the experience for a minute.

MOTHER   I'm not feeling afraid of him. I'm afraid *for* him. There wasn't murder in his eyes, there was fear—like I was in his way, and he didn't want me there. [*Ms. W. begins to cry and the therapist gently strokes her arm. Mr. C. comes over and hugs Ms. W. as she cries. The therapist's increased proximity to the mother has encouraged the stepfather to move closer to his wife.*]

Later in the session Mike tells his version of the story to Joan, the other team member. Joan introduces a sense of the absurd so that Mike can hear what he edited from his story.

MIKE   I'd been up all night watching the movies *Hell's Angels* and *Forbidden Passion*. In the morning we went to visit my cousins. I saw Paul for the first time in two and a half years. He was like a brother and lived with us for about five years. Chris kicked him out because my parents couldn't handle him. When I came home from my cousin's house, Mom yelled at me to mow the lawn and pick up brambles. I was hungry and asked for a sandwich. She just laughed and told me to make it myself. I dropped a pickle on the floor and she pulled me down by the hair to pick it up. She wouldn't listen to me. She kept laughing. I told her if she kept laughing, I'd take the birch switch away from her.

JOAN   Let me see if I've got this straight. I hear that a volatile family got into a fight over a pickle on the floor. And you lost it—ran around with a chain, hollering and swearing. Your mother was pulling your hair. I don't know what else was going on, but you ended up pushing your mom and trying to choke her to death. Now that's pretty crazy shit— like what you'd read in a newspaper. What does it seem like to you? Is it better than TV? What's going on? Where do you come up with ideas like this? It's intriguing to me. Does someone tell you to do this? Do you have friends outside telling you to "off" someone? Do you ever find yourself talking to yourself and wondering what it would be like to do something like that? [*Mike denies all these questions sheepishly.*]

Mike, know what I think? You're really a good guy who's playing the part of a bad dude. You've been miscast. What you really want to be in is a family love story where everyone loves everyone: Mom loves you and so does the girl next door. Your stepfather cares about you as if you were his own son. Your stepbrother looks up to you, and Mom and your stepfather are totally boring in their affection for one another. Sure, sometimes they get mad at each other, but they work it out. They don't use you as the one to express the anger.

Now in this play Mike, scene one has got to be your telling your mom how much you love her and how very, very, very sorry you are for hurting her. Can we start with that? [*Mike, looking relieved, says "yes."*]

Historical and current stressors. After the crisis was addressed, the family shared more information with the team. There had been a history of intergenerational abuse in the family. Ms. W. was sexually abused by her brother and sister, but her mother had refused to believe her disclosure to her. Mr. C. has hit Ms. W. during arguments. Both Mr. C. and Ms. W. have always punished Mike and Roger by hitting or slapping them. Further information also emerged from the family regarding the shifting composition of household members. The in-home team's initial impression was that the household had for a long time consisted of mother, her son, stepfather, and his son. The team learned, however, that Ms. W.'s mother, Ms. W.'s brother, and Ms. W.'s nephew had also been household members. For five years Ms. W.'s nephew, Paul, lived with the family and had a close relationship with Mike. When Paul acted out at the age of 14, Mr. C. sent him to live with another uncle. After home-based services began, Ms. W.'s 49-year-old brother moved from the home. One month later Ms. W. was hospitalized in a psychiatric unit for one week. Following this event, Ms. W.'s mother was moved from the household to a personal care facility. The emergency page to the home-based team from Mr. C. occurred three weeks later.

Strengths of family members. Ms. W. has demonstrated the ability to deal with stress without alcohol. She can set limits on her tendency toward excessive caretaking. For example, she took responsibility for asking her brother to leave the household and placed her mother in a personal care facility. She is painfully honest with herself. Mr. C. cares about Ms. W. and wants to be respected as her partner. He works hard to provide financially for the family. Mike behaves responsibly outside of the home. He is frequently hired by neighbors to do outdoor work because he is reliable and competent. He shares his music cassettes with his stepbrother. Roger is able to understand that he has been Dad's "favorite" and the impact this has on Mike. He appreciates Mike's taste in music.

Hypotheses. Working with the family's crisis created more trust between the family and the in-home team. Consequently, assessment information emerged that was essential for the team to develop more accurate hypotheses about the meaning of Mike's violent behavior. These hypotheses included:

1. Mike feels covertly supported by his stepfather in his display of violence toward his mother.
2. There is limited sexuality between stepfather and mother, which encourages a coalition between mother and son; before moving from the household, Ms. W.'s brother and her mother may also have regulated intimacy and volatility in the parental relationship.
3. Family members use aggressive behavior as a way of increasing proximity in a very disengaged family system.
4. Mike feels that he is the outsider to the overt coalition between his stepfather and stepbrother.
5. Mike worries that the repetitive "shape-up or ship-out" message from his stepfather will result in his being thrown out, like his cousin Paul was; Mike tests his mother to the ultimate limits to see if she loves him as much as Mr.C.

Treatment interventions. This crisis in the family provided an opportunity to alter family patterns, as described by the following interventions:

1. The family's conversation was shifted from the focus on gaining control of Mike's behavior to exploring the affective issues in the family that created this situation.
2. Mike was asked if he felt that Mr. C. had replaced him in his mother's affections. When Mike said "yes," he was

asked how he felt about that. The team worked slowly to guide Mike and Mr. C. into talking about how their relationship had developed and how it had been regulated by Ms. W. and Roger.

3. Mike's assaultive behavior was redefined as one horrible but forgiveable example of how the entire family had used violence to solve problems and increase closeness. Mike apologized to his mother and made reparation. The family developed a list of "Thou shalt not" rules for family communication (no violence, name-calling, etc.).

4. A plan was created with the parents wherein they would call the police if Mike *or* Roger displayed potential volatility. Roger was included in this plan because the parents wanted to highlight the responsibility that each boy had not to provoke the other.

5. The importance of Mr. C. and Ms. W. working together in a strong parental alliance was emphasized; sessions were held with the parents to discuss alternative disciplinary approaches.

6. A therapeutic alliance was developed with Mike through individual sessions, in which he was encouraged to express his feelings appropriately and negotiate ways to meet his needs with his parents.

7. Conjoint sessions were conducted with Ms. W. and Mr. C. to help them learn how to communicate their needs to one another and how to negotiate conflict without triangulating Mike or Roger.

8. Family sessions were used to discuss possible age-appropriate recreational activities for the boys to reduce feelings of isolation and boredom; also, family recreational activities were designed to promote pleasurable connections among family members.

HYPERACTIVE/IMPULSIVE CHILDREN AND ADOLESCENTS

Diagnostic Description

Attention-deficit/hyperactivity disorder (ADHD) is a syndrome comprised of a cluster of symptoms that includes inattentiveness, impulsivity, and hyperactivity. A child need not display all core symptoms; that is, he or she may be inattentive but not hyperactive. There is no single profile of an ADHD child, as significant variability occurs in symptoms, responses to treatment, and prognosis. Children with ADHD can differ in performance at any given moment, on any day, and at any developmental stage. Four times as many boys present with ADHD than girls. Intellectual functioning is somewhat lower in children with this disorder. The diagnostic criteria for ADHD should be viewed in terms of what is considered "developmentally appropriate" for the child's chronological age. For example, a two-year-old would not be expected to sit still for 20 minutes, whereas an eleven-year-old would.

According to the *DSM-IV* guidelines, to qualify for a diagnosis of ADHD the child must exhibit at least six symptoms of hyperactivity and/or impulsivity and/or at least six symptoms of inattention. Generally, *hyperactive* children are unable to sit still or play quietly. They may talk, fidget, squirm, climb, or run about excessively. Easily distracted, the child often loses or forgets things and may not seem to be listening when spoken to directly. Close attention is not paid to details and careless mistakes are often made. Routine activities requiring sustained attention (such as schoolwork or homework) are difficult. The organization and completion of tasks are problematic, especially if instructions have involved multiple steps. *Impulsivity* causes the ADHD child to act before thinking. Thus the child may blurt out in class, not wait his or her turn, and fail to plan goal-directed actions. The use of poor judgment may result in the child putting him- or herself in dangerous situations or not controlling antisocial impulses, such as stealing or lying. In addition to these symptoms, other temperamental and behavioral problems may exist in ADHD children, including low frustration tolerance, excessive demands for attention, difficulty getting along with others, difficulty adjusting to new situations and following rules, school underachievement, low motivation, and poor self-esteem (Barkley, 1990).

The severity of the ADHD disorder ranges from mild to severe, depending on the number, intensity, and persistence of symptoms exhibited and resistance to therapy. According to the *DSM-IV* criteria, difficulties in developmental functioning caused by ADHD symptoms must occur in more than one social context (e.g., home, school, or peer group), present before the age of seven, and persist for at least six months. However, many ADHD children and adolescents also experience associated problems, such as learning disabilities, oppositional behaviors, conduct disorders, mood disorders, or anxiety disorders. Differential diagnosis is often difficult since each problem influences and interacts with the others, and the relevance of any one problem may change over time. An accurate diagnosis helps to identify which of the problems are most important and which can be treated effectively. Therefore, while most children with ADHD have learning difficulties, the possibility of specific coexisting learning disabilities must also be assessed.

Learning disorders may affect a child's ability to perceive, integrate, remember, or express information. The ability to learn depends on the way a child's brain receives and processes information. A diagnosis of learning disorder (LD) occurs when the child's performance on individually administered, standardized tests in reading, mathematics, or written expression is significantly lower that what would be expected, given the child's age, education, and level of intelligence (American Psychiatric Association, 1994). Bogas (1993) highlights the significant interplay between behaviors common to children with ADHD and those with learning disabilities: "While we can track discrete cognitive functions such as memory or language processes in a child, . . . these functions are not self-contained but, rather, are influenced by temperament, family/social and educational factors" (p. 387). She recommends a multimodal diagnostic and treatment approach involving biomedical, psychoeducational, and family systems.

Case Vignette: "Kay" *

"Kay," a seven-year-old Caucasian girl who had been adopted at age two, was referred for home-based services by Child Welfare Services because her adoptive family could no longer cope with her longstanding disruptive behaviors. These included not completing chores or following house rules and locking the cat in a car without food or water. Frequent complaints from the school centered on Kay's impulsive and distractible nature, her inattentiveness and

---

*Liane Kuhns and Rosemarie Witt were the therapists in this case.

lack of appropriate social skills, and her serious deficits in language skills, including reading and writing.

The referral to mental health home-based services was precipitated by a family crisis in which Kay locked the family cat in her adoptive 17-year-old sister's car on a hot summer day. The cat nearly died and the car's interior was destroyed. Her sister issued an ultimatum to her parents that if Kay did not leave the home, she would. Feeling torn, the adoptive parents met with Child Welfare personnel with the intent of having Kay removed from the home. The parents were urged to try mental health home-based services before pursuing other legal options. The "D." family had been functioning in a highly satisfactory manner prior to Kay's adoption, but incorporating a child with these difficulties had created an imbalance in the family relationships.

Historical and current stressors. Kay was adopted at the age of two by Mr. and Mrs. D., a working-class Caucasian couple in their early thirties. The only information given to the adoptive parents was that Kay had been abused and evidenced behavioral problems. At the time of the adoption, the D.'s daughter, Joan, was 12 years old. The decision to adopt was made after Mrs. D. had a hysterectomy. Kay's developmental history as a preschooler was characterized by problems with attention span, low frustration tolerance, demands for attention, and difficulty adjusting to new situations. The adoption agency told Mr. and Mrs. D. that these symptoms were to be expected because of Kay's abuse.

Strengths of family members. Both Mr. and Mrs. D. are conscientious parents who had attended adoptive parent education meetings to facilitate Kay's transition into their family. They sought information about the potential effects of abuse on Kay's development and had demonstrated a great deal of tolerance for her disruptive behaviors during her preschool years. Both spouses hold stable jobs and enjoy good relationships with friends and extended family. They demonstrate a strong marital commitment to one another.

Joan is a bright, sensitive girl who initially welcomed the role of being a big sister to Kay. At 17 years, she is active with her friends and is planning to attend college.

A physically appealing little girl, Kay excels at video games and memorizing comic lines from the television show "The Simpsons." In a one-to-one, low-stimuli context with adults, she attends well.

She is always apologetic when she has shown poor judgment, such as when she hurt the cat.

Observed family interaction in the home. Mrs. D.'s heightened involvement with Kay during the initial family interview was quite apparent. Depending upon Kay's behavior, the mother would alternate between protectiveness and strong expressions of anger and frustration. She appeared to experience Kay's disruptive behaviors as a personal attack on herself. In listening to the mother's story, the therapist began to understand her reality. Day after day, she carried most of the responsibility for Kay's care, behavioral management, and emotional support. Mrs. D. seemed to be at a point of exhaustion and near-despair.

While both parents described Kay as negative, self-centered, and highly uncooperative in response to routines and requests, they argued over whether, and how, to discipline her. Mr. D. often felt that his wife tended to exaggerate Kay's misbehaviors. Looking for support, Mrs. D. had turned to her daughter as her confidante in complaints about Kay. The parents' greatest frustration stemmed from a mutual conviction that Kay was willfully being "bad." Their anger had led them to impose severe consequences on Kay for various misdemeanors and for resisting doing her chores and homework. For example, Kay's punishment for having nearly killed the cat and ruining the interior of Joan's car was that she had to clean Joan's room weekly for one year. During an individual session, Kay told the therapist that her parents were always angry with her and blamed her "for everything."

Hypotheses. The opportunity to observe Kay in the home with her family, in the school with the teacher and classmates, and in the community with her friends provided essential assessment information. Targeted hypotheses were then formulated as follows:

1. Kay's symptoms may be manifestations of an undiagnosed attention-deficit/hyperactivity disorder and a learning disorder, complicated by unresolved life experiences related to adoption and past abuse.
2. The D. family's response to Kay's symptoms has created a pattern wherein the mother shoulders most of the responsibility for Kay, the father provides minimal support, and

therefore Joan has assumed the supportive role with her mother, minimizing her support to Kay.

3. The parental conflicts over discipline reflect lack of clarity about the meaning of Kay's symptoms. Since the parents had been told that Kay's problems were related to her pre-adoption history, the possibility of ADHD or LD was never considered by the school or family.

Treatment interventions. The expectations and goals of treatment were initially focused on obtaining a comprehensive assessment by qualified professionals of Kay's cognitive/educational/behavioral/interpersonal strengths and weaknesses so that the family and school could be realistic in their expectations. Although Kay's behavioral and temperamental characteristics fluctuated, they would continue over a lifetime if an ADHD/LD diagnosis was accurate. Therapeutic goals with the family focused on changing the emotional "climate," strengthening the functioning of the family as a unit, and giving the parents tools to help Kay function and cope optimally in her environment. In a parallel fashion, the school context would need to be assessed to determine processes that might be helping or hindering Kay's functioning.

At the suggestion of the home-based therapists, the parents made a decision to have a comprehensive assessment conducted at a nearby medical center specializing in ADHD/LD. Kay was prescribed Ritalin, and the medication dramatically altered her behavior. Empowered by a fuller understanding of Kay's symptoms, the parents became more realistic in their expectations of her and the mother was able to depersonalize her response to many of Kay's behaviors. At Kay's request the parents arranged for karate classes, which provided a much-needed outlet for her energy as well as an enjoyable means of increasing her self-esteem, concentration, and personal safety skills. Kay, in turn, had fun teaching her parents her newly acquired skills.

Some of the family interventions introduced by the home-based team that were particularly appreciated by the parents included:

- supporting the parents' efforts to obtain a comprehensive evaluation for Kay
- conducting discussions with the parents aimed at promoting

agreement about realistic expectations for Kay's abilities to better control her behavior, limit-setting, and consistent disciplinary methods (using behavioral techniques)

- providing weekly respite for the mother by implementing out-of-the home recreational activities for Kay with one of the therapists
- inviting the parents to join the home-based team in attending an out-of-town conference on adoption issues
- increasing more positive sibling interaction with Joan
- working individually with Kay on affective issues by creating adoption rituals and enacting exercises that helped her explore and express her feelings
- designing individual tasks for Kay, aimed at promoting her ability to self-monitor, plan ahead, and anticipate consequences (compiling a list of coping skills for her to use, such as journal writing and going for walks, and teaching her assertiveness skills with peers).

The home-based team also worked closely with the assessment specialists, school personnel, and the family to ensure an appropriate educational milieu. Kay received individualized study skills instruction in a special resource class for children having learning disorders. Additionally, a daily reward system was implemented in all her classes with emphasis on self-monitoring and social skills development.

Case examples in this chapter typify the clinical challenges encountered by the mental health home-based therapist. There are no "quick fixes" or simple cures. By listening to the family's story and observing the minute-to-minute feedback in every transaction during sessions, a therapist begins to formulate hypotheses about the child's symptoms and the family's organization. Working in collaboration with the parent(s), a plan is developed for treatment intervention. In order to meet the clinical challenges of these high-risk families, the in-home therapist needs both supervision and training, which we will discuss in the next two chapters.

CHAPTER 6

Supervising the
Home-Based Therapist

> Supposing you were sitting on a train standing still in a great railroad station and supposing the train on the track next to yours began to move. It would seem to you that it was your train that was moving, and in the opposite direction. The only way you could tell about yourself, which way you were going, or even if you were going anywhere at all, would be to find a point of reference, something standing still, perhaps a person on the next platform; and in relation to this person you could judge your own direction and motion. . . . All you need to do is see your point of reference.
>
> —Madeleine L'Engle, 1972

THE STRESS THAT COMES FROM conducting intensive in-home services can be overwhelming and may lead to rapid burnout. The home-based therapist requires a supportive context in order to manage the many pressures that emerge during the close and sometimes volatile interactions with families and the community. The supervisory relationship is both the critical context of support for the home-based therapist and the pivotal factor in shaping the treatment process. The guiding ecosystemic concept is that both the supervision and the therapy emerge from an interconnected web of relationships involving the client, family, treatment team (supervisor, home-based therapist or team), program agency, community helpers, and, when possible, trainers (see Figure 6.1). The supervisory relationship provides a "point of reference" that encourages the therapist's creativity in constructing a total ecosystem that assists families in utilizing their own resources and those of the community more effectively.

185

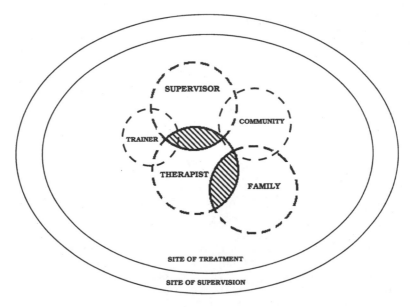

Figure 6.1
ECOSYSTEMIC STRUCTURAL MODEL OF SUPERVISION

ASSUMPTIONS OF ECOSYSTEMIC
STRUCTURAL SUPERVISION

There are two basic assumptions underlying an ecosystemic structural model of supervision. The first assumption is that a supervisor has a particular orientation to therapy, which can be clearly articulated to the supervisee, who will undergo his or her own process of selecting a model of therapy. For example, a supervisor endorsing the ecosystemic structural model assumes that families who present for therapy have evolved a relational context around a symptom or problem, which obstructs successful mastery of developmental and/or extrafamilial challenges (Minuchin, 1974). The second key assumption is that isomorphism or parallel process occurs between one's clinical model and supervision model; that is, the supervisory process should follow from the same principles that govern the therapeutic process (Connell, 1984; Haber, 1996; Liddle, Breulin, Schwartz, & Constantine, 1984; Liddle & Saba, 1983). Just as the therapist's primary goal is to create an optimal therapeutic context, the supervisor's primary goal is to create a supervisory context that will actualize both the supervisor's and supervisee's potentials. In both therapy and supervision, change occurs only in the context of a meaningful relationship. Therefore, the same interpersonal skills used in therapy need to operate in supervision. Growth can occur in a nonthreatening, noncompetitive "holding environment" within which the supervisee experiments with new behaviors, develops increased autonomy, and exhibits an openness to learning (Friedman & Kaslow, 1986; Schwartz, 1988). The supervisor will create change experiences for supervisees, who, as therapists, will create change experiences for families.

There are many other examples of parallel process in therapy and supervision. Just as the therapist assesses both the strengths and the nonadaptive patterns of interaction involving family members and extrafamilial others, the supervisor looks for both competencies and maladaptive patterns of interaction involving the therapist, family, community, and supervisor. Supervisors must attend to the distinctive characteristics of supervisees (race, ethnicity, gender, sexual orientation, age, religious background, lifestyle, educational and professional experience, variability of learning styles, etc.), who, as therapists, need to be responsive to a family's unique characteristics. Mutually developed supervision goals and accountability evaluations will guide the supervisory process, just as collaborative goal-setting and ongoing evaluation shape the treatment process.

WHAT IS SUPERVISION?

Supervision can be defined as "an intensive, interpersonally focused . . . relationship in which one person is designated to facilitate the development of therapeutic competence in the other person[s]" (Loganbill, Hardy, & Delworth, 1982, p. 4). Supervision is a dynamic process that develops out of the relationship between supervisor and supervisee. Within this evolving relationship, Holloway (1995) notes that "the supervisor and supervisee will negotiate a personal way of using a structure of power and involvement that accommodates the supervisee's progression in learning" (pp. 41–42). Supervisors and supervisees enter a relationship at differing developmental levels in relation to personal history as well as the mastery of family therapy (Kaslow, 1986). The supervisory process occurs over time in a developmental spiral that alters the complementarity of the relationship. For example, in supervising a less experienced therapist, the supervisor may initially assume a more directive, hierarchical style to meet the beginner's needs for structure and immediate knowledge. Over time, however, as the supervisee gains competence and desires more autonomy, the supervisor must shift to a more collaborative, less hierarchical role. Supervisors become ineffective when they do not shift their role from "expert" to "collaborative partner," an accommodation that acknowleges the supervisee's increased expertise. With a more experienced therapist, mutual discussion can help a supervisor gauge the optimal levels of intensity, interaction, and autonomy. Both inexperienced and experienced therapists and their supervisors are responsible for ultimately developing a collaborative learning alliance.

The parameters of the supervisory relationship must be clearly defined and understood by both parties. A supervisory relationship should be ongoing and occur within a consistent time frame. The ultimate goal of supervision is the clinical socialization of the therapist, as evidenced by knowledge, clinical skills, and ethical public practice (Bernard & Goodyear, 1992). Supervisors need to maintain clear boundaries between professional development and personal growth or therapy. If this boundary is blurred, it may result in the supervisee's becoming excessively dependent, confused, and unclear about his or her professional role in relation to the supervisor.

After exploring the supervisee's expectations of supervision, the supervisor should clarify what the process will entail and define his or her expectations for the supervisee. In establishing a supervisory contract, the personal and professional goals of the supervisee should also be discussed. It is important to understand why the supervisee has chosen the context of home-based services for professional development. What distinguishes the supervisory relationship from other clinical relationships (i.e., therapy, clinical training) is the requirement of mutual accountability and evaluation. The supervisor has the responsibility to ensure that the supervisee is clearly informed regarding performance expectations and supervisory goals, criteria and methods of evaluation, and parameters regarding confidentiality in supervision (Holloway, 1995). Developing a baseline of what a supervisee needs from supervision based on job expectations is an essential first step to establishing a supervisory contract.

The orientation training checklist developed by Dunlap (1996) and found in Appendix H describes baseline knowledge needed by newly employed in-home therapists. This checklist serves as a preliminary supervisory contact, since it clarifies the new hiree's existing skills versus those skills that will be addressed within supervision. For example, a new staff employee should know basic job expectations stemming from the agency's policies and procedures. Understanding program components unique to home-based services (respite, family support, emergency service) is a job expectation. Computer skill proficiency is assessed for drafting required medical records and patient correspondence. Practitioners need to know what type of clinical information is emphasized by the program and what clinical interview skills are required. An ecosystemic approach emphasizes evaluation of current individual and family functioning and historical information (e.g., genograms, critical life event timelines). The ability to integrate assessment information when constructing a treatment plan and to write effectively is essential. A new in-home therapist needs to know community resources and their locations. Working in a team-delivered service requires mastering team issues.

The fact that the supervisor is in a position of authority and evaluation raises issues of power and hierarchy in the supervisory relationship. Since the supervisor's job is to "impart expert knowledge, make judgments of the supervisee's performance and act as a gatekeeper in the profession" (Holloway, 1995, p. 43), the supervisor's position in the supervisory relationship is, by definition, a hierarchical one. Holloway (1995) describes two types of power that are inherent in the role of supervisor as evaluator—reward power and coercive power. For example, a supervisor can provide rewards by validating performance ("You have done an excellent job!") or dispensing punishment ("You are on probation"). However, the power differential may take different forms, depending on the degree of attachment and fit between the supervisor and supervisee (Holloway, 1995). The ongoing interactions between these individuals allow them to mutually influence each other. Power that develops through interpersonal involvement is more effective than coercion. If the supervisory relationship develops in a strong and positive fashion, the power of both participants will be enhanced. The most important factors determining the levels of involvement in the supervisory relationship over time are the personal characteristics of each individual and relevant contextual factors.

CONTEXTUAL FACTORS AFFECTING SUPERVISION

The meaning of our experiences and expectations is unconsciously shaped by our culture. Falicov (1988) has defined culture as "those sets of shared world views and adaptive behaviors derived from simultaneous membership in a variety of contexts, such as ecological setting (rural, urban, suburban), religous background, nationality and ethnicity, social, class, gender-related experiences, minority status, occupation, political leanings, migratory patterns, and stage of acculteration, or values derived from belonging to the same generation, partaking of a single historical moment, or particular ideologies" (p. 336). Since a supervisor and supervisee will always differ regarding their life histories, experiences, values, styles of living, and methods of communication, supervision can be considered a "cross-cultural" endeavor even when both parties are members of the same culture.

Supervisors must value individual difference and freely demonstrate this value in supervision. In a therapeutic system formed by the therapist, family, and supervisor, it would be unusual to have every one of the same race, ethnicity, and socioeconomic status. Supervisors who do not want to assume the position of "cultural blindness" should be alert to the prevalent cultural minimizations that occur frequently in supervision and therapy. The tendency to deny differences by adopting the universal construction that "everyone is the same" is a common blind spot (Smith, 1981) that can prevent helpers from sensitively reading feedback that reflects important differences in communication styles, beliefs, motivations, and values (Ryan & Hendricks, 1989). According to Hardy and Laszloffy (1994), "Race is always an organizing principle in therapy. . . . Since the importance of race is often minimized, most therapists do not acquire the skills and sensitivities necessary to 'see' and 'talk' about the racial subtleties in therapy" (p. 15).

Supervisors can increase cross-cultural awareness in their supervisees by discussing the variability that occurs in every therapeutic system and exploring the supervisee's particular way of viewing his/her own values, ethnicity, and culture. Examining what role these factors have played in the supervisee's personal development and how they may affect clinical practice can be both educational and sensitizing. This is particularly helpful before exposing the supervisee to therapeutic work with clients from other cultural backgrounds. Once cross-cultural clinical practice begins, Cook (1994) suggests such supervisory questions as: "At what point did you notice the client's race? What did you think about it? How did you feel about it? What did you do in response to the client's race? How did you feel as a (supervisee's race) person in relation to the client? How do you think the client responded to your racial appearance?" (p. 138). As the supervisor and supervisee become more comfortable discussing cross-cultural issues, their relationship will become more authentic and the supervisee will become more responsive to racial issues in therapy. The challenge for the supervisor is to model an appreciation of individual differences that does not make anyone "feel different" (Montalvo & Gutierrez, 1988). Discussion of cultural identity issues should serve the purpose of establishing trust and connection within a relationship rather than promoting distance.

Other important contextual factors that influence the supervisory relationship are: gender, personal qualities, experience level of the supervisor, and agency characteristics. Both Haber (1996) and Holloway (1995) offer extensive discussion on these topics.

SUPERVISORY GOALS

Once the parameters of the relationship have been defined, the supervision begins. The areas of competency that should be enhanced by supervisors of home-based therapy include case conceptualizations, family therapy, case management (i.e., knowledge of, and connections with, community resources, family advocacy channels, and interagency involvement), use of family support services, crisis intervention, team-building (if services are provided by teams), emotional awareness, self-evaluation, and professional role development.

Becoming a family therapist requires the development of perceptual, conceptual, executive (Tomm & Wright, 1979), affective, and cultural thinking (Falicov, 1988) skills. Perceptual skills are generally the most basic of these skills. Beginning home-based family therapists first need to learn how to see patterns, recognize sequences of interactions, and read feedback in family and community sessions. Supervisors who wish to teach these skills need to observe the therapist's in-home or interagency sessions. If camcorders are not available for therapists to use in the field, an in-office videotaped session or role-played session will suffice. If neither of these modalities is available, the supervisor can teach perceptual skills through analysis of family therapy teaching videotapes (if the agency has audiovisual equipment).

Once perceptual skills have been acquired, they need to be understood within a conceptual and cultural framework. To facilitate this goal, the supervisor can recommend appropriate literature and discuss the application of ideas during clinical case discussion.

Skill in conducting therapy can only occur through clinical practice. Through years of clinical experience, therapists develop a repetoire of skills from which interventions are created. These skills relate to *content* interventions (what to do with verbal material), *process* interventions (what to do with nonverbal, behavioral material), and simultaneous *content-process* interventions (what to say and do with verbal and nonverbal material concurrently). The basic executive skills taught to home-based therapists include:

- forming a collaborative relationship with the family and extrafamilial helpers
- changing perceptions by redefining (reframing) problems in interactional terms
- utilizing family strengths by creating enactments to promote new patterns of behavior
- boundary-making (e.g., establishing clear rules of interaction such as family members talking for themselves, individuals talking to each other rather than about each other, designating who talk to whom about specified issues) (Minuchin & Fishman, 1981)
- unbalancing (i.e., challenging the distribution of power and

influence within family relationships by intentional therapeutic side-taking) (Minuchin & Fishman, 1981)

- creating intensity (i.e., emphasizing a therapeutic message through repetition, extending the time of a new interpersonal transaction, or using a novel therapeutic style that helps to focus the family's attention) (Minuchin & Fishman, 1981)

These skills can be honed by reviewing in-home videotaped sessions and engaging in demonstration role-play, through phoned-in directives during an in-office one-way mirror session, or through demonstration by the supervisor during an in-home session observed by the therapist.

Experienced supervisees generally require supervision that helps them to recognize the finer nuances of family process; create themes, metaphors, and focus "on-the-spot" in sessions; develop conceptualizations that more thoroughly capture the complexity of the family's dynamics; incorporate theory and interventions from other models, when appropriate; begin to articulate their own developing models; and expand the use of self in the therapeutic process.

Supervisory goals for both beginning and experienced supervisees should also include fostering awareness of their affective responses to others and increasing comfort levels with a wide range of emotional expression. Reviewing videotaped sessions, with an emphasis on the therapist's self-evaluation of affective issues, is one way to approach this goal. Other effective supervisory methods include devising role-playing scenarios wherein the therapist either experiences the feeling state of another or practices the expression of an unfamiliar affect.

Most of the supervisory goals described thus far relate to therapists working singly in a family therapy practice in any treatment context. Using a two-person team to provide home-based family therapy to high-risk families has many advantages, however. Peer support is crucial when faced with the intensive needs of multi-problem families and concerns about safety issues in off-site locations. Practically speaking, teamwork also means that there is always clinical coverage if one therapist is sick or on vacation. Furthermore, the inherent diversity of teamwork gives supervisors greater flexibility in creating a therapeutic fit with families. Supervisors can create *fixed teams* to make scheduling easier or *flexible teams* to match family needs with team expertise, style, etc. The use of flexible teams creates the opportunity for staff to learn from each other and to eliminate the possibility of anyone feeling "stuck" with an undesirable partner. Another advantage of using teams relates to two common clinical challenges experienced during in-home therapy: induction and maintaining a clear direction and focus in the session. Assigning one therapist to take the lead in a family session and the other to assume an observer role reduces the team's vulnerability to induction. The team can agree to take timed breaks during the in-home session so that the observing team member can let the lead therapist know if therapeutic focus has been lost or induction is occurring.

In a team-delivered home-based service, supervision needs to address issues of team-building and potential triangulations. Like an "arranged marriage," team-building involves negotiating issues of power, conflict, intimacy, developmental differences, variations in personal style, and differing world views about family values, the practice of therapy, and lifestyle. By using planned exercises, supervisors can help teams clarify their values, develop honest communication, negotiate team boundaries, clarify accountability issues (Dunlap, 1997), and become aware of isomorphic processes between the team, family, supervisor, and other in-home program team members. The process of team-building with "fixed" team assignments is less complex than in programs using "flexible" team arrangements. Here staff retention becomes an important variable to ensure the optimal time for team-building.

CLINICAL CHALLENGES OF SUPERVISEES*

A *challenge* is defined as "the quality of requiring full use of one's abilities, energy, resources" (*The American Heritage Dictionary*). What constitutes a clinical challenge will be unique to each thera-

---

*Many of the ideas in this section were generated by faculty of the Philadelphia Child Guidance Center's Family Therapy Training Center during discussions about supervision in 1992. The faculty included: Marion Lindblad-Goldberg, Andrew Fussner, Gordon Hodas, Ann Itzkowitz, Wayne Jones, and Ruth Sefarbi.

pist's self-perception in the moment regarding what to do in a given session with a specific family, presenting with particular clinical problems and idiosyncratic family processes. Not only does the therapist have to decide "*what* do I do *when*," but also "*how* do I do what and when, given my therapeutic style and level of experience?" An additional question is, "*Can* or *may* I do this, given the rules and parameters of *where* I'm conducting the session?" Therapy always involves rapid decision-making in response to the minute-to-minute verbal and nonverbal feedback that occurs in every clinical encounter. Ultimately, this decision-making process is influenced by a therapist's self-knowledge and the skills he or she brings to the clinical encounter, as well as the constraints and possibilities existing in a given treatment context.

The therapist's challenge becomes the supervisor's challenge, given that the therapeutic system encompasses the family, therapist or therapists (if a team is used), supervisor, and their interrelationships. First the supervisor assesses the therapist's challenge through feedback received from case discussion, observation of videotaped in-home sessions, agency sessions, or direct observation of in-home sessions (see Figure 6.2). With *case discussion* the supervisor cannot personally "see" the relationships between the therapist(s) and family members but only "hear" about them, filtered through the perceptual subjectivity of the therapist. What is visible is the therapist(s)'s relationship to the supervisor and, when there is more than one therapist, to each other. The more distant the supervisor is from direct observation, the less likely it is that he or she will be able to assess accurately the supervisee's challenge. The exception to this scenario is when the supervisor already knows the therapist's capabilities with a diverse range of families through previous opportunities for direct observation. Case discussion with team therapists provides the additional information of what each team member has observed about his or her partner's relationship with family members. Given a good relationship between team members, this source of data can increase the accuracy of the supervisor's assessment.

Observing sequences of interaction on videotape allows the supervisor to see clearly who did *what*, *when*, and *how*. What is missing from this modality, however, is the opportunity for the supervisor to suggest interventions and then observe the supervis-

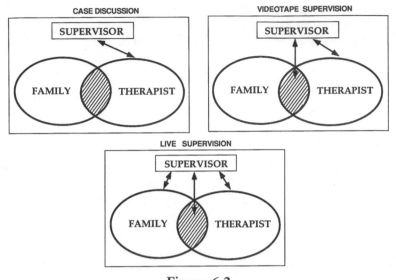

Figure 6.2
POSSIBLE CHANNELS OF OBSERVATION AND
COMMUNICATION BETWEEN SUPERVISOR AND THERAPIST

ee's response. Thus, it is strongly recommended that home-based treatment include *live supervisory sessions* scheduled either at the family's home or at the agency. Not only will these sessions enhance the supervisor's understanding of how the family and therapist(s) interact with each other, but the supervisor can also see how the supervisee incorporates feedback. During a home session, the supervisor can let the family know that there will be periodic "consultation breaks" during the session. During these time-outs the supervisor typically makes suggestions, which the therapist then implements with the family.

If an observation room with a one-way mirror is available at the agency, weekly three-hour *group supervision meetings* can include at least one live supervision session. If a large room is used, the supervisee can conduct the session in front of colleagues. The family takes planned breaks, leaving the room so that the supervisor can give directives to the therapist and elicit the group's input. Live supervision is an excellent way for the therapist to receive immediate corrective feedback and for the staff to learn perceptual and conceptual family therapy skills. Since staff rotate on the crisis service, this teaching tool allows them to become familiar with their colleagues' families. Given the myriad of challenges experienced by home-based clinicians, the supervisory tools need to be diverse.

Using these supervisory modalities, an important goal of supervision is to expand a therapist's style of contact and intervention when faced with personal clinical challenges. The clinical challenges experienced by therapists relate to their therapeutic response when confronted by events occurring in a therapy session. Therapy is, by definition, an encounter of the close kind. "A family therapist cannot observe and probe from without. He must be a part of a system of interdependent people . . . while maintaining the widest possible use of self" (Minuchin & Fishman, 1981, p. 2). For example, to truly "know" a family, the therapist must become part of the family, experiencing family members unique pain, patterns, and ways of being. Simultaneously, however, neutrality must be maintained so that the therapist does not become overly attached to one perspective over another. Knowing how to respond to both the family's feedback and one's internal reactions is vital to relationship-building, assessment, and treatment. While some therapists are skilled in knowing how to process their feelings and thoughts and discern what action to take, others have a narrower range of expertise. An effective therapist needs to be like a pliable pretzel—able to bend and twist, flexibly responding to varying family styles, emotions, and behaviors.

An effective supervisor is sensitive to the therapist's struggle to master the anxiety of doing therapy and is aware that a therapist's stylistic tendencies rigidify during anxious moments. Anxiety is particularly heightened during the initial encounters between therapist and family. Consequently, the therapist's efforts to reduce anxiety may be counterproductive to relationship-building. It is the supervisor's job to "contain" the trainee's anxiety in response to what the family presents by providing feedback that normalizes or detoxifies the anxiety. This supervisory feedback ideally alters the therapist's affective, cognitive, and/or behavioral responses. These alterations, in turn, shift the family's reactions to the therapist. The two most common responses to anxiety that challenge home-based therapists are being "in the head" or "in the heart." How the supervisor alters the trainee's anxiety is described in subsequent case examples.

IN THE HEAD

The therapist having an "in-the-head" response becomes, in essence, a wallflower at the family's dance. Experiencing the family from a distance, the therapist's little gray cells conduct their own dance. The range of these "in-the-head" responses may include several of the following observations. Therapists become captured by the seriousness of their hierarchical role as *therapist* or *educator*; emotionally divorced from their own inner child and its quality of affective responsivity; closed rather than selectively disclosing; chess masters preoccupied with figuring out the most correct moves; surgeons in love with technique; overdependent on intellectualization, resulting in limited creative energy and/or freedom of movement (i.e., sitting rigidly). The supervisor is challenged to create a supervisory process that will help "heady" therapists to think in metaphorical terms, thereby experiencing the similarities between their own life situations and those of family members; become more related in their communication; exhibit curiosity and spontaneity; discover their own pathways of understanding and caring about another's situation, feelings, and motives; and move toward alternative ways of responding, especially with family members who exhibit the same characteristics.

Clearly, the supervisor must first be sensitive to the complementarity in the supervisory relationship. If the supervisor's response is also "in the head," change will not occur; to the degree that the supervisor is too emotionally reactive, the therapist will become even more intellectualized. An optimal supervisory style is flexible, providing appropriate affective and cognitive responses as needed. For example, the supervisor may use a playful style to create a context that allows "in-the-head" therapists to experiment with new roles through the use of humor and play. Because this context has different rules and expectations of behavior, supervisees' anxieties about acting silly or looking ridiculous are usually reduced. Supervisory enactments can be designed wherein therapists experience the joy of spontaneity and creativity. As Duhl (1983) says,

"These metaphoric, yet real experiences, become the pardonable excuses for dropping one's normal self or 'proper' behavior or the image of 'I'm not a person who . . . ' while trying something different" (p. 270). The following case illustrates the supervisor's interventions while working with an "in-the-head" therapist.

Case Vignette: "Mike"

"Mike," a 29-year-old Caucasian social worker with five years of clinical experience at a Veterans' Administration hospital, had been working for six months in a mental health home-based services program. His supervisor, "Eve," was a 40-year-old Caucasian social worker with six years of experience in family therapy and four years of experience as a supervisor. Eve and Mike had established an effective supervisory relationship over the six-month period. Eve had been working with "Marion," a 45-year-old Caucasian psychologist, as her consulting supervisor for four years. Eve viewed Marion's consulting role as helping her "to modify [her position as supervisor] in the therapeutic system by offering a new perspective" (Haber, 1996, p. 137). Similar to the role of a trainer (see Figure 6.1), the consultant's input acts as an external feedback loop into the therapeutic system composed primarily of the supervisor's relationship to the supervisee and family. If the supervisor supervisee-family reach an impasse, the consultant can use her meta-vision to introduce ideas that may transform this therapeutic system.

During Eve's supervision of Mike she observed that his general style in sessions with various families tended to be intellectualized, polite, and somewhat reserved. While pleasant, his affect was bland and without humor. He always spoke in a steady rhythm with little inflection. He appeared to be most comfortable in the centralized role of the professor, telling people quietly what they should do. In every in-home session, Mike never moved from his chair once he sat down. Mike's style did not present a challenge for him or for the supervisor until his initial visit with the "B." family.

The "B." family was composed of mother, age 44 years, father 40 years, Pete, 14 years, and the identified patient, Tom, 12 years. This Caucasian, middle-class family had been referred for home-based services following a five-year involvement with a program for children with developmental disabilities, where Tom had been in individual therapy. The referring psychologist was concerned about Tom's intense anger toward his brother, expressed repeatedly in the threat, "I'm going to get a .357 magnum and blow his fucking guts out!" Mr. and Mrs. B. wanted in-home services because of Tom's aggressive behavior toward his brother at home and with peers at school.

The family's history revealed that Tom was diagnosed in infancy as having developmental delays because of low motor tone, slow motor development, and underreactivity to auditory and visual input that made it hard for him to engage and stay engaged. Mr. B. interpreted these findings as evidence that his son was "retarded." Subsequently, father became depressed and began seeing a psychiatrist for medication. An evaluation of Tom at the age of six years indicated average intellectual functioning with an unspecified learning disorder. Despite these evaluative findings, Mr. B. remained depressed about his son. This depression was reinforced by Mr. B.'s mother, who likened Tom to her son. Mr. B. had never allowed himself to express anger toward his mother, who had been a single parent and was quite controlling and critical of him. The nonadaptive family pattern observed in the first in-home interview involved a coalition of Mrs. B. and Tom versus Mr. B., Pete, and the grandmother. The conflict between Tom and Pete mirrored the parental conflict. The repetitive interactive cycle existing since Tom's preschool days was as follows: The grandmother, the father, Pete, or the school would criticize or condemn Tom; the mother would protectively defend Tom and attack the grandmother, her husband, Pete, or the school. Tom would respond in an immature or aggressive way in the family or school. Subsequently, he would be criticized again by the grandmother, the father, Pete, or the school, and the cycle would continue.

Except for Pete and Tom's shooting critical darts at each other before the session began, the family's affect was flat during the interview. Mrs. B. complained that she was tired of always having to handle her sons' fighting by herself because her husband was either at his mother's house or, when home, glued to the television set. She announced that since teenage boys need a father, she would no longer play the role of a single parent when she already had enough to do around the house. Following this proclamation, she picked up her knitting and kept to herself. Mr. B. then monopolized the rest of the interview, speaking in an intellectualized, monotonous drone that eventually put all the family members virtually to sleep (including the dog!). Furthermore, the content of Mr. B.'s negative monologue focused on the inadequacies of everyone in the family (especially Tom) and his pessimistic predictions of Tom's future (i.e., "he'll end up in jail"). The father acknowledged that he never engaged in any activities with either of his sons and that, as his wife had said, his free time was spent either at his mother's house or watching television at home. Mike's polite attempts to interrupt Mr. B. so that he could talk with Mrs. B., Tom, or Pete proved futile.

While reviewing the videotaped in-home session, Eve asked Mike what his feelings had been during the session. Mike said he felt paralyzed and requested that he receive one-way mirror supervision at the agency for the B. family's next family session.

The discussion between the consultant and supervisor about the family session highlighted the themes of paralysis and affective deadness in the family and the nonadaptive coalitions. It was hypothesized that Tom's aggressiveness was a way of trying to provoke the family, especially the father, to life. The similarities between Mike's therapeutic style and the father's style in the session explained why Mike had felt challenged; both would need to shift in order for the family to come alive. The consultant asked Eve about the range of Mike's behavior with his male colleagues. Upon reflection, Eve was surprised by her realization that with his male colleagues, Mike was humorous and assertive in setting up touch football practices with them during lunch hours. Following the consultant's suggestion to create a spontaneity enactment, Eve bought Mike a large yellow rubber duck. She asked him if he could show her and the staff how to play "as if" touch football in the interview room used for one-way mirror supervision. Throughout this hilarious event, Mike loosened up and displayed considerably more affect, humor, and assertiveness than in other encounters with Eve.

In planning the in-office family session with the B. family, it was agreed that the session would use enactments designed to interrupt the coalitions in the family and strengthen Mike's relationship to the father. Initially, Mike would meet individually with Mr. B. and then include Tom and Pete in the session. The consultant and Eve would meet with Mrs. B. behind the one-way mirror, allowing her to observe Mike and her husband and sons. Additionally, informal rapport could be established with Mrs. B. The session's *process goal* would be to create more interaction between Mike and the father, and between the father and his sons. The *content goal* would be to explore possible ways for the father to initiate recreational activities with his sons, especially Tom. It was suggested to Mike that, when meeting with the father, he should play around with the yellow duck and, if possible, initiate a spontaneous game of catch while they talked. Mike liked this idea, saying, "If I sit down in the session, I'm dead."

When Mr. B. saw Mike playing with the yellow duck, he laughed and readily agreed to a game of catch. During the game, Mike and the father talked about recreational activities that the "men" of the family might enjoy. When the boys came into the session, they were astounded to see their father laughing and running around with the yellow duck. They quickly entered what became a spontaneous game of "as if" touch football, with Tom and Pete enthusiastically teamed against Father and Mike. As the game progressed, the boys united in their elated efforts to devise devious maneuvers that would defeat the adult team. Since the interview room was small, everyone inevitably bumped into each other, amidst laughter and humorous teasing. At one point the father called a time-out to show Tom how to kick the yellow duck more effectively for a touchdown. When Tom scored a winning touchdown, everyone cheered. Behind the mirror, Mrs. B. enjoyed the spectacle. Her enthusiasm led her spontaneously to buzz into the room (using the phone-in mechanism) to encourage her husband's team. When she saw her husband help Tom with his kicking skills, her eyes misted and she said softly, "Tom has always wanted his father to be there for him." At the end of the session the mother gave each of her "men" a hug and suggested they celebrate the boys' victory by going out for pizza.

In subsequent in-home sessions with the family, the themes of play and humor, rather than paralysis and anger, continued. The supervisor's interventions gave Mike permission to expand his therapeutic style, enabling him to become more related and collaborative with the family.

IN THE HEART

The "in-the-heart" response spans a wide range of positive or negative feelings a therapist may experience within a family encounter. When a therapist perceives and appraises a family event as benefical, positive feelings ensue and therapeutic functioning is enhanced. Conversely, negative feelings are the response to what is sensed and appraised as harmful and lead to less effective functioning. Positive feelings include enjoyment, fondness, happiness, appreciation, respect, hopefulness, helpfulness, caring, and empathy. On the negative side, therapists sometimes feel frustrated, angry, overwhelmed, disappointed, scared, sad, and helpless.

Extreme reactions to a family, a family's history, or presenting clinical problems constitute the clinical challenge for "in-the-heart" therapists. Therapists who are emotionally overreactive in their style may also experience excessive feelings of responsibility for helping, protecting, and taking away the pain of others. Family members may experience this intense responsibility as an invasion of their interpersonal boundaries.

Sometimes a therapist's excessive emotional reactivity relates to perceived similarity between traumatic events in his or her past and those described by the client, such as having a parent with mental illness, abusive parenting, or incest. Highly sensitive issues like these need to be handled in the therapist's own therapy and not in supervision. More often, similarity of experience occurs around events such as marriage, giving birth, raising children, illness, divorce, or death. In these instances, supervision can help the supervisee to distinguish between his or her situation and the family's therapeutic needs. One category of "in-the-heart" responses occurs when the therapist encounters an unexpected confrontation or challenge from family members: "You are not helping me! I'm calling another therapist!"; "You are the expert—*you* make him take his medication." Termed an "in the face" experience (Hodas, 1992), the common affective response of the therapist is to feel inadequate, frustrated, or annoyed. In the heat of the moment the therapist may be unable to gather his or her thoughts and thus feel momentarily paralyzed. Hodas's (1992) advice to supervisors of "in-the heart" therapists is to underscore (1) the importance of depersonalizing the event and avoiding power struggles at such moments; (2) the conceptual understanding that some families project blame as a way of dealing with crisis; and (3) the ongoing importance of emphasizing collaborative teamwork between family and therapist.

Being aware of the complementarity within the supervisory relationship is very important when dealing with in-the-heart responses. If the supervisor is compassionate and empathic, the supervisee will be able to incorporate suggestions. However, if the supervisor feels negatively toward the supervisee or has an overly intellectualized style, the supervisee may say less and less but remain emotionally charged. This could lead to the supervisor's subtle withdrawal and, consequently, the therapist feeling abandoned. The following case example illustrates an "in-the-heart" challenge for both therapist and supervisor.

Case Vignette: "Ann"

"Ann," a 30-year-old Caucasian social worker, with eight years of postdegree clinical experience, worked for four years in the Department of Child Welfare's child protection unit. For the next four years, she was employed as a home-based worker at a mental health agency. Her supervisor, Barbara, was a 40-year-old Caucasian social worker with 10 years of clinical experience. The agency consultant, Marion, a 45-year-old Caucasian psychologist, had been Barbara's supervisor when she had enrolled in the Family Therapy Training Center that Marion directs. Subsequently, Barbara recommended the training program to Ann. During her first year of training, Ann's first pregnancy resulted in a miscarriage. Ann had become very depressed after the miscarriage, feeling that she had somehow failed, despite the strong emotional support she received from her husband, parents, training colleagues, and supervisors. Eventually, Ann's strong Christian beliefs helped her through this difficult time. As a second-year trainee, Ann was entering into her third month of a second pregnancy.

Both Barbara and Marion had established a positive supervisory relationship with Ann, whose strong interpersonal skills, intermediate-level skills as a family therapist, and eagerness to expand her professional growth made her a valued supervisee and therapist. Her colleagues at the agency and within the training program liked and respected her contributions. She was quite effective as an in-home therapist with all of her families. To maximize clinical productivity at her agency while enrolled in the training program, Ann sometimes used training sessions to evaluate families being considered for her agency's home-based services. Ann's clinical challenge occurred during one of these evaluation interviews.

Ms. Terry C. was a 20-year-old, African-American single parent who had never been married and lived with her two children, Billy, age four, and Dorothy, age three. Prior to the referral, Ms. C. had been staying in a shelter for battered women where she had sought refuge from her abusive boyfriend. The referral was made by Ms. C.'s caseworker from the Department of Child Welfare's child protection unit. The purpose of the referral was to help Ms. C. manage her children and deal with the abusive relationship with her boyfriend. The caseworker described Ms. C.'s mother as also being emotionally abusive to Terry, who was evicted from her mother's home when she became pregnant at the age of 16.

In planning for this evaluation session with the C. family, the goals were to begin establishing a relationship with Ms. C. and her children, to understand the mother's goals for treatment, to explain the home-based services, and to ascertain Ms. C.'s level of interest in the services. Ann was annoyed when the C. family arrived 45 minutes late because she had been looking forward to her full hour of one-way mirror supervision. Ms. C.'s consent to be observed by the training group was obtained. She and her children were then introduced to the supervisor and observers. Ann directed the family into the large interview room. Ms. C. and the children were dressed in warm coats and hats, since the interview took place in winter.

Upon entering the room, Billy and Dorothy, still cloaked in coats and hats, began running around, grabbing at the toys. Ms. C. sat down with her coat and hat on and immediately began describing her concerns to Ann. While the mother was talking, Billy jumped onto her lap. She stopped talking and said to him, "Say your name. Say your colors." As Billy responded, his mother smiled with pride.

Ms. C. then revealed that Billy's father had been electrocuted by lightning and had died the previous summer, in response to which Billy had begun wetting the bed. She continued to describe a litany of other traumatic events in a nonstop but bland manner. Throughout this process, Ann sat with her head down drinking from her coffee cup, saying nothing in response. She made absolutely no effort to connect with Ms. C.—not even to suggest that she might want to remove her hat and coat, since the room was warm. Ann appeared oblivious to the noise level and distractions created by Billy and Dorothy. Ms. C. then began describing a terrifying event when her boyfriend began choking her and she felt she was slipping into death. In a very detached manner, she continued to describe how she would kill him if he came around her again. Again, Ann continued to drink her coffee and said nothing. At this point the supervisor called Ann out of the room for a consultation. Unfortunately, this short 15-minute session needed to end because the next scheduled family was waiting to be seen.

Both the supervisor and the training group were extremely puzzled by Ann's unusual behavior in the session. Supervisees new to one-way mirror supervision and group observation can sometimes "freeze" in a session. Ann, however, was an experienced family therapist, well versed in the skills for doing an initial interview. How to explain Ann's behavior? Sometimes parallel process exists between the therapist-client relationship and the therapist-supervisor or therapist-supervisor-training group relationships. In Ann's situation, this was not happening. Ann had close, comfortable relationships with both her supervisors and her training colleagues. Another issue to consider was the possibility of anxiety about conducting cross-cultural therapy. Again, since Ann had worked extensively and effectively with other African-American families, this hypothesis was ruled out.

During the consultation with Ann, the supervisor asked her what she was feeling in the session. Ann expressed her annoyance that this "case" was not appropriate for family therapy supervision. She explained that she had worked with similar "cases" during her years with Child Welfare and that a battered woman such as Ms. C. was "hopeless" and incapable of change. She then launched into an impassioned tirade about how unfair it was that some women had no trouble having children even when they weren't ready to become mothers, as in the case of teenage mothers. The intensity of Ann's affect, coupled with the supervisor's knowledge of Ann's miscarriage and the fact that Ms. C. had been 16 years old when she had her first child, led the supervisor to consider whether Ann's interview with Ms. C. had triggered Ann's internal reactions. The discussion with Ann concluded with her insistence that the case be transferred back to Child Welfare.

With the cards clearly on the table, so to speak, the supervisor had several options. She could enter into a power struggle with Ann and insist on her continuing to act as therapist with the family. She could transfer the family to someone else. The most viable option in the supervisor's thinking was to go with Ann's resistance and then develop appropriate supervisory interventions. What she said to Ann was, "You are probably right because you have certainly had more experience with Child Welfare families than I have. Why don't I end the session with you, and over the next two weeks we'll think about the best recommendations to give to Ms. C." During the last few minutes of the session, the supervisor sat next to Ann and told Ms. C. how impressed she was with the children's comfort in this strange room and with Billy's knowing his name and colors. She empathized with Ms. C. about how painful and difficult things had been. She told Ms. C. that the group was going to think carefully about how to best help the family and that she would call her in a few days.

The supervisor was struck by the dramatic nature of Ann's in-the-heart response that had so paralyzed her in the session. She began to wonder if Ann's anxiety about the successful completion of her second pregnancy was related to her behavior with Ms. C. Was there a parallel process operating? Was Ann's feeling of hopelessness about Ms. C.'s "prognosis" a parallel expression of her self-prognosis for this pregnancy? How could this be handled in supervision without doing therapy with Ann?

The supervisor's hypotheses, coupled with her firm belief in Ann's underlying strength, led to the creation of the following supervisory interventions. At the next training session (on December 17), Ann spontaneously brought Christmas cookies for the training group and was promptly labeled the group's "giving spirit" by the supervisor. A role-play was developed wherein Ann would be the therapist whose goal was to reassure a pregnant adolescent (played by one of the other trainees) that not only would she be all right throughout her pregnancy, but she would also be a wonderful mother. Ann did an extraordinary job of empathizing and reassuring the "teenager" during the role-play and was strongly validated by the supervisor and group. The supervisor then told Ann that she thought recommendations should be given to Ms. C. in person. Rather than having a therapy session, however, perhaps Ann could design a special experience for the family, since the appointment would be on December 24. To prepare for this meeting, the supervisor suggested that Ann sit at home in the rocking chair given to her by her mother in preparation for the baby's birth, place her hands on her stomach, and imagine all the wonderful memories she had of being given to at Christmas. After doing this, she could turn her reflections to what kind of experience she might create for the C. family.

When the family came to their second appointment on Christmas Eve day, Ann asked the mother if she and the children would like to enact a nativity play. The mother's enthusiasm bloomed when she saw the costumes Ann had brought for everyone to wear. Ms. C. was to play the part of "Mary," Billy would be "Joseph," and Dorothy and Ann would be the angels who came to bring presents to the baby Jesus (portrayed by a doll). Ms. C. looked pure and beautiful as "Mary." Billy and Dorothy looked very appealing in their costumes. Ann had difficulty with her "angel" costume and Ms. C. helped her to achieve the right effect. Ms. C. then directed Ann to "bring presents to the baby Jesus" after she and Joseph had expressed feelings of wonder about their newborn son. At the end of the play, Ann and Ms. C. sang "Silent Night" and "Jingle Bells" with the children. With warmth and authenticity, Ann spontaneously proclaimed to her, "You were such a wonderful mother to baby Jesus and you did such a great job of teaching Billy and Dorothy the Christmas carols!"

This was an extremely moving experience for everyone, including the observation group. Ms. C. and Ann became "soul sisters" united in their shared spiritual beliefs. Before the family left, the supervisor called Ann out of the room for a consultation. Tongue in cheek, she asked Ann about transferring the family back to Child Welfare. Equally tongue in cheek, Ann replied, "Marion, you really don't know about Child Welfare families. I want to work with Ms. C. and her children. They will benefit enormously from in-home family therapy."

CHALLENGES OF HOME-BASED SUPERVISORS

These examples typify the resourcefulness needed by supervisors in dealing with the clinical challenges of their supervisees. In addition, the distinguishing features of a home-based treatment context add another level of complexity to the process of supervision. Typically, the role of supervisor requires the wearing of many hats. Supervisors must respond simultaneously to the exigent clinical demands of clients served, the needs of staff at varying levels of experience and clinical skills, the anticipations of community referents and resources, and the administrative expectations of agency directors, county, state, and managed care funders. Achieving a balance between clinical and administrative responsibilities within these multiple roles can be a difficult task, as will be seen in the following sections.

Balancing Administrative and Clinical Responsibilities

Home-based program supervision includes both administrative and clinical responsibilities, since the program director generally carries the dual role of clinical supervisor. Quality assurance standards for supervision reflecting the unique features and values of these CASSP programs have been developed for Pennsylvania's Family-Based Mental Health Services (Stern, 1993). Program directors must document their response to the following areas of inquiry:

1. Do you empower your in-home staff by building on their knowledge?
2. Are you available to your staff and able to provide them with guidance, support, and direction through your acquired experience?
3. Do you offer your staff opportunities for skill-building?
4. Are you networking with other child-serving systems, county programs, public health clinics, County Board of Assistance, pediatricians, family practitioners, local ministries, human service directors, and schools?

5. Does the program employ a hierarchical system with definitive roles?
6. Do you log supervision hours?
7. Do you use videotaped sessions of clients to provide feedback to staff?
8. Is each treatment plan signed off by you as the supervisor?
9. Do you focus on each staff person's strengths?
10. Do you focus on each staff person's weaknesses?
11. Do you encourage creative treatment planning by your staff?
12. Does the staff attend training on prescribed days?
13. Are you able to raise your staff's motivation by: (a) giving staff permission to set limits about health and safety issues, and (b) acting as a buffer when staff are stressed?
14. Do you receive supervision of your supervision?
15. Is technical assistance available to you with regard to budget preparation, rate setting, and other administrative tasks?
16. Is training available to you for improving your clinical, programmatic, administrative, and supervisory skills?

Quality assurance standards for supervision are highly recommended to provide support and establish performance evaluation criteria for program directors. However, effective supervision will be predicated on the support available to the supervisor as well as the supervisor's ability to organize time, thereby assuring a balanced response to both the program's requirements and the staff's needs. This is easier said than done, given the current demands of managed care documentation, program management issues, and the additional responsibility of providing off-site mental health services for high-risk families. On a daily basis, the supervisor monitors the referral process, case assignments, service implementation, and discharge planning. Weekly, the supervisor provides one hour of supervision to each home-based team and two hours of group supervision to all teams. The supervisor may also choose to observe and assess the staff's home and/or in-office visits at various stages of treatment. A significant amount of time is spent weekly in liaison work with other agencies to assure smooth case transition and access to other services. Clearly, the combined program director/supervisor role is a demanding one.

Assessing Training and Preventing Burnout

Newly hired staff need orientation training to become familiar with agency and program policies before initiating home visits. An example of an orientation training assessment for newly hired home-based therapists, developed by Dunlap (1996), can be found in Appendix H. Pairing a new staff member with a more experienced partner is one of the advantages of a team-delivered service. Knowing the experienced staff person's knowledge base and skills, the supervisor can have more confidence in sending a new hiree out in the field. When in-home services are individually delivered, there are no safeguards against unprofessional conduct unless the supervisor observes the off-site visit (Hansen, 1995). Requiring staff to use camcorders to videotape off-site sessions allows performance monitoring and reduces travel time for supervisors. When the use of stationary camcorders becomes familiar and viewed as "standard operating procedure" during in-home sessions, families generally forget they are being videotaped and interact in their characteristic fashion.

Supervisors should also recognize and address the stressors that are specific to these new jobs in the mental health field. Job stressors include heightened feelings of responsibility and being overwhelmed by the family's emotional demands, insecurity regarding clinical knowledge and skill level, and relatively low salaries. *Burnout*—the term used when a clinician becomes stressed and unable to cope—is most likely to occur in staff who feel overworked, unappreciated, ineffective, and unsupported. Clinicians become disappointed and sometimes cynical. Severe burnout occurs when there is a total imbalance of job stress in relation to job support. When a client suicide occurs within this high-risk treatment population, and such an emotionally charged event is not processed through supervision, program support, and healing rituals, the therapist's feelings of guilt and shame often create an inevitable decision to change jobs. The symptoms of burnout can include exhaustion, both mental and physical; hopelessness, helplessness, and low self-esteem; and frequent illnesses. One important way for supervisors to address burnout is to help staff develop effective ways of organizing their time and energy. Sensitivity to weekly scheduling is paramount. The nature of these mental health jobs causes staff to overfunction and develop "compassion fatigue."

The most critical supportive factor underlying success in home-based services is the ability of the program staff, including the director/supervisor, to function as a cohesive, collaborative team. Additionally, the program director should be part of the larger agency management team, so that responsibility is shared in the decision-making process of difficult cases (Wolf, 1990). Ideally, if everyone on the team is accountable and competent, the director can delegate responsibility and feel confident in the staff's ability to fulfill job assignments independently. The reality is that most programs have staff who are at different developmental levels relative to their longevity in the program. Generally, junior staff are teamed with senior staff, who help to mentor them. When effective clinical supervision is provided, clinical skills improve and even small successes with families are appreciated.

The most disruptive event in the life of a home-based program occurs when the director leaves. This happens frequently when there is no support for either the program or program director from the agency's executive director down through the levels of supervision to the program director. Similar to family development, such an event catalyzes a new configuration in the program: A senior staff member (or members) will be elevated to "take charge" until displacement occurs when the new director is hired. Programs that have had a series of new directors have either staff who have tightly bonded "for better or worse" or high staff turnover. It is important for a new director to appreciate the program's history and help staff "mourn" the departure of the previous director and/or staff members. A new director should establish his or her position of authority slowly, initially exhibiting sensitivity to, and appreciation for, the staff who held the program together in the absence of the program's "parent."

It is the supervisor's job to mold the staff into a collaborative, cohesive team, free from the perils of burnout. Weekly group supervision meetings need to be organized so that, in addition to reviewing clinical casework, there is time for coworkers to acknowledge and support one another's accomplishments and be empathic during difficult times. Sharing feelings and listening to others is simple to do, and very important. Encouraging humor and playfulness in staff meetings, as well as generally in the environment of the program, gives staff permission to be spontaneous and creative. One supervisor begins each staff meeting by asking staff to describe weekly examples of "Can you bottom this?" These hilarious "bloops" of in-home therapy moments allow the staff to move from feelings of "grin and bear it" to those of "grin and share it."

WEAVING IT ALL TOGETHER

The tapestry of home-based therapy is woven from the blending of many threads. The figures on the tapestry represent the family's stated needs and desires. The supporting threads are the myriad of available services and resources. The home-based therapist is the weaver who, in collaboration with the family, blends all the threads into an agreed-upon design. The supervisor guides the weaver's shuttle. The following case describes the sequence of home-based treatment referral, assessment, stages of treatment, and termination. The concurrent supervisory process is also presented as a counterpoint to the therapeutic endeavor. Helping any therapist to conduct a comprehensive assessment and then to design focused session interventions requires skillful supervision. When supervision is targeted for home-based therapists treating complex family situations and serious mental health problems, the challenge is even greater. While the various treatment components comprising mental health in-home services are essential resources, the integration of these components into the ongoing therapy adds another level of complexity. The art of home-based therapy supervision requires the ability to help therapists think and plan comprehensively yet maintain simplicity in their work.

CASE VIGNETTE: "NELL" AND FAMILY*

After completing a master's degree in psychology and four years of outpatient clinical experience, Nell was hired as a program director to begin the development of a new mental health home-based program. Prior intensive training at the Philadelphia Child Guidance Center's Family Therapy Training Center had given Nell a strong sense of confidence in her family therapy skills. During

---

*Nell Jackson was the therapist in the case.

her year of training, she was viewed as an extremely competent clinician. Warm and supportive with a diverse range of clients, she was also skilled in the art of challenge when clinically indicated. An unmarried Caucasian woman of 30 years, Nell exhibited a rare combination of humor, enthusiasm, intuition, and intelligence. She was always open to feedback and suggestions in supervision. These qualities made it extremely enjoyable to work with her. While in the initial stages of developing the mental health home-based program, Nell decided to treat a referred family so that she could experience home-based therapy as a deliverer before hiring and supervising program staff.

The Supervision Contract

Nell established a supervisory contract with Marion, who had been her training supervisor at the Philadelphia Child Guidance Center. The specified contract related primarily to her role as in-home therapist with a family. However, Nell had also expressed interest in supervisory issues that might arise when she would begin supervising the two-person teams in the home-based program. Thus a decision was made to create a triangle within the supervisory context by including a 32-year-old male Caucasian senior faculty member of the Family Therapy Training Center* as a co-supervisor. Creating a three-person supervisory context, with the accompanying diversity in gender, lifestyles, and professional disciplines, would potentially replicate issues Nell would be encountering in future supervision of her staff and, hopefully, demonstrate the successful resolution of these issues.

The supervision contract specified a two-hour bimonthly schedule with the co-supervisors. In addition, "as needed" phone calls would be made to Marion between formally scheduled supervisory sessions. The supervisory modalities used were case discussion and review of videotaped treatment sessions. The goals of supervision were to help Nell in the areas of case conceptualization, treatment intervention, and decision-making regarding the integration of in-

---

*Bruce Buchannan was the co-supervisor on this case. Some modification of the case and its supervision have been made to facilitate clear communication of ideas.

home program components. These components included crisis and family support services, case management, and advocacy with other service systems. A mutual agreement was made regarding evaluation. Nell would receive supervisory input targeted to her supervision goals within each period of supervision. At each subsequent supervision session she would, in turn, let the supervisors know which ideas had been most helpful to her.

Supervision: The Referral to Home-Based Services

The first supervisory session focused on Nell's description of the referral process for the "H." family. In September of 1988 Mrs. Sue H. called her Child Welfare worker expressing concern about the severe behavior problems of her 15-year-old stepson, Sam. The caseworker referred her to the county's community mental center crisis unit. After one crisis unit session on October 4 and one outpatient session on October 21 (both sessions with Mrs. H. and Sam), a psychiatric evaluation was conducted on October 23. The treating outpatient psychologist made a crisis telephone referral to the mental health home-based program on October 25. According to the referring psychologist, Sam was verbally abusive to family members and school personnel. He refused to attend school and hung out with a "bad crowd," with whom he smoked pot and drank alcohol at least twice a week. Sam refused to accept any authority and often "lived on the street," although he was encouraged to stay at home. Child Welfare Services was considering a residential placement for him. The diagnostic results (based on the *DSM-III–R*) from the psychiatric evaluation were: "Axis I: Overanxious Reaction of Adolescence; Axis II: Learning Disability; and Axis III: Rule Out Attention-Deficit /Hyperactivity Disorder and Conduct Disorder, Undersocialized Aggressive."

Following telephone interviews to establish a beginning collaborative relationship with the Child Welfare worker and the referring psychologist, Nell arranged an in-office meeting on November 8 with the professionals, Mr. and Mrs. H., and Sam. After explaining the home-based services, both Mr. and Mrs. H. expressed strong interest in the program. Sam said that he did not care one way or another about participating in the program as long as Nell didn't "rub him the wrong way." Nell's role as therapist and the roles and resource availability of the two other professionals were clari-fied for the family. Signatures were obtained for the release-of-information forms and consent for in-home session videotaping. The first in-home session was scheduled for November 15.

Goals for the Family Assessment Interviews

The goals for the initial family assessment interviews were planned during the first supervisory session. It was mutually agreed that Nell was to (1) form a beginning relationship with each person in the family; (2) obtain clear goal statements and treatment objec-tives from family members; (3) provide guidelines to the family for how treatment sessions and agency meetings would be con-ducted and when termination of services would occur; and (4) obtain comprehensive assessment information that would result in a clearly focused treatment plan. The assessment information included a family genogram, a timeline of critical life events, struc-tural maps of observed family relationship patterns, observations of individual functioning, and an eco-map.

Hearing the Family's Stories

The subsequent supervisory session with Nell reviewed her first eight treatment contacts, including: three sessions with the entire family; one conjoint session with the father and stepmother; three individual sessions with the father, stepmother, and Sam; one ses-sion with Nell and the school principal; and one session with Nell and the school district's director of special education. Initially, supervision focused on Nell's integration of information from the genogram and the timeline of critical life events obtained from the stories told by family members. Typical of in-home family histories, the stories unfolded like a Russian novel with multiple plots and subplots.

Sam's father, Will, is 41 years old, a high school graduate, and the fourth of five children from a Caucasian working-class family. His father had a history of alcoholism and occasional physical abuse directed at his wife. At the age of 19, Will married "Jane," who is 41 years old, also a high school graduate, and the youngest of five children from a Caucasian working-class family. Abandoned by her mother at birth at the same time her parents divorced, Jane was raised by two stepmothers during her father's subsequent marriages and divorces. Both stepmothers were reportedly physically and emotionally abusive to Jane.

One year after Will and Jane married, their first son, Will Jr., was born. Shortly after his son's birth, Will was drafted and spent six months in Vietnam. Furloughed due to an injury, Will refused to return to duty and was sentenced to eight months of imprisonment and five years of probation. Two years later a daughter, Jen, was born. Two years later Sam was born. Will worked as a cabinet-maker to support his family, and two years after Sam's birth, Jane began working as a nurse's aide. Will's mother died when Sam was in first grade. Sam was evaluated and placed in a special education class as a second-grader. Due to his distractibility and difficulties with impulse control, he was referred to the community mental health center, where Ritalin was prescribed.

During second, third, and fourth grades Sam's behavior problems in school increased. Concurrently, his parents were experiencing severe marital conflicts. Jane would impulsively flee with the children to relatives in another state, whereupon Will would follow and bring them back. The tension in the home was also experienced by Sam's older brother, Will Jr., who frequently fought with his father. The Child Welfare authorities were called by an anonymous neighbor to investigate. According to Will, his wife placed Will Jr. in a home, whereupon Will helped to secure his release. According to Jane, Will was instrumental in securing placement for Will Jr. During this period of turmoil, Sam began expressing suicidal ideation. Six months later his parents separated. Jane moved to an apartment for nine months until the divorce was finalized. Will was granted sole custody of the children because a court custody evaluation deemed their mother "emotionally unstable." Mother received visitation rights. One month after the divorce, Jane remarried; Larry, a divorcèe, and Jane moved to a distant state and maternal contact with 10½-year-old Sam ceased.

Three months later, Will Jr. left home at the age of 17, lived on the streets, and engaged in delinquent activity. During this time Sam became very fearful that his brother would beat him up, even though there was no history of aggressive assault by the brother. His paranoid anxieties may have led to his introjection of the tough and defiant behaviors of his brother as a role model. The brother subsequently married a 23-year-old divorcée with a five-year-old son from a previous marriage. After two years, the couple had another son, Kyle.

This troublesome confluence of events may have precipitated Sam's decompensation and progressive deterioration. He began refusing to go to school. If forced to go, he became unruly, threw furniture around, pushed teachers, and was consequently suspended many times. He also became very self-destructive—banging his head against walls and hitting himself with his fists. At the school's recommendation, his father approved Sam's hospitalization on an adolescent in-patient unit, where he was medicated with lithium and Mellaril. Following the hospitalization, Sam returned to junior high school. Shortly after returning to school, his paternal grandfather died. Three months after this event, his father married Sue, whereupon Sam began verbalizing his desire to join his deceased grandfather.

Sue's Story

Sue experienced many traumas growing up. She was sexually abused by many of her mother's male friends until she was 10 years old, at which time her mother abandoned her. She was then raised by a stepmother and her father, who also abused her and her sisters until he was charged with sexual abuse and sent to prison. Sue had a very positive relationship with her stepmother, who raised her after father's incarceration. At the age of 18 Sue began a relationship with Fred, whom she eventually married. After 24 years of marriage and seven children, ranging in age from 24 to 9 years at the time of the divorce, Fred left Sue for another woman. Three months after her divorce, Sue moved from her home state to another state. After a three-week courtship, she married Will and brought her two youngest children to live in Will's household.

At the time of the remarriage Sue was 43 years old, her daughter Sara was 12, and her son David was 9. Will was 38, Jen was 14, and Sam was 11. This blended family was definitely not the "Brady Bunch." Within six months Child Welfare authorities charged Sue with physical neglect of all the children. Sam's out-of-control behavior at school had escalated so dramatically that he was placed in a special education day school in another county. One weekend he became so uncontrollable that Sue handcuffed him, locked him in his room, and slapped him several times. Consequently, the Child Welfare authorities charged Sue with child abuse of Sam. Three months later Sue's first husband was awarded custody of Sara and David, who moved to live with him in another state. Seven months later Sam was again referred for psychiatric hospitalization due to his disruptive behavior. Ritalin was prescribed. Upon discharge, Sam was returned home. The out-of-county school refused to readmit Sam who, in turn, refused to return to his local public school. Within four months after Sam's expulsion from the out-of-county school, Sue moved out of the household to live with friends in another state and did not return to the H. household for a year and a half.

Within one month after her stepmother moved out, Jen (now 17 years old) became involved with her best friend's brother, Ted, who was 21. Ted began living with Jen, Will, and Sam. Ted developed a close relationship with Will, who felt he could count on Ted to help him around the home. Within that year Jen became pregnant.

When Jen was six months pregnant, Sue returned to the household in August and began working at a restaurant to increase the family's income. Will also attempted to augment his salary as a cabinet-maker by taking a second job as a security guard at a bowling alley. At the end of September, Sam's uncontrollable behavior prompted Sue to contact the Child Welfare worker and the referral process to the mental health home-based program began.

Supervision: Themes and Hypotheses from Historical Assessment Data

Given the complexity of the H. family's story, the supervisory focus became the simplification of this historical material by highlighting for Nell the essential themes and hypotheses. In reviewing the genogram (Figure 6.3), several intergenerational themes were noted: (1) divorce, remarriage, and/or cohabitation; (2) physical abuse or neglect and/or sexual abuse; (3) alcohol abuse; (4) aban-

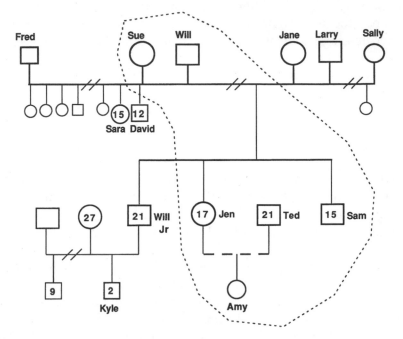

Figure 6.3
GENOGRAM OF THE "H." FAMILY

donment (e.g., Sue was abandoned by her mother; Sam's mother left him; a change in custody resulted in Sue's son, David, leaving his mother and moving to live with his father). The increase and decrease in Sam's symptomatology relative to critical life events (Figure 6.4), suggested a recurrent cycle. Sam's symptoms of anxiety, depression, rage, out-of-control behavior in school or truancy, and drug and alcohol usage were correlated with his feelings of loss and abandonment through such events as: deaths in the family; the threat, and subsequent loss, of his original family (parental conflict, marital separation, divorce, mother's remarriage and relocation to another state with no continued contact, brother's departure from the family); and distance in his relationship with father due to a number of factors (father's remarriage, addition of stepsiblings in the home, sister's boyfriend developing a close relationship with Sam's father, sister's pregnancy).

Figure 6.4
THE H. FAMILY TIMELINE

3/47	Will is born.	
2/47	Jane is born.	
6/66	Will and Jane graduate high school.	
9/66	Will and Jane marry.	
9/67	Will Jr. is born.	
9/67	Will sent to Vietnam for six months, injured, refused to return after furlough.	
4/68–12/68	Will serves eight-month prison term in another state and is given a five-year parole.	
1/71	Jen is born.	
12/73	Sam is born.	
12/75	Jane begins to work as a nurse's aide.	IP-2 yrs.
1/76	Paternal uncle (Sam's namesake) dies.	IP-3 yrs.
3/76	Jane has a hysterectomy.	
2/79	Paternal grandmother dies.	IP-6 yrs.
9/79	Sam is placed in a special education class as he begins second grade.	
9/81–12/82	Jane takes children to another state six times and Will brings them back. Sam begins medication with Ritalin. Complaints by school of no supervision of Sam at home.	IP-8–9 yrs.
1/83–10/84	Child welfare initiates residential placement of Will Jr. due to out-of-control behavior and a conflictual relationship with father.	
3/83	Sam expresses suicidal ideation.	IP-9 yrs.
9/83	Jane moves out of the home and a final marital separation begins; contact stops with Jen and Sam.	
6/84	Will and Jane divorce; Will granted sole custody and Jane receives visitation rights.	
7/84	Jane marries Larry and moves to another state.	IP-10½ yrs.

continued

Figure 6.4
continued

10/84	Will Jr. returns from placement, but leaves home and lives on the street.	
11/84	Sam referred for inpatient hospitalization due to uncontrollable behavior at school; receives medication (Lithium and Mellaril).	IP-11½ yrs.
1/85	Paternal grandfather dies.	
4/85	Will marries Sue who moves in with her two youngest children, Sara, 12 years, and David, 9 years.	
	Sam expresses suicidal ideation.	IP-11½ yrs.
9/85	Sam begins junior high school but is then referred by the school district to an out-of-county special education school for day students.	
10/85	Child welfare charges Sue with physical neglect of Jen, Sam, Sara, and David.	
11/85	Child welfare charges Sue with child abuse of Sam.	
12/85	Sara and David return to their father's home for Christmas in another state.	
2/86	Sole custody of Sara and David is awarded to their father.	
9/86	Sam is referred for inpatient hospitalization due to disruptive behavior; receives medication (Ritalin); upon discharge, the out-of-county special education school refuses to take Sam back and he returns to public school in his county; he begins a pattern of truancy or school misconduct leading to suspensions.	IP-13 yrs.
1/87	Sue moves out of the home.	
2/87	Ted (Jen's boyfriend) moves into the home.	
2/88	Jen becomes pregnant.	

Figure 6.4
continued

8/88	Sue moves back to the home.
	Will increases his work hours.
9/88	Sam increases his out-of-control behavior IP-15 yrs.
	at home, school, and in the community.
	Sam is permanently suspended from
	school and placed on home-bound in-
	struction.
	Sam is arrested for carrying a 3½ inch
	blade, but the charges are dropped.
	Sue contacts child welfare for help with
	Sam.
10/88	Sue and Sam are seen at the community
	mental health center; therapist makes a
	crisis referral to the mental health in-
	home services program.

Initial Family Visits: An In-Home Therapist's Narrative

The next phase of supervision focused on Nell's descriptions of the home environment and neighborhood, current family dynamics, Sam's individual functioning, and her relationships with family members. The following narrative describes Nell's first home visit.

It was twilight when I drove through this working-class neighborhood. The wooden houses (probably constructed in the 1940s) were small with tiny yards. Motorcycles were parked in many of the driveways—I'd heard this area was home to many of the Hell's Angels motorcycle gangs. Lots of teenagers in black leather jackets were hanging out on the street, but no one paid any attention to me as I left my car and tried to locate the house. The H.'s house needed paint, and the cement steps leading to the door were cracked. There was no doorbell or knocker, but I could hear the loud sounds of the TV coming from within. Mr. H. answered my timid knock on the door. I was led into the small, sparsely furnished living room that had a somewhat sterile flavor—no photographs or wall decorations. Mr. H. turned off the TV, helped me set up the camcorder, and placed a chair for me to sit next to him. He sat on an easy chair that clearly carried the implicit label "This is Dad's chair." Telling me to call him "Will," he introduced me as "Nell" to the other family members. I was struck by Will's large physical size in contrast to his gentle-looking face, which was shielded by a bushy black beard. He looked older than his 41 years. Like Groucho Marx, a huge cigar was firmly embedded in Will's mouth as he talked and was only removed when he needed to flick the ashes. Across from me on a couch sat his wife, Sue, a tired-looking but attractive 46-year-old brunette, and Will's daughter, Jen. Although her baby was due in a few weeks, Jen appeared younger than her 17 years. She giggled a lot and kept pulling at a large white tee-shirt that covered her big belly. On a chair next to her sat her boyfriend, Ted, age 21. Dressed in jeans and a work shirt, he appeared confident with his place in the home. Next to Ted sat Sam. Just two weeks shy of 15 years, Sam's long curly hair and freckled face gave him a vulnerable, younger look despite his tall, lanky build. He watched to see if I would react to his black tee-shirt that proclaimed defiantly: "Reach out and Fuck someone."

As I attempted to become comfortable with the family members by asking what activities they enjoyed and what they wanted me to know about them, many of their individual strengths and stressors were revealed. Will said he was working overtime on two jobs but felt satisfied because he enjoyed fooling around with the other guys at work. Leaving his second job at the bowling alley at midnight, he would often stop off at the local pub for a "few pops" before coming home. During periods of relaxation at home, he enjoyed various home improvement projects.

My impression of Will was that he was a man of average intellect and few words who lived life as he knew it—basic, direct, honest, strong work ethic, and no psychological nonsense. I liked Will and felt comfortable with him. He also seemed to like my talking to him as an equal. I think it was important to him that I was respectful of, and deferential to, his authority.

In contrast to Will, Sue seemed very bright, psychologically sophisticated, and verbally skilled. Sue's boss had told her she was the best waitress the local diner had ever employed. Congenial with her customers, her tips were plentiful. Some sadness was expressed as she talked of missing her children and not having enough money to travel out of state to see them. She also felt isolated from friends and relatives, since no one she knows lives in her current state of residence. She let me know that she was an excellent organizer, knew the value of rules and consequences, and felt this family needed more structure. I liked Sue and felt empathic about her isolation from her children, friends, and family. I was also struck by the ill-defined nature of her role in the home. I noticed personality similarities between Sue and myself in her direct style, verbal skills, and intuitiveness. It would have been easy to spend the entire session talking with her. She appeared hungry for my attention.

In getting to know Jen, I underscored her diligence and motivation in attending prenatal classes as well as continuing her high school education in order to graduate. Ted was validated for having started a stable job at a service station and looking forward to becoming a father. I felt that Jen and Ted were positively involved with one another. Though an easy rapport was established with Jen and Ted, I didn't feel that my presence held great significance for them.

Sam immediately appeared to be comfortable with me and seemed to want to show off. I appreciated his candor, spunk, and humor, yet I also felt a strong sense of his pain. Sam claimed to have no hobbies or specific interests other than just wanting to be done with school, go to work, and make $11.00 per hour like his older brother. He said he knew something about mechanics and carpentry. He had helped his father make cabinets and the two had remodeled the front porch. He liked to play his stereo radio quite loud. At one point he contradicted himself, saying that he liked to go to school but that the school authorities "didn't want him." They kept throwing him out, which suited him quite well. He characterized himself as being friendly with people who don't rub him the wrong way—but if they do, he "just makes their life miserable." He has three good friends who look to him as their leader. They all like to hang out and "rock."

Sam impressed me as a boy who was full of bravado and threw words around to intimidate and convey an image as a tough guy. For example, he described himself as very brave and immune to pain. He reported several incidents in which he did not feel pain or cry when he'd been punched or stabbed (with a pencil). I had the feeling, however, that he had a great deal of anxiety and ambivalence about not really believing what he was saying about himself. His stories revealed significant impairment in his judgment and poor impulse control; at the same time, he seemed to be asking for limits. His thought process did not show any suicidal content, self-destructive tendencies, or paranoid ideation. He responded to the session in a relevant, albeit cocky, fashion, answering questions well, never using foul language, and stating his wishes and wants quite clearly. He felt he was going through a normal phase in his growing up and that his destiny had already been decided. Intellectually, his abilities appeared average. He related to his environment in a very concrete fashion. Limitations were noted in his capacity to elaborate his responses or demonstrate abstract concept formation, despite his level of intelligence. I wondered if he would have difficulty in learning abstract material and whether a vocational school would be more suitable to his current needs. I also thought that a neuropsychological evaluation might be appropriate. [After the session Nell reviewed the psychiatric evaluation and noted that the psychiatrist's assessment corroborated her observations of Sam.]

When asked what goals each family member had for the therapy, Will immediately conveyed his sense that relationships were fine between himself and Sue (except for their "scraping" now and then), Jen, and Ted. Pointing a finger at Sam, Will said, "He's the one who has to change so he can live at home and go to school in our community." This overall goal statement appeared to have the consensus of all family members—except Sam. Will then simply and briefly outlined three treatment objectives: (1) Sam and Jen will learn to relate positively as brother and sister; (2) Sam will attend school regularly; and (3) Sam will take out the trash and wash dishes daily. Except for Sam's occasional defensive outbursts, family members listened respectfully while Will talked.

In contrast, Sue's litany of concerns extended over a 20-minute interval, during which all family members appeared disinterested. Sam and Jen began to giggle and tease each other. Will made no attempts to encourage others to be more respectful as Sue talked; nor did he verbally support any of her stated concerns. Sue began with a rather global problem definition: "It's everything—it's life!" When I asked her to be *a little more specific*, Sue expressed her desire for (1) more respect, cooperation, and support between family members; (2) more affection from Will; (3) more planned family recreational activities; and (4) more defined rules and consequences for Sam. Sue stated that her frustration with Sam made her often feel like "beating his butt."

Jen and Ted said that they would like help with financial planning in preparation for their future. Ted also said he wanted Sam to stop borrowing his audiotapes and clothes without asking. He expressed his concern about Jen's safety, since on one occasion Sam had threatened to hurt the baby by kicking Jen in the stomach. This incident was thoroughly discussed and the family ultimately agreed that Sam was venting his frustration and was not seriously intending to harm Jen or the baby.

When Sam was asked about his goals, he again stated that he did not want to go to school or to change any of his family relationships. What he most wanted to do was to "rock" with his friends.

Supervision: Family Dynamics and Directions for Change

The supervisors highlighted Nell's excellent relationship-building with family members, her emphasis on family strengths, and her astute observations of individual functioning. Given the complexity of the family assessment data, what Nell needed from her supervisors was a clear conceptualization of the family's dynamics. First, the current nonadaptive relationship patterns in the family were discussed (Figure 6.5). The core triangle organizing relationships in this family was composed of Will, Sam, and Sue. Neither Will nor Sue was confronting the obvious marital problems, and, indeed, both partners covertly allied with one another to avoid issues dealing with intimacy and conflict. They detoured their feelings of marital dissatisfaction around Sam's problems. Disunited as spouses and as parents, their parental authority was greatly comprised. Sam, meanwhile, had become quite artful in "splitting" the parental dyad, and in doing so, created a position of power for himself within the family. Sometimes Sam would be in collusion with his stepmother against his father, or vice versa.

As the in-home therapy began, there was a noticeable quality of distance in Sam's relationship to his father, which apparently

Figure 6.5
"H." FAMILY STRUCTURAL MAPS

Nonadaptive structural maps of the "H." family. This diagram illustrates that in both of Will's marriages to Jane and to Sue, conflict is detoured by attacking Sam.

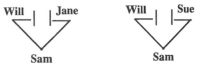

Nonadaptive structural maps of Will's, Sue's, and Sam's relationships. The overinvolved stepmother-stepson relationship relates to an underinvolved father-son relationship. Further, parental conflict between stepmother and father undermines parental authority, resulting in the son's having more power than either parent.

propelled Sam closer to his stepmother. Since she experienced herself as the "outsider" in this family, she, in turn, pushed for more closeness with Sam. These patterns of power and proximity and distance, however, were clearly not working. Sam's out-of-control behavior appeared to be a cry for more involvement with his father. A repeating behavioral cycle was noted: To the degree that his father was distant and abdicated parental authority, Sam would become out-of-control; to the degree that Sam became uncontrollable, his stepmother would become more involved with him; to the degree that his stepmother was overly active in controlling Sam, the father remained distant and passive as both parent and spouse. Consequently, Sam's adolescent needs for nurturance from his father were unmet. Feeling abandoned by his father, Sam would become uncontrollable in the hope that his father would eventually display nurturance and provide the controls and limits Sam desperately needed.

Given this understanding of how the current family patterns were maintaining Sam's difficulties, Nell now knew what changes to pursue. Perhaps she could encourage Will, as the biological parent, to assume the active parental role with Sam. Sue could be encouraged to support her husband in his new role and hopefully establish a closer relationship with him. In this way she could define a role for herself in the family, since it was clear that neither Jen nor Sam accepted her role as mother. Sue would need to make a commitment either to be there for Will and the family or to leave. The supervisory discussion also helped Nell to become more aware of the potential pitfalls facing her as a therapist. She could easily become inducted into the family's core triangle.

Supervision: Ecosystemic Dynamics and Directions for Change

Finally, the supervisory discussion turned to the information garnered from the ecomap (Figure 6.6), the timeline, and the sessions held with school personnel. The nonadaptive relationship patterns between the family and key outside systems were examined. Strategies for improving these relationships were suggested. For example, although Will had complied with the recommendations from previous mental health representatives (inpatient pro-

Figure 6.6
ECO-MAPS OF THE "H." FAMILY

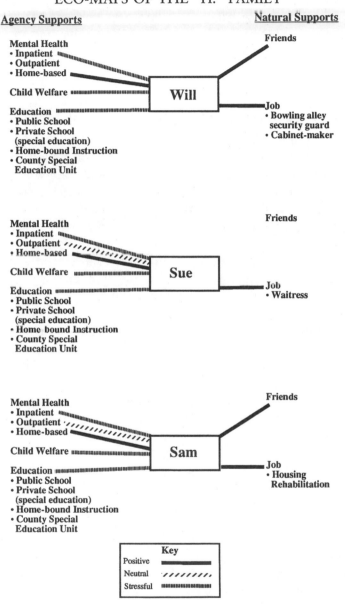

Agency Supports

Natural Supports

Mental Health
• Inpatient
• Outpatient
• Home-based

Child Welfare

Education
• Public School
• Private School
  (special education)
• Home-bound Instruction
• County Special
  Education Unit

Will

Friends

Job
• Bowling alley
  security guard
• Cabinet-maker

Mental Health
• Inpatient
• Outpatient
• Home-based

Child Welfare

Education
• Public School
• Private School
  (special education)
• Home-bound Instruction
• County Special
  Education Unit

Sue

Friends

Job
• Waitress

Mental Health
• Inpatient
• Outpatient
• Home-based

Child Welfare

Education
• Public School
• Private School
  (special education)
• Home-bound Instruction
• County Special
  Education Unit

Sam

Friends

Job
• Housing
  Rehabilitation

Key	
Positive	▬▬▬▬
Neutral	///////,
Stressful	▥▥▥▥▥▥

grams), he did not view these experiences as helpful. Nell might want to explore with him his hopes or fears regarding this new mental health service. Since Will had not worked in partnership with the other mental health therapists, perhaps having him experience his parental power in the treatment planning process would prove helpful.

The historical relationship with the Child Welfare System had left Will feeling his hands were tied as a parent. In fact, he attributed his lack of assertion in disciplining Sam to a fear that Child Welfare might label him as an abusive parent and remove his son from the home. Sam, however, seemed to be begging for his father to take an assertive stand with him. Perhaps a Child Welfare worker could be invited as a "guest" to the therapy and demonstrate disciplinary techniques to Will that were deemed acceptable.

Relationships with the public school personnel and the school district's special education unit were very negative. The immediate problem was that the principal did not want Sam attending the high school where he served as principal. After issuing numerous suspensions because of Sam's uncontrollable and/or truant behavior, the principal had finally placed Sam on home-bound instruction. Unfortunately, the only time the home-bound instructor could come to the home was during Will's two-hour break between his two jobs. From Nell's perspective this was problematic if a critical family relationship goal was to increase Sam's time with father. The supervisors suggested that perhaps a "creative" psychiatrist from Nell's agency could draft an official recommendation to the principal. Considering Sam's lack of educational motivation and need for limits, an immediate intervention was needed. The official recommendation would propose that the most beneficial educational experience for Sam would occur under his father's supervision. Thus, Sam's "schooling" should consist of spending time with his father, both at home and at his father's evening job at the bowling alley. Nell felt the principal would enthusiastically endorse this recommendation, since his sole concern was that Sam not return to his high school. The psychiatrist's official report would eliminate the principal's responsibility for securing a temporary school placement. The long-term goal, however, would be to find a school situation that would be responsive to Sam's learning disability, motivate him, and simultaneously enhance his low self-esteem.

Locating an appropriate school placement was now the responsibility of the special education unit. The director of special education was frustrated because she could not recommend a long-term school placement without Sam having a psychological evaluation. Her intent, however, was to seek another out-of-county special school. The director viewed Sue as negligent for not bringing Sam to the necessary evaluation sessions. Sue, in fact, had not brought Sam to the sessions because neither Sam nor his father wanted him to return to a special education private school, particularly in another county. In the supervisory discussion it was suggested that Nell continue to develop her own relationship with this key educational decision-maker and then advocate for Sam's referral to the local vocational school. It would be necessary to "grease the wheel" with this school professional before arranging any meetings between her and the parents. Securing a vocational school placement would undoubtedly serve Sam's educational and emotional goals, as well as his father's desires, better than a special school placement. However, the recommendation for the excellent vocational school located in Sam's county would have to be strongly supported by the director of special education.

Nell left her third supervision session with a clear understanding of what changes within the family and between the family and school would be necessary to prevent Sam's placement. She was prepared to design her individual, conjoint, and family sessions with clear content and process goals. Content goals would address the affective concerns within the family; process goals would be based on knowledge of what changes in relationship were needed. She now had a blueprint for creating enactments between family members designed to alter the nonadaptive relationship patterns. However, the most important goal for future family sessions would be to develop a shared meaning with the family about the problem definition. Would Will and Sue understand that many of Sam's problems were embedded within their own interactions? Would they agree to change these interactions in order to help Sam? This crucial session would entail developing a collaborative treatment plan with the family that would be consistent with the family's stated goals and concerns yet move in a direction of change based on a shared understanding of the problem definition.

Supervision: The Beginning Phase of Therapy

In reviewing sessions, the supervisors concurred that Nell's collaborative treatment planning meeting with the family was a pivotal moment. Within this session Nell shared her understanding of how the critical events of loss and change occurring in Sam's life were related to the escalation of his difficulties and emphasized that the most important people to help him now would be Will and Sue (by her supporting Will), since the professionals had not been helpful. This reframing of the meaning of Sam's problems had a profound effect, particularly when combined with an enactment that created more closeness between Will and Sam by having them talk together without interference from other family members. Will told Sam that he would commit to helping him by spending more time with him and "getting on his butt" if he did not wash the dishes, take out the trash, be nicer to Jen, and most importantly, go to school. Within an enactment between Sue and Will, Sue agreed to diminish her disciplinary role with Sam and shift to supporting Will's parental authority. Will, in turn, agreed to be more appreciative of Sue's commitment to be there for the family. The collaborative treatment plan was then developed and agreed upon by all family members. A calendar was given to the family to record any progression made weekly toward each of the treatment objectives.

Jen and Ted appreciated Nell's encouragement that they be viewed as their own "family unit." They readily accepted Nell's referral to the community mental health center for help with their financial planning. Their daughter, Amy, was now one week old and Nell had given the family her videotape of Amy's family birthday celebration.

In an individual session Sam finally told Nell where he went when he was truant from school. He had formed a relationship with a contractor, Todd, who was renovating a home in a nearby neighborhood. Todd had asked Sam and Max (a new friend of Sam's who, coincidentally, was attending the county's vocational school) to help work on the renovations. Todd was impressed with

Sam's carpentry skills. This new information provided a wonderful opportunity to create an enactment of Sam's demonstrated competence. Together Nell, Sam, Max, and Todd planned a surprise visit for Will to the renovated home; the visit was videotaped and subsequently shown to all family members. Sam proudly toured the home, showing his father all the work he had done, and Will was amazed. Further, when Todd told Sam's father what a responsible, conscientious young man he had as a son, Will beamed with pride. This was father's *first* experience with an outsider praising Sam's accomplishments, and Nell was very touched.

In reviewing other sessions, the supervisors learned that the agency psychiatrist with whom Nell worked had sent the principal his official recommendation that Sam "go to school" with Will at the bowling alley. The principal had agreed. Sam was currently adhering to the agreement to go with his father to the bowling alley.

Nell had also worked hard to establish a strong alliance with the director of special education, talking to her at length about Will and Sue's commitment to Sam's well-being and why it was important to them to have Sam educated in their county. Nell emphasized the negative effect on Sam's self-esteem when the neighborhood boys made fun of him every time he had taken the school's yellow bus to the "school for crazy, retarded kids" in the other county. She told the director how proud Will was when he saw the carpentry work Sam had done in the renovated house and the positive impact this had had on Sam's self-esteem. Once the director agreed to consider a school within the county, Sue promptly brought Sam to the psychological evaluation sessions. The special education director finally appeared willing to support a referral to the vocational school in Sam's county.

Within the supervision, Nell was strongly validated for her excellent work. Despite all the potential obstacles, the family and other systems were clearly moving toward change. It felt like a honeymoon period. Would the family be able to sustain these significant changes? Nell was encouraged to congratulate the family for its efforts, but also to suggest that change sometimes occurs in a zigzag fashion; families can move forward, even when some backward steps occur.

Reframing a Crisis

Marion received an urgent call from Nell and a crisis supervision session was held. Sam's behavior had suddenly deteriorated. He was having explosive fights with his father and refusing to go with him to school (i.e., the bowling alley). In a session with Nell, Sam told her that during the last few weeks of Jen's pregnancy, unbeknownst to Will and Sue, Jane, the biological mother of Jen and Sam, had begun telephoning her daughter. Jane's son, Will Jr. (the only child she had been communicating with for the past five years), had told her about Jen's pregnancy. During one of these calls Sam had gotten on the phone and told his mother that his father didn't love him and that his stepmother beat him regularly. In a state of impulsive anger, his mother told him that her and her husband Larry would come and rescue him. They would kidnap him and take him back to their home in another state.

Nell was in an extreme state of emotional agitation. Recognizing this as an in-the-heart reaction, the supervisors quickly intervened to move Nell to an in-the-head mode of functioning. First, they reframed the "crisis" as a long overdue opportunity to have Will and Jane meet together as co-parents. Together they could create a plan that would satisfy Sam's needs. Calmly, they continued to outline the specific steps Nell would need to take.

First, Nell would ask Sam to have his mother call her so that she could meet with her and Larry when they arrived. Nell would also express her sincere interest in getting to know Sam's mom. Second, Nell would let Sam know that she would be discussing Jane and Larry's upcoming "visit" with Will and Sue, whom she would help to understand that Sam's provocative statements to his mother were his way of expressing how desperate he was for contact with her after a five-year period of silence. Nell would let them know that reestablishing a relationship with his mother was critical to Sam's long-term emotional development. She would also let them know that in cases of divorce, it was not unusual for a teenager to want to live with a noncustodial parent to reestablish a relationship. The crucial question would be raised whether Will could consider the possibility of supporting a decision for Sam to live with his mother, if it turned out to be in Sam's best interest. Nell would emphasize that an impulsive kidnapping event would not be helpful to Sam. Rather, she would hope to slow things down and create a thoughtful planning process between Jane and Will regarding Sam's future educational needs and living arrangements. She would need to elicit Will's agreement to meet with Jane to discuss these important issues. Finally, knowing Sue's tendency to impulsively leave the home during periods of turmoil, Nell would ask Sue to make a commitment to stay and support Will.

By the end of the supervision session, Nell herself was no longer in crisis because she had a clear plan of action. Also, just as she knew she would be on 24-hour availability call to the family during this process, Marion had reassured her that, as supervisor, she, too, would be constantly available by telephone to Nell. Marion requested that Nell call her for phone supervision after talking with Sam, Will and Sue, and Jane. Both supervisors let Nell know that every session throughout this crisis period would be carefully planned with regard to specific content, process, and outcome goals.

Providing Support and Reassurance

In the calls to her supervisor, Nell reported that Sam was very enthusiastic about her meeting with his mother. Nell scheduled a meeting with Jane and Larry the day they arrived. The session with Will and Sue had been difficult. Will was very hurt by Sam's perceived rejection. Sue comforted Will by sharing how she had felt when her two children had returned to live with their father but also that she knew how much they had missed him. She suggested to Will that it would be good for Sam to develop a more realistic portrayal of his mother. She reassured Will that his demonstrated love and commitment to Sam over the past five years could never be erased, even if Sam chose to live with his mother. Appreciating how Sam could be emotionally harmed by an impulsive kidnapping, Will agreed that he would meet for a co-parenting session with his former wife.

Dealing with Induction

There were two essential outcome goals for the in-office session with the mother and stepfather: (1) Jane and Larry would agree to work in the best interest of Sam; and (2) Jane and Larry would agree that Jane should meet with Will the following day to discuss a future plan for Sam. Nell's in-session goals were to establish a strong collaborative alliance with both Jane and Larry, to maintain a neutral position regarding Sam's future living arrangement, and to call Marion at any point in the session if Nell felt she was not being effective.

Twenty minutes into the session with Jane and Larry, Nell left the room and called Marion. Nell was extremely angry at Jane for having abandoned Sam and not owning up to this. Also, Jane was strongly critical of Will and Sue's parenting efforts, and Jane was determined to remove Sam from this situation immediately. Furthermore, Larry's continual defense of Jane's behavior was infuriating to Nell. It was obvious to the supervisor that the goal of establishing collaborative relationships with the couple would not happen without supervisory intervention.

In processing the sequences of the interview with Nell, it was clear that a symmetrical escalation was occurring between Nell and the couple. The more Jane and Larry would criticize Will for Sam's behavior and justify why they had been unavailable to Sam for five years, the more Nell defended Will. Marion recognized that the crux of the problem was Nell's loss of neutrality due to her being inducted into Will's role. She tried several ways to shift Nell's negative perceptions of Jane and elicit an empathic response. Knowing Nell was a feminist, she reminded her of the movie *Kramer vs. Kramer*, which had presented a no-blame view of women who made the decision not to raise their children. Surely, Nell was not blaming Jane for the decision not to raise Sam? Nell remained angry. Marion then appealed to Nell's own desires as a woman: "Would you have wanted to stay in the marriage to Will?" Nell hesitated as she imagined the ever-present black cigar dangling from Will's mouth. Sensing Nell's momentary hesitation, Marion highlighted how painful Jane's decision must have been. She emphasized comments Jane had made in the session that indicated her concern for Sam during the ten years she had raised him. Finally, she helped Nell to see how promptly Jane and Larry had responded to Sam's current cry for help and their commitment of time, money, and effort to fly in to "rescue" him.

When Nell returned to the session, her expanded perspectives allowed her to become truly empathic to Jane's position. She regained her neutrality about where Sam should live and collaborative relationships were formed with the couple. Strongly supported by both her husband and Nell, Jane made the decision to meet with Will the next day to discuss co-parenting decisions.

The Controlled Encounter

Both supervisors benefited from the work by Isaacs, Montalvo, and Abelsohn (1986) in planning with Nell the in-office co-parenting session between Will and Jane. One outcome goal for the session was that Will and Jane would agree to work together as co-parents in the best interests of Sam. A second outcome goal was that Will and Jane would sign an agreement specifying (a) each parent's assignments over the next two months regarding the exploration of alternative custody arrangements and optimal school placements for Sam; (b) their mutual willingness to take turns telephoning each other every Sunday to discuss school and custody updates and reports on Sam's behavior that week; and (c) their mutual willingness to enforce the rule that Sam could only talk to a parent about issues related to that parent, thereby reducing Sam's attempts to split their parental alliance. A final outcome goal discussed with Nell would depend on whether an adequate co-parenting process was established during the session. If the session went well, Will and Jane would be asked to meet with Sam the next day to share with him their parental decisions.

The primary process goal for the session was for Nell to assume a hierarchical and centralized position as therapist. She would set clear boundaries for when Will or Jane could speak to her or to each other during the session. Nell would also maintain the rules for their interaction, which would be presented as the session began. These rules included adhering to a maximum of 90 minutes for the session and, allowing for planned breaks during the session if a cooling down period was necessary. The content goals for the session would involve Will summarizing Sam's experiences over the past five years and giving a current update, and Will and Jane making the necessary decisions on how to proceed with future issues of custody and educational placement for Sam.

In subsequent supervisory discussion of the session, Nell characterized her experience as therapist with the metaphor, "I was like the bridge over troubled waters." Despite frequent escalation of conflict between the divorced couple—wherein Jane would flee from the room, be followed by Nell, calmed down, and return—Nell was able to keep the parents on track. This was accomplished by clear boundary-setting and the repetitive appeal for them to work in the best interests of Sam. After the agreement was signed, a session with Jane, Will, and Sam was scheduled for the next day.

A Crisis within a Crisis:
Use of Family Support Service Monies

During the previously described supervision session, Sue and Will called into Nell's beeper. Sue's oldest daughter was at her out-of-state home in a body cast due to a recent car accident. Unable to take care of herself, she wanted her mother to come live with her for the next month. Sue felt divided by the simultaneous pull of her commitment to support Will and her daughter's need. Both Will and Nell supported Sue in the decision to respond to her daughter's needs. In turn, Sue was supportive of Will's meeting with Jane and Sam at their home for the next session. Reestablishing the mother-daughter relationship would no doubt help Sue relax in her stepmother role with Sam, and providing concrete assistance was viewed as furthering his treatment goals. Therefore, a decision was made to use family support service monies to pay for Sue's plane trip to her daughter's home. Monies were also allocated to pay for daily long-distance telephone calls between Will and Sue so that they could continue to maintain a sense of closeness and support of each other's parenting efforts.

The Family Reunion

A plan for the in-home session with Will, Jane, and Sam was devised by Nell and her supervisors. The session's central theme was the family's need for balance in their efforts to both love and control. During the first half of the session with mother, father, and child, it was predicted that all would have an emotional reaction to their reunion in the original family home. The goals for this part of the session would therefore be based on the theme of parent-child love and would involve the following enactments:

1. Mother and father would tell Sam how much they each loved him and that they wanted to do what was best for him as parents.
2. Jane would share with Sam her reasons for leaving five years ago and explain that her lack of contact did not reflect a lack of love but, rather, an avoidance of pain.
3. Both parents would tell Sam that they were exploring the best living situation for him and were open to abiding by his choice.

The second half of the session would deal with the theme of control and would involve the following enactments:

1. The parents would clearly state what their mutual expectations were for Sam's behavior at home and school, regardless of where he lived.
2. The parents would demonstrate to Sam that they were working together on his behalf as parents by shaking hands.
3. The parents would discuss the written agreement they had signed and emphasize that Sam could not "play them off" against each other in the future.
4. Nell would try to use some of the spontaneous process material in the session to simulate a crisis wherein Sam might lose control and the parents would need to take charge.

In the subsequent supervisory session it became apparent that this session had been the turning point in treatment. Clearly, Sam had never experienced his parents as a united team. Not only were previously unspoken but highly charged affective issues dealt with, but Nell had also done an outstanding job of creating a control enactment. When Sam defiantly left the room saying that he was going to refuse to go to "school" with his father to the bowling alley, both parents got up from their seats, brought him back to the room, and made it very clear that they would not tolerate this rebelliousness. As Jane said, "I may not be here, but I'm going to back your father up all the way!"

Interagency Meetings, Informal Resources, and Use of Respite Services

During the middle phase of therapy, sessions were scheduled on a less intense basis (about three hours weekly). Supervision focused on Nell's goal of getting Sam back in school. A series of sessions was held with Will and Sam to prepare them for the meetings with the vocational school personnel. Will and Sam needed to clearly articulate their ideas regarding the most effective ways of integrating Sam slowly into the new school experience. The plan they developed incorporated the following ideas: (1) Both Will and Sam needed to feel they had supportive allies in the new school environment; (2) both Will and Sam felt that reentering school should occur gradually for Sam, beginning with an hour a day, moving to a half day, and finally a full day; (3) Sam wanted the vocational school to credit his work with Todd in the home renovation as part of his required school attendance; ideally, the school would allow Sam to "go to school" with Todd one full day a week. These negotiations with the school proved successful.

Another issue discussed in supervision was Will's expressed need for respite. With Sue still absent from the home, Will was working triple-time as father and in his two jobs. As Will said, "I feel stretched like a rubber band that's about to break." He wanted to go camping with some of his male friends but was concerned about leaving Sam unsupervised. In a session with Will and Sam various options for respite were discussed. Sam had the idea that perhaps he could stay with his friend Max (who also attended the vocational school), but whose family was short on money. A subsequent session was held with Max's parents, Will, and Nell to negotiate how respite monies could be used to support transportation, food, and entertainment for both Sam and Max during this week. The outcome of this informal respite was positive. Both father and son had gotten a well-deserved break from all their hard work over the past months.

It was noted that a parallel process was occurring both in the work with the family and in supervision. In the therapy Will had become the definite leader in treatment decisions, with Nell in the role of facilitator. Similarly within the supervision process, Nell was now telling the supervisors what her treatment decisions were, and the supervisors were supportive but no longer needed to be directive.

Supervision: Termination

Treatment sessions with the family were scheduled for one hour per week during this period. With Sue's return home and strongly reestablished in a supportive role with Will, Nell no longer needed to be in that role. Sam was now going to school every day as well as washing the dishes and taking out the trash. Jane had gradually decreased her weekly conversations with Will, and it became clear that she no longer wanted Sam to live with her. However, she continued to maintain contact with Sam by telephone and was always supportive of Will's actions. It was time for Nell to say good-bye to the family. A closing celebration planned by the family was held at the bowling alley with Nell, Will, Sam, and Sue. It was fitting that the team of Will and Sam resoundingly defeated the team of Nell and Sue. Nell recapped all the changes the family had made, which had also been highlighted in the weekly calendar given to them in the first family interview. She then told each what she had learned from him or her about the hidden strengths of families and gave each a gift that symbolized his or her unique strength. Sam's gift was a red tee-shirt with a heart containing the message: "Reach out and love someone."

The supervision was also ending. A closing discussion focused on a mutual evaluation of the supervisory process and the expansion of Nell's range of competence with this new treatment model. Both supervisors expressed their appreciation to Nell for teaching them so much about the satisfaction and struggles of home-based therapy.

Summary of Treatment Sessions

The treatment of the H. family covered a period of four months, with session scheduling being the most intense during the first two months. Fifty-three meetings were scheduled: 39 at the home, 4 in the office, 3 in the community, and 7 at the public school, special education unit, or vocational school. During the entire treatment, there were only two cancellations by the therapist and none by the family.

An in-home visit was generally designed to include time for a combination of individual, dyadic, triadic, or family sessions as determined by treatment needs. Thus an in-home visit could range in duration from one half-hour to three hours. There were 22 *individual* sessions with Will, 10 with Sue, and 8 with Sam. Will and Sue had 10 *dyadic* sessions, Will and Sam had 18, Sue and Sam had 4, Sue and Jen had 2, Will and Jen had 2. Will, Sue, and Sam had 6 *triadic* sessions; Sue, Jen, and Ted had 1; Will, Sam, and Jen had 1; Will, Sue, and Jen also had 1. Five *family* sessions were held with Will, Sue, Sam, Jen, and Ted. Three sessions were held with family members in the community (2 at father's bowling alley and one at Sam's renovated home project). When Jane and Larry came into the area, 1 dyadic session was held with them and 1 was held with Will and Jane. Will, Jane, and Sam had 1 triadic session. Seven treatment meetings and seven phone sessions were conducted with various school personnel. In summary, one year of therapy was compressed into four months.

A telephone follow-up interview was conducted with Will and Sue three years later. Sam had graduated from vocational school and was working in Todd's construction company; Jane and Ted had attended Sam's graduation. After Jen had graduated from high school, she, Ted, and their three-year-old daughter had moved into a nearby apartment. Will's oldest son and his family had become frequent visitors to the H. home. Sue's children were maintaining contact with her by telephone and occasional visits.

CHAPTER 7

Training the Home-Based Practitioner

> ... mastery is staying on the path. But the journey of mastery eventually takes you beyond fundamentals to levels of subtlety and skill that exist at the further reaches of your potential.

> —George Leonard, 1987

NATIONWIDE, A NUMBER OF diverse new initiatives, programs, and services has proliferated to serve families and children, based upon consensual principles of effective practice; that is, practice should be child-centered, family-centered, community-based, collaboratively community/consumer planned, and culturally competent (Combrinck-Graham, 1995). The success of these programs depends on the understanding, knowledge, skills, and attitudes of the managers, supervisors, and front-line staff implementing them. Unfortunately, little is being done nationally either to define essential competencies or to support training initiatives that would ensure effective implementation of family-centered service reforms (Cohen, 1996).

Conducting home-based therapy with high-risk families whose children and/or adolescents exhibit severe emotional disturbances is stressful and emotionally demanding. The job requires the practitioner to have an extensive knowledge base, well-developed clinical skills, maturity, and the ability to assume a significant amount of responsibility. Typically, however, the home-based practitioner is a master's or bachelor's level clinician who has had little formal training in family theory, family therapy skills, or home-based

243

family service practice. Often, the practitioner's supervisor lacks formal training in these areas as well. This is not surprising, since traditional professional schools at both the undergraduate and graduate levels rarely incorporate instruction on family-centered therapy or home-based practice in their curricula.

Concern about performance when conducting or supervising home-based therapy is prevalent among practitioners (Christensen, 1995; Cottrell, 1994). Limited skill level increases fatigue, morale problems, and staff turnover. Tracy, Bean, Gwatkin, and Hill (1992) operationally defined burnout as a practitioner's decision to change jobs within six months and found that the average length of stay in family preservation jobs was 18 months. According to one program director, the loss of a worker represents several thousand dollars, given the investment required in job orientation and supervision to help the worker acquire beginning skills for in-home work (L. Hoge, personal communication, 1997). A key variable in preventing burnout and increasing job satisfaction is the opportunity to enhance one's professional knowledge and develop treatment skills that are job relevant (Tracy et al., 1992). A survey conducted in 1990 by Pennsylvania's Office of Mental Health compared staff turnover in two major service areas: mental health home-based services and intensive case management services.* While mental health home-based services staff received job-related training, intensive case management staff did not. After a two-year period, there was 200% staff turnover within the intensive case management services, compared to zero turnover by the mental health group. Despite the need for training home-based services staff in a systemic perspective, the lack of available literature reflects

---

*Case management is *one* program component available to families during the period they are served by mental health home-based services. Families who are *not* receiving mental health home-based services may be referred for intensive case management services. These services are provided to families having a child whose severe emotional disturbance necessitates involvement with multiple systems of care. Intensive case management is provided through an individual, the case manager, who collaborates with the family in identifying and obtaining necessary services. The case manager may act merely as a consultant and resource person to the parents or, at the other extreme, may identify services, make referrals, provide follow-up, and be the family's advocate in obtaining services for the child. Unlike the home-based practitioner, the intensive case manager *does not provide treatment*, but rather connects the child or family to treatment resources. Intensive case management services are extended to families from the identified child's entry into the mental health system and, in some instances, may continue until the child reaches adulthood.

the novelty of this new practice area (Gorman, Lockerman, & Giffels, 1995; Sugarman & Masheter, 1985; Zarski, Pastore, Way, & Shepler, 1988).

THE PENNSYLVANIA MENTAL HEALTH HOME-BASED SERVICES TRAINING EXPERIENCE

Establishing a State Training Initiative

As a result of the federal-level Children and Adolescent Service Systems Program (CASSP) initiative through the National Institute of Mental Health (NIMH), Pennsylvania's Bureau of Children and Youth Services, Office of Mental Health, funded a major children's mental health initiative in 1987, at an annual cost of $2.03 million. This initiative put into operation the CASSP philosophy by providing start-up monies for mental health in-home services to providers in 10 counties statewide. Since that time, mental health in-home programs have been developed to serve all 64 counties in the state. These programs are located in both public and private agencies and institutions in a variety of social and political contexts with diverse urban, suburban, and rural client populations. (See Chapter 3 for how to plan and implement mental health in-home programs).

In addition to program costs, monies were allocated to create a statewide training and evaluation initiative in 1988. Both were conducted through a subcontract with the Philadelphia Child Guidance Center. State regulations were developed that specified a training requirement for all programs. The evaluation initiative was completed in 1996. By 1993 the proliferation of programs statewide had resulted in a subcontract with a second training provider to serve the state's western region; the Philadelphia Child Guidance Center continued to provide training to the remaining three regions. Currently, the training for mental health home-based services is funded by each agency's program.

Both the training model and the program evaluation design are congruent with the ecosystemic structural family therapy approach used in service delivery. The state selected the Philadelphia Child Guidance Center because the values underlying the Center's clinical and training models were congruent with the CASSP philosophy.

Another selection factor was the Center's reputation for providing highly competent training. Also, the Philadelphia Child Guidance Center had implemented mental health home-based services in 1980 and the trainers were familiar with this new type of service delivery.

Training Format and Target Groups

When new programs were developing throughout the state, training was targeted to every level of staff from the top administrators to home-based practitioners. Training began with an overview of mental health home-based services provided to regional, county, and agency program directors, as well as county CASSP representatives. The focus of this initial training was to build supportive relationships with top-level administrators, to educate them regarding the principles, values, and assumptions of a systemically-oriented, family-centered treatment approach, as well as to have them directly experience the training approach that would be used with home-based program staff. Since the development of new programs has been completed within the state, overview training for top administrators is no longer necessary. Currently, new program directors are mentored by agency supervisors who are familiar with the program's administrative issues.

Each program's director and front-line staff receive training at a geographically accessible regional training site approximately 2 days per month for a total of 17 days per year over a 3-year cycle. Approximately 200 home-based program staff are trained yearly. All new staff and program directors also attend 3 days of start-up training. Thus a total of 54 days of training is provided to program staff within the 3-year period. Additionally, scholarships are given for a 3-week summer family therapy practicum sponsored by the Philadelphia Child Guidance Center's Family Training Center. In selecting applicants for these scholarships, priority is given to those program directors who have no formal training in family therapy and who need to develop and/or strengthen their case conceptualization abilities and clinical skills. Each year from 1988 through 1997, 2 training days focusing on supervision issues were provided to program directors.

Tailoring Training Curriculum to Meet Consumer Needs

The training curriculum was originally developed by a committee composed of parent advocates and child service system providers, including mental health professionals and paraprofessionals working in home-based, outpatient, and inpatient programs. While the curriculum was being prepared, site visits were made to the first 10 in-home programs funded and an assessment of the staff members' clinical skill levels was conducted. Over the past 10 years the original curriculum has undergone continual refinement through feedback from curriculum committees composed of the program directors and in response to yearly research evaluation reports describing characteristics of the population served.

It is critical that a home-based curriculum emphasize the necessary knowledge and skills that will have optimal relevance to the in-home service consumers. The evaluation initiative for Pennsylvania's mental health home-based services was particularly helpful in identifying these needs, as it included data presenting a statewide overview of family demographics, characteristics of identified patients and their families, and the prevalence of types of problems addressed. For example, annual research reports described a profile of the 1,968 families served and evaluated (Dore, 1994, 1996).

The racial composition of families served reflects the overall racial composition found in the state of Pennsylvania. Of families served statewide, 84% are Caucasian, 7% are African-American, 4% are of Hispanic origin, just over 1% are Asian, less than 1% are Native-American, and 3% are composed of members of varied races. Educational levels of both male and female parents are higher than national norms (68% of the mothers and 69% of the fathers have at least high school diplomas), while reported incomes are lower (36% less than $10,000; 35% less than $20,000). The family structures are as follows: 38% of the households have two biological parents; 36% involve single-parent households (23% mother only, 13% father only); 26% of the households include a nonbiological adult (17.6% involve remarried parents, with 14.2% stepfathers and 3.4% stepmothers, and 8.4% involved mothers with live-in male partners).

The largest percentage of youth referred for in-home services are in their early teens, although referrals cover a range from preschoolers to young adults. Twice as many males as females are identified patients, who are also likely to be the oldest child in the family. About 61% of the identified patients and 30% of their siblings have experienced out-of-home placements before in-home services began. Based on 600 of the 1,968 families evaluated, over 82% of the referred identified patients have experienced prior mental health treatment and about 17% have also been involved with the Child Welfare, Juvenile Justice, and drug and alcohol systems. The mental health problems of children and adolescents treated in the home-based programs cluster most heavily in a few specific categories: adjustment reactions (aggression), oppositional disorders, conduct disorders, and attention deficit disorders. Thus, nearly 80% of identified patients are characterized by disturbances in overt behavior—externalizing disorders. Children and youth diagnosed as having major mental illnesses account for about 15% of home-based patients, which represents a substantial proportion of the most disturbed children in the population. Many of the identified patients also exhibit multiple disorders. It is not surprising that over half of children and adolescents entering home-based treatment are functioning at levels ranging from "clear interference" to "major interference" in daily life, as measured on the Global Assessment of Functioning Scale for Children included in the *DSM-IV* (American Psychiatric Association, 1994).

Results from the Family Assessment Device (Epstein, Baldwin, & Bishop, 1983) indicate that, at referral, most of the identified patients view their families as more impaired than do other family members, particularly in the areas of communication and affective responsiveness. Mothers consistently voiced concerns about how roles are allocated within the family, while fathers tend to see their families in a more positive light than other family members. Siblings are often in general agreement with the identified patient about problems in family functioning but tend not to perceive things as negatively as the identified patient does. Based on 600 of the 1,968 evaluated families, many parents themselves have sought help— about 42% of mothers and 36% of fathers had received prior mental health treatment. Of these parents 17% of mothers and 7.7% of fathers had experienced psychiatric hospitalizations or drug and alcohol residential placements that took them out of the home.

The nine most frequent problems addressed by home-based clinicians (listed in order of prevalence) were: (1) inadequate parenting skills, (2) acting out behavior of a child, (3) school-related problems, (4) problems in family communication, (5) lack of responsible behavior in a child, (6) lack of respect for authority in a child, (7) weaknesses in the parental subsystem, (8) difficulties in the parent-child relationship, and (9) aggressive behavior by a child.

Curriculum Content

The formal curriculum represents learning modules deemed relevant to Pennsylvania's mental health home-based service practitioners and consumers. Relevancy was determined both by curriculum committees composed of program directors and research evaluation reports providing information on family demographics and prevalence of clinical problems described by families and home-based clinicians (Dore, 1994, 1996). The congruence between the organization of curriculum content, the particulars of the families served, and the distinctive features of Pennsylvania's mental-health in-home services can be seen in Table 7.1.

New staff and/or program directors attend three days of start-up training where essential introductory information is provided. For example, after a trainer reviews the CASSP principles, home-based program components, and ecosystemic model that characterize Pennsylvania's home-based services, the theme of relating to parents as partners is highlighted by having a parent-educator (previously a consumer of in-home services) instruct new program hires on what they can learn from parents and how to support parent advocacy. Understanding the legal rights of children in mental health, education, juvenile justice, child welfare, and developmental disabilities is also crucial when working with multisystems-involved children and adolescents. Additionally, new personnel need to recognize the importance of team building (in a team-delivered service) and of avoiding the professional fatigue that can be endemic to home-based practice.

Twenty-four of the ongoing training modules that are based on program issues or evaluation information are taught by Philadelphia Child Guidance trainers, eight days yearly over a three-year period. The basic theme underlying all of these modules is "how

Table 7.1
PENNSYLVANIA'S THREE-YEAR MENTAL HEALTH
HOME-BASED CURRICULUM*

Modules Based on Program Principles and Issues
  Start-up Training
  • Overview of Mental Health Family-Based Services
  • Learning from Parents**
  • Supporting Parent Advocacy**
  • Children's Legal Rights
  • Working with Two-Person Teams
  • Avoiding Professional Fatigue
  Ongoing Training: Modules Taught by Family Therapy Training Center
  • Ecosystemic Structural Family Therapy: Theory, Assessment, and Intervention
  • Linking Child Service Systems: Strategies and Cautions
  • Teaching Parenting Skills in Context
  • Sibling Issues
  • Use of Family Rituals in Family Therapy
  Ongoing Training: Modules Taught by Agency or Community Resources
  • Accessing Available Resources
  • Safety and Liability Issues
  • First Aid and Cardiopulmonary Resuscitation
  • Facilitating Support Groups
  • Medication Possibilities for DSM-IV Diagnoses
Modules Derived From Statewide Demographics of Consumers
  Radical Composition of Consumers
  • Developing Cultural Competence
  Family Structures of Consumer Families
  • Working with Couples
  • Creating an Adaptive Divorce
  • Clinical Issues in Single Parent Households
  • Clinical Issues in Remarried and Cohabitating Families
  Age Distribution of Identified Patients
  • Families with Young Children
  • Children in the Middle Years
  • Working with Adolescents

---

*Developed by Marion Lindblad-Goldberg, Ph.D., 1989.
**This module was taught by a parent-educator.

continued

Table 7.1

continued

Modules Based on Type and Prevalence of Clinical Problems
in Consumers
   Assessment and treatment of:
   • Attention-Deficit/Hyperactivity Disorder
   • Oppositional Defiant Disorder
   • Family Violence
   • Child and Adolescent Depression and Suicide
   • Parents with Mental Illness
   • Substance Abuse in Families
   • School Problems
   • Sexual Abuse
   • Children with Special Needs
   • Physical Illness in Families
   • Pre-Placement, Placement, and Post-placement Issues

to" implement an ecosystemic structural approach in the assessment and treatment of families referred for in-home services. For example, using this approach means that practitioners need to know how to teach parenting skills in the context of a family session, respond to sibling issues, use family rituals to create and sustain change, and develop appropriate linkages to and interventions with other child service systems. Also, since the service population reflects diversity in culture, family structure, and age distribution of identified patients, the home-based clinician needs to know how to: respond with cultural competence to each family; work with couples; develop interventions with divorced, single-parent, remarried, or cohabitating families; and appropriately respond to the developmental differences of preschool, middle years, and adolescent clients. Home-based therapists require a solid clinical knowledge of the type and prevalence of clinical problems found in families served by home-based programs. The therapists need to understand assessment issues and be able to plan treatment interventions for families having parents with mental illness and children or adolescents presenting with attention-deficit/hyperactivity disorder, oppositional defiant disorder, depression and suicidality, school problems, substance abuse, sexual abuse issues, special needs, and pre- and post-placement issues. Knowledge and interventions pertaining to family violence (i.e., domestic violence, physical or sexual abuse, etc.) must also be mastered by the home-based therapist.

The remaining modules in the curriculum are taught by specialists within each home-based program's agency or community. These modules reflect a worker's need to know how to access available resources on a family's behalf, handle safety and liability issues in the home and community, and administer first aid or cardiopulmonary resuscitation when necessary. Agency or community psychiatrists who administer medication to clients served in the home-based program are good resources to teach staff about *DSM-IV* diagnoses and appropriate use of medication. In-home programs that want to provide support groups for children, adolescents, or parents benefit from local expertise in group facilitation.

In addition to the formal curriculum, nine days of clinical case consultation are provided yearly over the three-year training cycle. Home-based therapists present videotaped excerpts from in-home sessions and written case presentations during these training days. Training consultation is based on specific case consultation questions formulated by home-based therapists in concert with their supervisors. A typical case consultation training day scenario is presented later in the chapter.

THE TRAINING MODEL

What Is Training?

Supervision has been defined as an "an intensive, interpersonally focused . . . relationship in which one person is designated to facilitate the development of therapeutic competence in the other person[s]" (Loganbill, Hardy, & Delworth, 1982, p.4). What distinguishes the supervisory relationship from other clinical relationships is the function of mutual accountability and evaluation. In contrast, training aims to support and supplement the supervisory relationship by bringing a new perspective to both supervisor and supervisee, generally in a larger context involving many supervisors and supervisees. Using a family analogy, the trainer has the role of grandparent, while the supervisor is like the parent to the child who is represented metaphorically by the supervisee. The parent's responsibility is to promote a parent-child relationship that will support the child's emerging competence and growth within the context of acknowledged rules and expectations. The grandparent's role is to support the parental hierarchy and parenting process. Grandparents also provide wisdom, encouragement, and respect to the parent and child as well as to other parents and grandchildren in the family.

As can be seen in Figure 6.1, the trainer's input acts as an external feedback loop into the therapeutic system composed primarily of the supervisee's relationship to the supervisor, family, and community. The trainer is a part of the therapeutic system and yet separate from it. This positioning allows the trainer to have an objectivity and a wider perspective than either the supervisor or supervisee who are each influenced by their relationship with each other and their relationship to the family. Quite simply, the trainer is less likely to be influenced by the emotional field of the family or the supervisory relationship. The trainer looks through a wide-angle lens and sees the larger picture; the supervisor looks through a regular lens and focuses on a smaller part of the picture.

Training Goals, Methods, and Evaluation

The principles and processes of the training model are parallel to those found in the mental health home-based service model. Training groups, like the families served, have significant diversity. The profile of a typical training group shows diversity in age, culture, defining county characteristics that impact on each program, educational experience, and theoretical orientation. Within the three-year training cycle, the training group comes to represent a three-generational family with third-year, second-year, and first-year trainees.

Just as service delivery occurs in the home, training is conducted in the "home" regions of the trainees. The emphasis on working with multiple systems that have an impact on the family's life is replicated in the training design by providing initiatory training to representatives from the region, county, and agency who will be involved in regulating, funding, and (ideally) supporting the home-based program.

The Philadelphia Child Guidance Center's Family Therapy Training Center has developed a way of training home-based therapists that parallels our clinical work. The collaborative style of our trainers is guided by the assumption that the knowledge of the trainees has equal importance to the ideas the trainer offers. The trainer's goal is to expand the trainees' existing competencies in terms of knowledge and clinical skill. The methods used during the presentation of formal curriculum modules include a brief lecture, demonstration of a competency through discussion of the trainees' cases, and role-play practice. For example, the module, "Use of Family Rituals in Family Therapy," focuses on the competency of designing family rituals that promote or support change within family relationships. The brief lecture describes and illustrates, through videotaped home-based case material, various rituals of celebration, healing, and membership that are used in the process of family therapy. Trainees are then asked to design a ritual for one of their home-based families. Role-play is used to provide the trainee with "skills" practice in how to co-evolve and implement a ritual with a simulated home-based family. At the end of a formal curriculum module, we have found it helpful to have trainees complete evaluations that rate the degree to which the experience increased their knowledge and to describe the three most important ideas or interventions they learned that could be applied to their own clinical work.

During a clinical case presentation training day, the training goals are to increase skills in case conceptualization, treatment planning, and treatment intervention. The methods used include written case presentations, group resource sharing, demonstration of a trainee's skills through videotaped case segments, role-play practice, and group consultation. Over the years we have refined a clinical case presentation outline, which was originally developed by one of our trainees (Archaki-Stone, 1989) (Appendix I). Adhering to this outline greatly enhances strengths-based case conceptualization and treatment planning skills. The format encourages the trainee to organize complex assessment information, develop clinical hypotheses, and generate treatment goals, objectives, and methods of intervention. The consultation questions posed by the trainees serve to focus the training group's consultative feedback as described later in the scenario of a typical clinical case presentation training day.

Treatment intervention skills are developed through a strengths-based demonstration process. Instead of discussion of what a trainee does with a family, videotaped segments of in-home sessions are presented. The first segment presented by the trainee illustrates a moment with a family that displays the trainee's competence in enacting a clinical skill. The second segment presented demonstrates a trainee's difficulty in implementing a desired goal within a family or interagency session. Following the trainee's videotaped presentation, a role-play is developed to replicate the family session where the trainee felt challenged. Through the mutual coaching of the trainer, the trainee's supervisor, and the group, the trainee has the opportunity to demonstrate competency by practicing alternative intervention skills. At the end of each training year, 23 clinical skill competencies measuring a trainee's perceived growth are evaluated by the training provider (Appendix J).

Training days are viewed as necessary "respite" to preserve the morale of the in-home workers and to create a time and place for them to reflect on their work. Program directors arrange back-up for the crisis service so that the space and time for training can be preserved. A cohesive training group becomes a natural source of collegial support, since other agency staff are not familiar with unique ups and downs of in-home work. When one home-based program was being dissolved because of political conflicts within their county, the anxious staff sought solace from the training group. They also shared their coping humor by passing out official notices announcing: "Due to current financial restraints, the light at the end of the tunnel will be turned off until further notice." Each group manages to exhibit its own brand of humor. Graduation rituals are conducted to celebrate a trainee's graduation or to punctuate the end of the training year. Often trainees present videotaped skits that hilariously depict "moments" during the in-home therapy process or creative efforts that "roast" the training procedures.

A Typical Clinical Case Presentation Training Day Scenario

At a typical clinical skills training day, Nan and Jay, a new in-home team, in concert with their supervisor, presented a case to the trainer and the 40-person training group. The patient, Evan, was an eight-year-old Caucasian boy who lived with his biological parents. Child welfare initiated the referral to mental health in-home services following a truancy complaint from the school district in December. Evan's attendance record indicated that 44 unofficial school absences had occurred since September. The school was very involved in removing every obstacle given by the parents as reasons for Evan's lack of attendance. The school had gone so far as paying a neighbor (whose son also attended the school) to drive Evan to school on the days when the neighbor's job schedule made this possible. Understandably, the school was concerned with Evan's parents' lack of responsibility in addressing the attendance problem.

While viewing the videotaped initial family session, training group members could observe directly the team's experience in the family's small, cramped, two-bedroom apartment. Jay told the group that conducting sessions in the family's living room was like performing "psychological aerobic therapy" because of the abundance of exercise equipment and stacks of psychology books. Only mother was initially available as the interview began. She described her theories about Evan's behavior and referenced her comments using several psychology books. Eventually Evan walked into the living room and turned on the TV full blast. When mother turned it off, the son turned it on again and the two of them began wrestling with the TV remote control. In frustration, Evan slapped his mother in the face. Mother promptly walked out of the apartment, leaving Evan with the home-based team. When Jay called to the father who was in the bathroom, father said "What do you want me to do about it? It's his mother's fault—she raised him." Dad then left the apartment to go bowling and told the team to "lock up" when they left. The team went to their car, called their supervisor for advice, and subsequently located a neighbor to stay with Evan until one of the parents returned. When Nan called the next day, mother never mentioned the incident. When Nan raised the concern that Evan should not be left at home without supervision, mother blamed father for Evan's behavior.

The team's consultation questions for the training group were: (1) Why is the team more concerned about Evan's truancy than his parents? and (2) How can the team get the parents more invested in the therapy process? After dividing the training group into four discussion groups, the trainer asked each group to reflect on the observed team/family interaction from the videotaped in-home session and to review the written case presentation, especially the genogram and timeline data. The groups' task was to develop hypotheses about the meaning of Evan's truancy and to generate responses to the team's consultation questions. The trainer synthesized the groups' comments and provided specific feedback to the team and supervisor.

The discussion groups all agreed that the meaning of Evan's truancy was clearly related to the abdication of parental responsibility for his behavior. The more difficult question to answer was: Why had Evan become an "orphan" in his own family? The case presentation information revealed that the wife's infidelity early in the marriage had caused father to doubt whether he was Evan's biological father. Consequently, father had never developed a relationship with Evan and had abdicated responsibility to mother to raise him. Mother, however, was convinced that her husband was Evan's father and infuriated that he would not believe her. After eight years of functioning like a single parent to Evan, mother adamantly refused to raise Evan by herself. She began working a day job 7:30 A.M. to 1:00 P.M. while father worked from 2:00 P.M. until 10:00 P.M. Returning home after her job, mother immersed herself in reading psychology books or exercising. Without parental support, Evan was like a car with an empty gas tank. By staying at home, rather than going to school, he seemed to be looking for opportunities to have some interaction with his neglectful, abdicating parents—especially his father.

The training group's response to the first consultation question was that the in-home team had become as inducted into feeling responsible for Evan as the school had in response to the void created by the lack of parental responsibility. Interventions suggested to remedy the team's dilemma included the following ideas:

1. A multisystems meeting, scheduled with the child welfare caseworker, the school counselor, the in-home team, and the parents, could be conducted with the goal of providing a unified message that the parents were responsible for insuring Evan's school attendance and that the school would

file truancy charges if Evan did not begin to attend school in one week.

2. Following the multisystems meeting, the team could meet with the parents in their home to express their concern about the legal consequences that would ensue if Evan did not go to school and to let the parents know they would support the parents' efforts.

3. Given the intractability of the school attendance problem, the team might expect that the most significant, immediate intervention for the parents would be a crisis precipitated by a court hearing during which a fine would be imposed on the parents.

4. Jay might want to move slowly in developing a relationship with father and ultimately plead with him to forgive his wife and end their power game so that he could become a father to the son who so clearly worshipped him.

5. Creating a strong alliance with the mother, Nan could attempt to help her to forgive herself for past infidelities, forgive her husband for his lack of trust in her, and recommit herself to becoming Evan's mother.

Following the group's discussion, the trainer created role-plays for Jay and Nan to practice the skills they would need to connect with each parent.

Two months later, Jay and Nan and their supervisor shared follow-up information on this case with the training group. Initially, the parents had refused to come together in assisting Evan to go to school following the multisystems meeting. After the court hearing, however, when the judge told the parents they would be fined $500 for every day of school that Evan missed, the process of the in-home therapy changed. Supported by their respective alliances with Jay and Nan, husband and wife began discussing the betrayals each had felt within their marriage and the impact this had had on their parenting of Evan. The wife asked her husband to forgive her and told him that she wanted to recommit to the marriage and to parenthood. The husband, in turn, forgave his wife. A ritual was created wherein mother went on a two-week church retreat to meditate and prepare herself for her new commitment. During the period when mother was at the retreat, Jay supported father's development of a closer relationship to his son and father's insistence that Evan go to school. When mother returned from the retreat, she and father worked together to insure Evan's school attendance.

Certification

Certification procedures were first developed in response to Medicaid funding issues for B.A.-level workers. The mental health home-based services were being provided by a team-delivered service composed of two practitioners, one at the master's level and one at the bachelor's level. Since both members functioned as equals in the provision of therapy and other service functions, an agreement was made that Medicaid would reimburse them at the same rate during the three-year training cycle. Upon completion of training, however, a certification procedure was needed so that a B.A.-level worker could be deemed "equivalent" in clinical skills to the M.A.-level worker, thereby securing the same reimbursement rate for both workers. Consequently, the Philadelphia Child Guidance Center's Family Therapy Training Center was asked to develop a certification process. This consisted of a written exam covering the formal curriculum and trainer ratings of videotaped segments of each trainee's work that demonstrate 23 clinical skill competencies. Currently, the Pennsylvania CASSP Training and Technical Assistance Institute, in collaboration with the Family Therapy Training Center and others, is developing new certification procedures that include an exam covering the formal curriculum and consumer satisfaction questionnaires for clients served by particular in-home practitioners. Efforts are being made to incorporate this certification into managed-care credentialing requirements for staff providing public sector mental health.

Training Challenges

This training initiative was ambitious and required agency directors and staff to learn to do things in very different ways. Inevitably there was some initial resistance to, and difficulties in, implementing the original plan. One of the initial areas of resistance was the use of home videotaping. There were several programs that took much longer to accept this method as a viable learning tool. Once staff from other programs began to endorse the taped interviews as extremely useful, however, their resistance gradually dissipated. A second area of difficulty has been the complex logistics involved in transporting the training staff all over the state for the training sessions. Changes in train schedules, flight schedules, and increases in airfares present constant obstacles. Much more planning and travel time is needed than originally anticipated, including making allowances for bad weather and other unforeseen circumstances. Also, funding changes, beginning when Medicaid funding was extended to in-home programs in 1991, have meant that the scheduling of training needs to reflect sensitivity to current job expectations for home-based practitioners. These clinicians now have to demonstrate more accountability in maintaining a specified number of weekly client contacts—irrespective of a shortened work week due to a scheduled training day or national holiday. Careful planning insures that training days are scheduled every two weeks and efforts are made not to schedule a training day during a work week shortened due a national holiday.

Considerations in Seeking Family-Centered Training

States and agencies that recognize the crucial relationship between staff skill development and effective family-centered practice pose common questions regarding what issues should be considered when designing a training initiative. The following questions and responses are based on numerous training contacts implemented with states and agencies.

What philosophical and organizational issues need to be examined by the state or agency before initiating family-centered training? An organization's theoretical orientation(s), procedures, hierarchy, and traditions are generally interwoven with the treatment services being provided. Many mental health services focus on the pathology of the identified patient and offer treatment approaches that address these deficits. One cannot conduct family-centered training within a context that does not support a family-centered treatment philosophy. Family-centered treatment requires a unifying theoretical model that is ecosystemic, goal-oriented, short-term in duration, and emphasizes engaging the resources of families and other social systems—such as the ecosystemic model presented in Chapter 2. This approach includes making use of professional resources with differing theoretical orientations (for example, psychiatrists whose orientation is to the individual and psychologists or social workers whose orientation is to the social context) but within the framework of a unifying theoretical model—which itself must be congruent with the service delivery model. This provides clearer intervention guidelines for therapists. More typically, there is not a unifying theoretical model for service delivery and/or training (as occurs in many state or agency training projects), and trainees receive various learning modules from trainers representing diverse theoretical orientations. Somehow the trainee is expected to integrate these eclectic experiences—a daunting challenge for a new therapist.

Adopting a theoretical model based on ecosystemic structural family theory has direct logistical, financial and practical consequences for both service delivery and training in agencies:

- Intake, medical records, and treatment policies may have to be modified for whole families to be seen. Will there be space? Evening hours?
- To what degree can the agency support the staff in terms of training and providing equipment (e.g., one-way mirrors, adequately-sized observation rooms and audio connections between these rooms, videotaping and playback equipment, camcorders for use in home sessions)?

Who is to be trained? This question is crucial. The authors advocate training "from the top down": that is, building supportive relationships with organization decision-makers and training them to understand the basics of a family-centered systemic orientation, using the same training format their staff will receive. We also recommend providing intensive clinical training to supervisors who are committed to staying with the agency and who will eventually become trainers to other staff. Alternatively, it may be more cost-effective for agencies to hire a trainer to work with a heterogeneous group of supervisors and staff together. When this occurs, it is important to design the training day (as indicated by the Pennsylvania training experience) so that the seniority of supervisors vis-à-vis staff is recognized. For example, a separate break-out activity for supervisors is scheduled either before the training day begins or during lunch time. Also, if the training group is divided into small discussion groups, supervisors are often appointed as discussion leaders. A crucial principle to remember is that *training supplements ongoing supervision* and the supervisor-supervisee relationship must be supported. In determining which staff members to include for training, several factors should be kept in mind:

- Include staff who work closely together programmatically (for instance, M.A. and B.A. members of a team).
- Do not make the training groups too heterogeneous in terms of job function (for example, intake workers and senior-level clinicians).
- Family-centered treatment will be most effective if every level of personnel is trained (administrators through front-line staff).
- Make an effort to incorporate into a family-centered model the resources of the "old guard"—that is, long-time agency staff who feel comfortable in what they already know and may be resistant to learning new methods.

What are the staff's training curriculum needs? The question "What to train whom for what?" should be addressed by first conducting an assessment of the staff's knowledge and family intervention skills. It is advisable to have representative staff members help the administration carry out this assessment in a way that is nonthreatening and nonjudgmental to staff.

How long does training take? Administrators should recognize that skill acquisition is a process that occurs over time. In Pennsylvania our three-year cycle totaling 54 training days has empirically demonstrated growth in clinical competence over this time period. Decision-makers should be aware that random workshop and/or conference attendance does not *necessarily* enhance clinical skills. If time-limited family intervention training is provided, provision should always be made for ongoing post-training consultation to ensure continuing growth.

How can administrators seek training services? In preparing a Request for Proposal (RFP) for family-based training services, it is extremely important for administrators to first articulate their philosophy and values with clearly stated objectives. The philosophy should emphasize the importance of family-centered programs involving four major components: an ecological perspective; a family systems perspective; the importance of developmental stages; and a commitment to preserving families.

Other critical information provided in the RFP should include criteria for evaluating the training proposal. Administrators will want to evaluate the clarity and appropriateness of the proposal's training objectives, teaching methods to be used, methods of assessing training outcome, and the trainer's qualifications. The RFP should also indicate what audiovisual equipment and facilities (e.g., one-way mirror/observation rooms, teaching space) will be available to trainers.

Quality training can be provided by both individuals and organizations who specialize in training and have traveling faculty. In looking for someone who can do quality training, it is important to differentiate between individuals who *provide supervision* and those who have had *experience as trainers*. A qualified trainer is both an effective family therapist and supervisor *and* has been training for at least 10 years. The qualified trainer is someone who has excellent skills for dealing with group process and can readily translate complex knowledge for both paraprofessional and senior professionals alike with humor, respect, clear communication skills, warmth, and charisma. Probably the best way to select a trainer is to have the final candidates conduct a short training session with some of the potential target groups as part of the selection process. If that is not possible, then identify every agency on the candidate's résumé where he/she has provided similar training and contact those agencies for recommendations. Keep in mind that a qualified trainer is a specialist who represents the highest level of clinical and teaching competencies. Excellent trainers cost money. Cheaper training is not better training. True cost-effectiveness is realized when an expert trainer facilitates the development of high-level skills in staff with skills ranging from entry-level positions to more advanced positions.

Probably the most significant measure of training efficacy is the demonstration that families have been helped to achieve desired goals for their troubled children. The next chapter examines the process of evaluating treatment outcomes in home-based services.

CHAPTER 8

Evaluating Treatment Outcomes in Home-Based Services

Our therapists from the home-based program helped our family learn better ways of managing Melanie's behavior. They were always reachable in a crisis, like the time Mel ran away. They also put us in touch with other parents of children like Melanie. That helped us to feel less alone with our problems.

–A follow-up interview with a mother, 1990

When Tim and Karen [home-based clinicians] first came to our house, I thought to myself, *How are they ever going to help us out of this mess?* We had been struggling with Jeff's problems for so long, I figured this would just be one more futile effort to make things better. But it wasn't long before they had found a really good school program for our son which made a big difference in his behavior. That helped our family relax a little and begin to look at how we reacted to Jeff's behavior in unproductive ways.

—A follow-up interview with a father, 1992

Before we started home-based services, I was ready to give up. I had already called Child Protective Services once to tell them I was afraid I was going to hurt David. They're the ones who put me in touch with the home-based program. It was so good just to feel like I was not all alone, that the home-based team was on my side.

—A follow-up interview with a single mother, 1995

THESE REFLECTIONS, and many others like them, were told to us by parents whose families received home-based services in Pennsylvania. Nowadays asking parents and consumers whether mental

264

health services were helpful is an accepted part of service planning. A decade ago, when we were first planning the evaluation of Pennsylvania's new home-based initiative, there was a lot of discussion among researchers and evaluators as to whether the opinions of service recipients were really a worthwhile addition to an outcome evaluation protocol. Fortunately, we have come along way in the years since. It is now recognized that those who have received mental health services are among the best judges of the adequacy of service delivery, and most outcome evaluations *do* elicit participants' point of view (Evans, Armstrong, Thompson, & Lee, 1994). Parents are able to tell us what worked about home-based services and what could be improved. As a result, we are able to make adjustments to our program model to better meet the needs of the families we serve in Pennsylvania—but more about that later.

Evaluating client outcomes in treatment is increasingly a requirement for delivering clinical services in the mental health system (Schalock, 1995). Both public and private funders of services to children with serious emotional disturbances are making accountability by service providers a central concern. Like other forms of children's mental health services, home-based programs must be able to demonstrate that they are effective in meeting program and treatment goals. Funders often specify the types of data home-based programs must provide to satisfy these requirements. However, these are frequently descriptions of clients served and accounts of services provided rather than true indicators of treatment outcomes. Monitoring service delivery, while an important first step in evaluating treatment outcomes, does not indicate whether the model implemented is effective or which clients benefit most from the treatment provided.

A home-based program that is able to move beyond indicators of program implementation to develop methods of measuring treatment outcomes is in a better position to respond to demands to prove effectiveness and to counter threats to funding support (Sederer & Dickey, 1996). In Pennsylvania, the Division of Children's Services in the State Office of Mental Health was successfully able to stave off a legislative effort to cut back funding for its home-based programs in the early 1990s by demonstrating results from its ongoing evaluation of home-based services. These findings indicated that only about 25% of children in families receiving home-based services had experienced a psychiatric inpatient placement in the year following treatment termination, as compared with 80% in the year prior to participating in a home-based program. In those placements that did take place, lengths of stay were shorter and placement was more likely to be deliberately planned rather than occurring as a reaction to a crisis. These data were so persuasive to legislators that funding for Pennsylvania's home-based programs was expanded rather than cut that year.

The proliferation of outcome evaluations in the mental health field testifies to the importance of demonstrating the effectiveness of a particular form of treatment for a particular type of problem or issue with a specified client population. The purpose of outcome evaluation is to demonstrate the relationship between goals and objectives of treatment, the treatment model employed, and results for clients (outcomes). Policy-makers, funding bodies, program planners, administrators, and clinicians must therefore have a clear understanding of program goals, the outcomes sought for families and children, and some consensus as to how those goals are to be attained (the treatment model). It also requires that program directors take initiative in demonstrating the effectiveness of their treatment models by measuring outcomes for the targets of change, be they families, children, or larger service systems.

Evaluating treatment outcomes of home-based programs that employ family systems theory requires an evaluation methodology that is sensitive to the multiple dimensions of change sought in this ecosystemic context (Klein-Walker & Crocker, 1988). At the same time, however, general principles of outcome evaluation also apply. Organizational obstacles to implementing outcome evaluations in home-based services are the first challenge to be overcome.

PREPARING FOR OUTCOME EVALUATION

All agency-based evaluations require a thoroughgoing understanding of organizational behavior (Rossi & Freeman, 1993; Schulberg, 1981). This is particularly true when those in charge of implementing outcome evaluations are "outsiders"—i.e., consultants hired by funding sources or agency administrators to evaluate an agency's program or service. While the outsider role has certain distinct advantages (discussed later in this chapter), it is also fraught with opportunities for running headlong into organizationally-based barriers to successful evaluation of treatment outcomes. And, while the internal evaluator may be more aware of the "land mines" of organizational politics, it is always critical to recognize and take into account those organizational characteristics that preclude or support successful evaluation.

First, the evaluator must consider overall *agency ideology*, as each type has important implications for the evaluation endeavor. Organizational theorists (Brager & Holloway, 1978; Hazenfeld, 1992; Scott, 1983) have categorized primary agency ideological orientations as (a) campaign based, (b) client centered, (c) process focused, and (d) venerational. *Campaign ideology* expresses an agency's deep commitment to a particular social mission. Such organizations usually take an adversarial stance with regard to the status quo. Because these organizations are committed to social change, they are usually open to the use of outcome evaluation to further support their battles against conservatism and conformity. However, such organizations are also likely to reject any evaluation findings that do not support their cause. Programs that espouse a new or radically different treatment technology often represent a form of campaign ideology. Staff enthusiasm for the new technology and commitment to changing how treatment for a particular problem or issue is carried out can easily co-opt the evaluation. In such organizations the evaluator can present outcome evaluation as a process of fine-tuning the treatment technology.

Agencies or organizations characterized by a *client-centered ideology* emphasize the rights and interests of the recipients of services. Such agencies are often open to exploring ways to optimize service effectiveness through outcome evaluations. They are receptive to evaluation research and likely to implement study findings. Conversely, *because* of their emphasis on service delivery, they are often loathe to spend precious funds on evaluation that could otherwise be used to provide additional services to their clientele. Presenting outcome evaluation as serving the best interests of clients is an important strategy with such an organization.

Organizations with *process-focused* or *venerational ideologies* are less open to conducting outcome evaluations and implementing the findings. Adherence to a process ideology suggests that the agency commitment is to the technology, to "the way we do things here." Venerational ideology, as the name suggests, emphasizes "the way we have always done things." Both of these ideologies tend to be found in older, more established organizations that have long filled a particular niche in the service system and may feel no particular pressure to change. Both organizational types are often resistant to implementing any kind of outcome evaluation of their programs or services. It is usually only when outside forces, such as funding sources or managed care companies, pressure them for service accountability that they reluctantly open their doors to the perusal of the evaluator. Even when that occurs, such organizations are likely to present significant barriers to the unwary evaluator. These organizations have a collective self-image to protect and can find myriad ways to sabotage any evaluation efforts that might call their ideology into question. Presenting outcome evaluation as central to their survival—as it often is in today's highly competitive and fiscally-driven environment—is necessary in such organizations.

Understanding the overarching ideological orientation of the host organization is but a first step in evaluating home-based services. Once the ideology is understood, however, the researcher is in a better position to comprehend and manage organizationally-based resistances to implementing an evaluation protocol.

Structural characteristics (Scott, 1983) of organizations can also have significant impact on the evaluation process. Highly complex organizations containing a wide variety of occupational specialties are usually more open to conducting and implementing evaluation of treatment outcomes, particularly if these specialties require a high degree of professional training (Hage & Aiken, 1970). For example, hospital-based psychiatric outpatient clinics, which are characterized by the interaction of a number of highly competitive professional groups, generally foster an environment conducive to evaluation. Members of such organizations identify with, and draw status from, their professional identities rather than their organizational roles. They bring new information into the organizational environment from their outside professional contacts and are more willing to question accepted treatment methods and to explore innovative alternatives.

Complex organizations such as public child welfare agencies, in contrast, are frequently staffed with individuals who have similar levels and types of education and training and can be difficult environments in which to conduct evaluation of treatment outcomes. Staff members' primary identification is with the agency, not with a professional organization that exposes them to new ideas and technologies. And there is no profession-based competition within the agency to enhance a climate of knowledge-building.

The *centralization* that characterizes bureaucracies such as public child welfare agencies is also a barrier to evaluation implementation. Bureaucratic structures are inherently resistant to change and staff members tend to view program evaluation as a thinly-disguised attempt to ferret out procedural misconduct (Scott, 1983). Such organizations are also highly formalized; work roles and relationships are tightly structured and governed by written rules and regulations. A high degree of formalization inhibits individual initiative and encourages conformity—characteristics that discourage the implementation of changes introduced by evaluation of treatment outcomes.

MAKING THE EVALUATION HAPPEN

Overcoming Barriers to Evaluation

Despite these potential organizational obstacles, it is possible to conduct evaluation in almost any kind of organizational setting by first observing a few simple rules. First, *it is essential to identify and utilize the organizational self-interests of key critical and supporting actors within the agency.* Understanding the behavior of organizational members from a power-politics perspective (Gummer, 1978) is helpful in this process. The power-politics perspective contends that each member of an organization seeks to enhance his/her position by controlling as many resources as possible. The higher the position in an organization, the more control the individual exerts over necessary resources, such as money, personnel, clients, and community sanction. However, according to this theory, even those at the top of an organization continually seek to enhance their positions by accruing additional resources.

The evaluator has potential resources to offer organizational members at all levels. Evaluation findings that demonstrate effective client service can be used by agency heads to garner more funding and additional community support. Such findings can also be used by program managers to barter for additional resources for their programs within the organization itself. Clinicians can utilize findings of treatment effectiveness to support claims of clinical skill and enhance opportunities for advancement within the organizational structure. When evaluation outcomes are negative, demonstrating little or no association between the treatment and achievement of outcome goals, findings can be used to advocate for additional staff training or additional program resources identified as necessary to enhance service provision. Negative findings can also be used to negotiate new referral criteria in order to focus services more directly on those who appear to benefit.

When researchers are mindful of the importance of engaging organizational actors at all levels—from administrators to program managers to clinicians—in planning the evaluation design, the potential for garnering additional resources is an unacknowledged but powerful incentive for member participation. This point speaks to the need for evaluators to *recognize their power and potential as organizational change agents.* The introduction of an outside evaluator, or even an insider-initiated evaluation effort, has the potential for interfering with the status quo, or, in the language of systems theorists, upsetting the organization's homeostasis. No matter how resistant the organization is to incorporating evaluation findings into its treatment model, introducing the idea of conducting agency-based evaluation itself initiates change. Program staff members who have begun to critically examine their treatment goals are different staff members from who they were prior to beginning this process. Even if the evaluation is never implemented, staff members have started to explore their practice. Once started, this process cannot be reversed and must eventually lead to an outcome, perhaps to completion of the evaluation task at some later time, or to a staff crisis that releases the tension generated by the aborted self-examination.

In considering the self-interests of key actors at different organizational levels, Caputo (1985) points out the compounding factor of the inherent conflicts between the roles and functions of clinicians, administrators, and researchers with regard to agency-based research. If evaluation of treatment outcomes is considered a form of research, the same dilemmas may be said to apply. Researchers, according to Caputo, are primarily interested in knowledge-building—in understanding the relationships between specific events. *Evaluators* are interested in identifying the relationships among treatment goals and objectives, services delivered, and client outcomes. *Clinicians* are interested in learning what types of interventions work best with which kinds of clients—the specifics of practice—and not in developing knowledge for its own sake. *Administrators* are concerned with implementing the agency's mandate for service delivery; they must bring together the human and material resources required to carry out the organization's purpose and function.

We suggest, however, that these differing perspectives are not inherently conflictive. While academic researchers may have traditionally focused on knowledge-building as a separate and rarified activity, evaluators are mandated to address issues of effectiveness that preclude the kind of esoteric "head in the clouds" research that has characterized such endeavors in the past. Contemporary evaluators acknowledge the importance of taking time to understand agency based-practice (Bickman, 1987; Oetting, 1982). In the past many outsiders studying clinical practice have been ignorant of its intricacies, particularly on the applied level. As a result, their evaluation methods were often inappropriate and failed to capture the nuances of direct service delivery (Schulberg, 1981). Today it is unthinkable that a program evaluator who is not also a clinician would neglect to spend at least as much time becoming informed about the service technology as in setting up a research protocol or collecting data (Family Resource Coalition, 1993; Pecora, Fraser, Nelson, McCroskey, & Meezan, 1995).

Involving Agency Staff

The key to successful agency-based treatment-outcome evaluation can be found in taking the time and effort to involve staff at all levels. As one authority on program evaluation states, "Instead of being an expert who does evaluation, the evaluator should be a consultant to program staff who are doing evaluation to meet their own needs" (Oetting, 1982, p. 64). The time taken in meeting and talking with agency staff members about the services they provide and their research questions concerning those services is time well spent. By involving those staff members most directly affected by the evaluation effort and forming collaborative relationships based on mutual trust and commonality of purpose—*and* listening to their anxieties about exploring their own practices—the evaluator can go a long way toward preventing the sabotaging that sometimes occurs in evaluation projects.

Most agency clinicians are willing teachers, *if* evaluators are open to learning. Attending clinical case conferences, viewing videotapes of treatment sessions, accompanying home-based therapists on their visits, attending staff training sessions, asking for relevant reading materials (and actually reading them!), and reading process recordings in case records are all ways the evaluator can become familiar with agency services and the treatment technology employed. These activities also demonstrate to staff members a respect for their professional expertise, an important ingredient in enlisting their cooperation in planning and implementing an evaluation of treatment outcomes (McCroskey & Nelson, 1989).

It is our experience that home-based clinicians as well as program managers nearly always have their own questions about how the service works. Helping staff members identify and formulate these as research questions, then relating them to the outcome evaluation, generates enthusiasm and commitment to the endeavor.

If some or all of an agency's staff are going to be involved in collecting data for an evaluation project, their investment is even more essential. Their advice and input in operationally defining process and outcome variables and developing the data collection protocol are essential to ensuring cooperation in data collection and obtaining insights into what procedures can reasonably be implemented, given particular programmatic constraints (National Center for Clinical Infant Programs, 1987). For example, if clients are in crisis during the first interview, it is probably unreasonable (if not unethical) to expect them to take time to complete self-assessment questionnaires. Or, if few clients have telephones, telephone follow-up contacts after service has been terminated are impractical and in-person follow-up interviews are necessary.

If staff members are involved in collecting data for the evaluation, they must be able to do this without significant additional burdens of time and/or paperwork. Most individuals who do "hands on" clinical work do so because they derive satisfaction from interacting with people, not paperwork. Most agencies, because of current funding requirements, already require clinicians to take on onerous amounts of record keeping. Adding to this burden will only generate hostility, not cooperation and collaboration.

It is usually not possible to collect treatment outcome data without some additional paperwork, however. Staff members' resistance to this demand on their time can be decreased by (a) giving them rewards for collecting the required data, (b) incorporating as much of the data collection as possible into routine record keeping, and (c) giving practitioners periodic summaries of research findings.

Rewarding Clinicians for Data Collection

Despite past studies purporting to show that clinicians are not interested in evaluating their practice and do not implement findings from treatment outcome studies (Gingerich, 1984; Mutschler, 1984; Saleeby, 1979), our experience has been otherwise. When practitioners feel that an evaluation is specifically designed to reflect *their needs as clinicians* and has direct relevance to *their practice with clients*, they are highly invested in the evaluation process (Campbell, 1987; McCroskey & Nelson, 1989). One way of enhancing this investment is to give practitioners immediate feedback in the form of information they can use in their clinical work with clients. For example, many instruments, such as the Family Assessment Device (Epstein, Baldwin, & Bishop, 1983) and the Beck Depression Inventory (Beck, Ward, Mendelson, Mock, & Erbaugh 1961), used as measures of change in evaluating treatment outcomes, also provide significant clinical information that can be used in the treatment process itself.

The Family Assessment Device (Epstein et al., 1983), a self-report instrument designed to be completed by all family members over age 11, gives clinicians information on how family members view themselves and each other on a variety of clinically important dimensions, including communication, problem-solving, affective relations, role allocation, and behavior control. It also tells clinicians how individual family members view their family as a unit on these dimensions. Anomalous responses by one or another family member provide important clues to family dynamics. In our study of home-based services in Pennsylvania using the Family Assessment Device, we found that mothers frequently rated their families as problematic in the area of role allocation, while fathers saw problems in the affective realm. From this finding we identified a common family pattern: an over-extended, overburdened mother/wife with a distant, non-participating father/husband who feels excluded from the emotional life of the family. Such a picture derived from an evaluation can supplement and support the clinician's own assessment and give direction to the treatment process.

There are other well-established standardized, self-report instruments designed to measure family functioning, which can give practitioners immediate feedback on specific areas of family distress or dysfunction (Sawin & Harrigan, 1995). The Family Environment Scale (Moos, 1974) and the Family Adaptability and Cohesion Scale, third version (FACES III) (Olson, Portner, & Lavee, 1985) are two such instruments. The Family Environment Scale is a 90-item self-report true/false questionnaire measuring three domains of family functioning: social relationships among family members, the climate for personal growth, and family system maintenance. Within these three domains are 10 subscales measuring such aspects of family life as cohesion, expressiveness, conflict, achievement orientation, independence, moral-religious emphasis, organization, and control. Individual and family scores can be computed, as well as a family incongruence score, which indicates the extent of disagreement among family members in their perceptions of the family's functioning in these areas. The 27 items in the social relationship domain, consisting of the cohesion, expressiveness, and conflict subscales, can also be used as a measure of supportiveness in the family system.

The Family Environment Scale has been widely used in outcome studies, with the conflict and cohesion subscales most frequently predictive of various outcomes (Sawin & Harrigan, 1995). Higher cohesion and lower conflict are associated with more positive outcomes in these studies.

The Family Adaptability and Cohesion Scale (FACES III) measures two primary dimensions of family functioning: adaptability and cohesion (Olson et al., 1985). As conceptualized in this instrument, *adaptability* refers to the ability of family members to alter their relational structure in response to internal (developmental) and external (situational) demands. *Cohesion* describes the emotional bonding in a family. Four levels of each dimension are described by the FACES III instrument, two extreme and two mid-range levels. The most functional family interaction is labeled "balanced" and falls into the mid-range of adaptability and cohesion. FACES III has been used in a wide variety of family treatment outcome studies, including studies of juvenile offenders and their families (Henggeler, Burr-Harris, Bordiun, & McCallum, 1991), adolescent drug abusers and their families (Friedman, Tomko, & Utada, 1991), and marital violence (Lehr & Fitzsimmons, 1991).

Teaching clinicians to administer and score instruments like these at intake and termination not only provides information on family dynamics and outcome data for the evaluation but also gives clinicians immediate feedback on their families' levels of functioning as well as progress in treatment along specific dimensions. Our experience is that clinicians become very engaged in discussing findings on these measures with one another, and through these discussions are able to provide us with new perspectives on family dynamics that, in turn, enhance our data analysis.

Incorporating Data Collection into Record Keeping

Computerized management information systems (MIS) provide an important opportunity for incorporating evaluation data collection into routine agency record-keeping procedures. Particularly since the introduction of managed care, agencies providing mental health services are increasingly required to collect service data on a regular basis and to provide managed care oversight companies with monthly reports on service provision. Ability to demonstrate faithful implementation of a well-specified treatment model is the cornerstone of outcome evaluation. Using service data that capture the clinician's case-related activity in time-limited segments (such as 15-minute increments) and identifying the objective of that activity is one way of demonstrating implementation of the model as specified.

For example, one of the specifications for home-based services is that the family contacts take place in the family's home or in community settings, rather than clinicians' offices or clinics. MIS service data often specify where family contacts took place and the nature of the contact (whether it was in person or by telephone), which family members participated, and whether collateral individuals, such as teachers, were involved. These data, already part of the routine reporting system, can be used in an evaluation to assess fidelity of the implemented program to the intended treatment model. A finding that the majority of contacts in a home-based program were taking place in clinicians' offices and involved contact only with the index child would suggest that the treatment model is not being implemented as intended, rendering the findings regarding treatment outcomes in a home-based model spurious.

Another specification of the home-based model is that treatment involves not only therapeutic intervention with the family as a whole, but also development of a stable, supportive network for the family that will endure once treatment is terminated. The number and nature of collateral contacts made by the home-based clinician, as noted in MIS data, provide one easy way of assessing level of activity around network development. Using MIS data—a method that is already imbedded in ongoing agency record keeping—is a nonintrusive way of gathering evaluation data that limits demands on agency staff.

Providing Periodic Summaries of Findings

A third method for effectively involving practitioners in the process of data collection is to present them with periodic summaries of evaluation findings. If the planned intervention is working well, these summaries lend support and recognition to clinical staff who are often overworked and underpaid. If there are problems in implementation of either the evaluation protocol or the treatment itself, periodic summaries are an effective way of identifying necessary mid-course corrections before the planned period of evaluation is completed. These periodic summaries, if delivered to staff in person by the evaluator, also provide an opportunity to reinforce personal connectedness and allow staff members to ventilate their (expected) annoyance at aspects of the data collection effort. No matter how committed practitioners are to the evaluation, it is still an extra demand on their time and energy to participate. They need the opportunity to complain occasionally, to have direct input in the interpretation of the findings, and to receive recognition for their collaboration.

Engaging Staff Collaboration

A final way of ensuring commitment to the data-gathering process (albeit one that does not happen frequently) occurs when a staff member (usually a supervisor) becomes so engaged in the evaluation endeavor that he or she seeks to become a more direct collaborator with the evaluator. In our experience, this has always been a productive partnership. One home-based program director, for example, was curious about how families' perceptions of their functioning differed from those of the clinicians who treated them. She was willing to add a clinician observation instrument that corresponds to the Family Assessment Device to the evaluation protocol. The clinicians in her program were inspired by her interest in their perspective on families, and they, in turn, became more engaged in the evaluation effort.

Another program director wanted to use two different self-report measures of family functioning in her program and compare the findings on each to see which was more predictive of treatment outcomes. As long as such "add-ons" do not compromise the evaluation design, the enthusiasm and cooperation they engender far outweigh any extra effort for the evaluator.

Involving Other Constituencies

In addition to agency administrators, program directors, and clinical staff, many evaluators advocate involving service recipients in the planning of outcome evaluations. Currently there are federal and state policy mandates to include representatives of target populations in program planning in the mental health arena (Friesen & Koroloff, 1990). When program planning also includes mechanisms for demonstrating program effectiveness, as it ideally should, the opportunity for consumer input is naturally present. Increasingly, under the influence of the NIMH CASSP initiative, parents of children with serious emotional disturbances have become key participants in all levels of planning, implementing, and evaluating services. The input of parents, and even older adolescents who have experienced serious emotional disorders, in regard to setting program goals and objectives, as well as designing services required to meet those goals, can be invaluable.

Advocates of consumer participation in outcome evaluation research include consumers' input in the data collection process and, above all, in the interpretation of findings. Parents whose families have received home-based services may be more willing to give honest reports of their treatment experiences in a follow-up interview with another parent than with a clinician or agency administrator. Because of client confidentiality issues, releases for such parent-to-parent contact would have to be obtained at program entry, but this is true with any type of evaluation procedure.

Including consumers such as parents and older teens in discussing and interpreting evaluation findings can help evaluators and program personnel gain a new perspective on these data. Family members who have coped with serious emotional disturbances in a child as well as participated in home-based services may have very different interpretations of outcome data than those who see the program from a service provider's point of view. In our experience in Pennsylvania, parents are important commentators on the service model as well as on elements of treatment. It was through their comments that heightened emphasis was placed on network-building and enhancement of social supports as program goals. Some families felt abandoned when their home-based clinicians terminated services and expressed the need for stronger linkages with alternative community resources.

If home-based services are funded through a state or county mental health system by state legislation, it is also important to include representatives of the funding body in evaluation planning. Input into the kinds of outcomes useful for future funding considerations is invaluable, as is the goodwill generated when funders are directly consulted. Funders are also more likely to take outcome evaluation findings seriously if they have had a hand in determining which outcomes are important to assess.

Assigned or Assumed Roles

One aspect of carrying out outcome evaluation seldom addressed in the research and evaluation literature is the other roles evaluators may find assigned to them in an organization. The introduction of an outsider, such as a therapist, into a well-established family system affects the system's dynamics. The system works to "co-opt" the outsider by assigning a role that is nonthreatening to the established order of business (Combrinck-Graham, 1990). Agencies operate in a similar fashion. It is not unusual for evaluators to suddenly discover that they are being treated as the agency historian, advocate, or given some other innocuous role that removes the implied threat of "evaluator." Needless to say, it is important for evaluators to maintain their autonomy as outsiders within the organizational system. The evaluator's tightly scheduled and highly structured role in the agency helps to maintain the necessary boundaries. However, if evaluators find themselves visiting the agency more often than originally planned, or staying longer than the time required by evaluation tasks, they should begin thinking about the boundaries of the current relationship.

One role that the outside evaluator may easily slip into is that of confidante. Particularly in the beginning phase of the evaluation process when the task is one of engaging staff in the endeavor, evaluators often find themselves the sounding board for all of the staff's complaints about administration or, more often, other community organizations with which they must collaborate in delivering home-based services. This is often displaced anxiety about the forthcoming evaluation project and should be treated as such by the evaluator.

At other times, however, there is a component to the voiced concerns that may have a negative impact on the evaluation itself and should be listened to carefully. In one agency, for example, evaluation planning meetings with clinical staff around identifying specific outcome goals revealed enormous disjuncture between staff's perceptions of the program's goals and those of the primary referring/funding source, a large public child welfare agency that contracted for home-based services. Clinicians saw their primary treatment goal as facilitating family stabilization and/or reunification, while the contracting agency often had the hidden agenda of demonstrating a family's inability to care for a child and the need for out-of-home placement. Because of communication difficulties between direct service staff in the two agencies and the lack of clarity in the intra-agency contract, clinicians felt that their work with families was frequently sabotaged by the referring agency.

This factor clearly had direct implications for an evaluation of treatment outcomes.

Managing Administrators' Ambivalence

In working with agency administrators, especially program directors, evaluators must recognize the ambivalence they are likely to face regarding outcome evaluation. Positive findings of treatment effectiveness will lend support to the agency's position in intra-agency contracting and add substance to claims on material resources; however, there is always the threat that evaluation findings will prove that the program and its services are ineffective after all.

Administrators' ambivalence can be managed in several ways by evaluators. First, the evaluation endeavor can be framed as an effort to discover how a program or service could be made *more effective*, not to prove or disprove program effectiveness. Which clients seem to benefit most? What mix of services leads to the best outcomes? This "frame" changes the perception of the evaluation process from one of good *or* bad programs, effective *or* ineffective services, to one that recognizes that all agency services and their delivery have room for improvement. The desire to improve programs and services suggests leadership that is secure yet risk-taking. After all, what is more all-American than self-improvement?

Second, it is up to evaluators to find ways for the evaluation process to meet administrators' needs, both expressed and unexpressed. As discussed previously, findings pointing to program success can be used to garner more resources both within and outside the agency. Even negative findings can be used in this way, if there is the possibility that additional resources can make a less-than-effective program more successful. In one research project involving a home-based program housed in a traditional mental health agency, the mere fact that evaluation of the program was being carried out and findings shared at agency-wide colloquia served to enhance the prestige of the program within its host organization. Initial resistance by the program director, who was well-aware of the lower status of her program in the organizational environment, was ameliorated when she realized that participating in the evaluation effort could potentially change the misperceptions of other staff members that her program existed primarily to give concrete services to families.

DESIGNING AND IMPLEMENTING
THE EVALUATION PROTOCOL

There are seven key steps involved in designing and implementing outcome evaluation of home-based services:

1. Clarify program goals/objectives.
2. Identify measurable treatment outcomes.
3. Specify treatment methods and techniques.
4. Specify measures of change.
5. Identify sources of data and select measurement tools.
6. Plan for analysis and interpretation of data.
7. Identify opportunities for presentation and dissemination of findings.

Obviously the content of these steps will vary according to program specifics, and each component must be fully "fleshed out" in order to create a meaningful outcome evaluation.

While designing a program evaluation ideally should be part of the program planning process, in actuality the program evaluator frequently comes into the picture after the program has taken shape. Not infrequently, programs developed in response to the identified needs of a particular clinic population are designed with broad, nonspecific, or unrealistic program goals. Perhaps the interventions to be used are not clearly defined, or their relationship to the desired program outcomes is unclear. Often an essential front-end activity of the evaluator is assisting program planners to specify outcome goals that are attainable, measurable, and reflect current intervention theory and research. Aspects of this activity are described more fully below.

In some cases, evaluators come on board after a program is actually up and running. It is much more difficult in these instances to influence program design, although, if it is a pilot period or if there are snags in the program's implementation, administrators and staff are usually open to restructuring program elements to make a sound evaluation feasible. When a program is underway, it is important to review the process of needs assessment, goal identification, and intervention selection with the program's designers, in order to insure conceptual integrity and theoretical coherence, which are the basics of evaluation design. At whatever stage in program implementation the evaluator enters the picture, key words in planning a program evaluation are *clarity* and *specificity*. Their meaning and application are discussed in the following sections.

Clarifying Program Goals/Objectives and Identifying Measurable Outcomes

Clarifying and specifying program goals and identifying valid and measurable outcomes in relation to the theoretical model of treatment employed by the agency or organization is a critical first step in designing an outcome evaluation. Without clearly defined goals it is not possible to conduct a meaningful outcome evaluation. Overall program goals are often set by policy-makers and funding bodies. In Pennsylvania, for example, state regulations issued by the Office of Mental Health defined three goals of home-based services: (a) to reduce the incidence of psychiatric hospitalizations and other mental health placements of children and youth; (b) to enhance families' ability to cope with a child or adolescent with serious emotional disturbance; and (c) to enhance the psychosocial functioning of all family members, including the child with serious emotional disturbance.

In considering goals like these, which are established by a funding agency, the first questions to be considered are: What is meant by the phrase, "enhancing families' ability to cope"? What observable and measurable action does it take to make that happen? While some outcome goals, such as "reducing the incidence of psychiatric placements," are easily measured, others must be broken down into operational parts or indicators. A measurable indicator of family coping, for example, might be reduction in the level of stress experienced in parenting an emotionally disturbed child, or it might be indicated by a change in overall family functioning, or by changes in behavior management strategies. This is where an ability to make connections among goals, treatment theory, and intervention strategies becomes critical. If the home-based program is based on family systems theory and the treatment is focused on changing family interaction patterns, like those we studied in Pennsylvania, then measuring changes in family functioning on a variety of dimensions would give an appropriate indication of enhanced family coping. However, if the home-based program draws on social learning theory and is directed toward teaching parents new child management methods rather than changing family interaction patterns, then measurement of changes in parenting skills would indicate enhanced family coping.

Similarly, in an outcome goal as broad and unspecified as "enhancing the psychosocial functioning of individual family members," it is crucial to identify which areas of functioning are important to the program's specific mission. For example, in the Pennsylvania evaluation, we believed that, based on prior research, the functioning of the identified patient would be a key variable in influencing treatment outcomes. Our hypothesis was that *the more impaired the psychosocial functioning of the identified patient at treatment intake, the more likely were post-treatment placement and/or continued family problems in coping.* We selected a measure of child functioning that was easily implemented and could provide a single-scaled score that allowed for intergroup comparisons as well as assessment of change over time. The Children's Global Assessment Scale (Bird, Canino, Rubio Stepec, & Ribers, 1987) corresponds to Axis V of the *DSM-IV* and is a required component in the psychiatric evaluation of children in Pennsylvania.

We also hypothesized that *families in which the parents had their own psychosocial difficulties, independent of those of the identified patient, would be more likely to experience ongoing difficulties post-treatment, including child psychiatric placement.* However, because the program was located in the child mental health system, the psychosocial functioning of parents was not open to our investigation. Instead, we used a "surrogate" indicator of parental functioning: parents' own involvement in the service system prior to engaging in home-based services. Thirty percent of mothers and about a quarter of fathers in Pennsylvania's home-based families had previous mental health or substance-abuse treatment histories. As we hypothesized, this turned out to be an important indicator of post-treatment problems in all areas of family life, not just in relation to child placement.

Specify Treatment Methods and Techniques

Once program goals have been translated into measurable outcomes, the next question is, "What will it take to make these changes happen?" In other words, "How are we going to get *there* from *here*?" The instrumental goals that guide home-based practice, and the facilitating goals that implement them, must now be developed (see Table 8.1). It is at this point that treatment theory becomes relevant (Chen, 1990; Powell, 1987). Because our model is based on family systems theory, in particular ecosystemic/ structural theory, it follows that strategies used to evoke the changes sought will be based on ecosystemic/structural principles.

A thorough review of research related directly to program goals is important at this point in evaluation planning (Rossi, 1992) in order to discover what other researchers have reported about achieving similar goals. For example, if one outcome goal is to prevent or reduce psychiatric hospitalizations, what factors have previous studies identified that precipitate child placement? Are these factors that could be changed through home-based treatment? If so, exactly how would that be done?

In our literature review we found that child psychiatric placements often result from mental health crises that bring children and parents to hospital emergency rooms. Because parents frequently do not have the know-how to diffuse these crises on their own, they search for help from medical personnel, who may be no more trained in crisis intervention than they. Unless there is a mental health professional on call in the emergency room, what often happens is a "band-aid" emergency admission to an inpatient psychiatry unit. Once the admission takes place, the child is often held briefly for observation and assessment, and then transferred to a longer-term facility. Some studies suggest it may be easier to enter a mental health facility than to exit one!

Research indicates that intervening at the point of crisis, before the child enters a mental health facility through the hospital emergency room, can prevent inpatient placements in a number of instances. As noted in Table 8.1, the instrumental goal relating to the outcome goal of placement prevention is stabilizing the family in times of crisis. Our strategies for doing so became the facilitating goals. These include setting up a 24-hour emergency response system for families receiving home-based services so that they can access a clinician immediately in a mental health crisis. Another strategy is to establish a system of respite care so that families and children could have time away from one another and therefore relieve some of the family tensions that frequently build under the stress of caring for a child with a serious emotional disturbance.

In order to meet our outcome goal of enhancing the family's ability to cope with their child, we drew on the research literature that addressed stress and coping patterns in families with children with special needs. While the literature on coping with a seriously disturbed child is limited, there are a large number of studies of families coping with children with other special needs, including developmental or physical disabilities and severe and chronic illnesses. This literature identifies a variety of well-documented strategies for effective family coping (Burr & Klein, 1994; Figley & McCubbin, 1983; Pearlin & Schooler, 1978). We drew on this literature to establish three instrumental goals related to the desired outcome: (a) increase the overall level of family functioning, (b) increase acceptance and support of the child with serious emotional disturbance, and (c) decrease environmental stress on the family.

Each of these instrumental goals is then operationalized into one or more facilitating goals specifying the activities designed to actualize it. Based on the research literature, to increase the overall level of family functioning, participation in family therapy and enhancement of family communication were selected as facilitating goals. Studies have found that open, direct, and supportive communication among family members is one of the strongest predictors of effective coping with a child with special needs (Figley & McCubbin, 1983).

Participation in a parent support group is the facilitating goal chosen to increase acceptance and support of the child with serious emotional disturbance, the second instrumental goal. Studies have found that parents and siblings who are connected with other families of children with similar problems are more accepting and better able to offer support to the child with special needs (Burr & Klein, 1994).

Environmental stress, which relates to our third instrumental goal, is a frequently-cited factor in the overwhelming stress often experienced by families of children with special needs. One facilitat-

Table 8.1

EVALUATION MODEL: HOME-BASED SERVICES FOR EMOTIONALLY
DISTURBED CHILDREN AND THEIR FAMILIES

Outcome Goals	Instrumental Goals	Facilitating Goals	Outcome Measures	Instrument/Method
Reduce incidence of out-of-home care for identified patient in participating families.	Stabilize family in times of crisis.	Establish 24-hour emergency response team.	Number, percent, and length of planned and unplanned out-of-home placements before and after program.	Intake and closing data, plus telephone follow-up administered 3, 6, and 12 months after termination.
Enhance family's ability to cope with emotionally disturbed child.	Increase family level of functioning	Assist family in meeting basic needs.	Family functioning before/after program.	Administer McMaster Family Assessment Device at intake and closing.
	Increase acceptance and support of child.	Participate in family therapy.		

Decrease environmental stress on family.	Participate in parent support network.	Parent assessment of progress on contracted treatment goals at 3, 6, and 12 months after termination.
Enhance coping and problem-solving skills of individual family members, including child.	Assist family in developing supportive service network.	Child's level of functioning before/after program participation.
Facilitate positive child behavior.	Teach family members new coping strategies and problem-solving techniques.	Children's Global Assessment Scale completed at intake and termination.
	Facilitate linkages with education system.	
	Help parents obtain more appropriate school placements for their children.	

ing goal identified to address this stress is to assist families in meeting basic needs. Because the target population for Pennsylvania's home-based programs is Medicaid-eligible families, there is often a wide variety of basic needs requiring attention. Clinicians not infrequently find themselves helping families apply for, and acquire, stable housing, food stamps, Social Security Disability benefits, and other forms of assistance before other, "softer" issues, such as family communication patterns or role allocation, can be addressed.

Acknowledging that many families of children with serious emotional disturbances require ongoing help and support in meeting basic needs, another facilitating goal is to develop a supportive network of community services and resources that would be available to families long after home-based services ended. Again, the research on families coping with children with special needs has found supportive networks to be a crucial factor in successful family functioning (Boss, 1988).

Teaching family members new coping strategies and problem-solving techniques, facilitating more positive linkages with school personnel, and helping parents advocate for appropriate school placements are the three facilitating goals designed to achieve the instrumental goal of enhancing positive behavior in the emotionally disturbed child. These goals are based on a systems theory perspective that enhancing the functioning of one member of the system (in this case, the child) will generate more positive responses from parents, sibs, and others in the environment—which, in turn, will reinforce and solidify the child's gains.

Specifying instrumental and facilitating goals in this way helps to focus the process of treatment and connect the program's philosophy to the outcome goals specified. The next step in the development of an outcome evaluation protocol is to identify (1) how the changes specified by the outcome goals will be measured, (2) sources of change data, and (3) the instruments or methods to be used to assess and measure outcomes.

Specifying Measures of Change

The guiding question here is "How will we know if the specified change has taken place?" Identifying specific outcome goals is crucial to any evaluation protocol attempting to answer this question. For instance, a reduction in psychiatric placements for identified patients can be demonstrated by simply counting the number of placements taking place within a certain period of time after treatment ends, or by tabulating the actual number of days spent in placement during that time. The resulting data may then be compared with some benchmark, such as: (1) the number of placements this same cohort of children experienced in an equivalent time period prior to home-based treatment; (2) the number of placements experienced by a control group of similarly-diagnosed children not treated in home-based programs (perhaps children in an outpatient therapy sample, who tend to have less complex treatment histories, less severe diagnoses, and more positive functioning overall [Dore, Wilkinson, & Sonis, 1992]); or (3) the average recidivism rate for children in the community who have previously experienced a psychiatric hospitalization (the best predictor of future inpatient treatment).

Methods suggested here for evaluating outcomes are predicated on the assumption that the evaluator is not using a controlled experimental design. That is, there is no random assignment of applicant families to home based services, with some families receiving no treatment or an alternative form of treatment that differs significantly from the home-based model. If such a design were possible, given agency resources and commitment, it clearly would be preferable and would result in a more scientifically rigorous evaluation of treatment effectiveness. However, such studies are complicated to manage and require significant commitment of time and resources to ensure that random assignment actually takes place and that the control condition is maintained. There are also frequent ethical concerns raised by program staff which, if not addressed adequately, can serve to undermine actual application of an experimental design.

Because this chapter is intended as a basic guide to treatment outcome evaluation and not as a handbook for evaluation research, it is assumed that random assignment and maintenance of a controlled condition are not economically feasible in most home-based programs. The alternative methods for structuring and carrying out outcome evaluation presented here are subject to both internal and external sources of invalidation (alternative explanations for outcomes other than treatment effectiveness) and will thus present more qualified findings. Without a randomly assigned control group, it can always be argued that any improvement in a child's functioning can be attributed to a naturally occurring process of maturation rather than to the effects of home-based treatment, or that increases in family functioning may have been caused by other significant events in a family's life, such as a parent obtaining a job after a period of unemployment or the departure of a mother's violent partner from the home. Findings from nonexperimental designs are said to demonstrate *associations* between variables rather than cause-and-effect relations. Methods of enhancing the reliability and validity of findings from nonexperimental designs, such as pre-/post-comparisons, are discussed in this chapter. In most cases they are of sufficient rigor to inform interested constituencies about outcomes for families receiving home-based services and to indicate factors associated with successful achievement of program goals.

Data Sources and Measurement Tools

Most authorities on outcome evaluation protocols recommend triangulation of data sources, just as in any research endeavor. This means using multiple sources for data on a given factor or variable. For example, if "child psychosocial functioning" is a variable in an outcome study, data on this variable would be gathered from several different reporters, or different indicators of psychosocial functioning would be used. A parent report instrument, such as the Child Behavior Checklist (Achenbach, 1991a), could be employed, along with the Teacher Report Form of the same instrument. There is also a youth self-report version for youth ages 11 to 17 (Achenbach, 1991b). Or, alternatively, a clinician observation rating of psychosocial functioning (such as we used in the Pennsylvania study), the Children's Global Assessment Scale (Bird et al., 1987), might be coupled with a parent rating, such as the Child Behavior Checklist, and a teacher rating, such as the Connors Teacher Rating Scale (Connors, 1969) for classroom behavior.

There are basically four different data sources used in outcome evaluation protocols: *clients* (parents, other family members, identified patient), *clinicians, independent observers,* and *archival data,* such as case records, court records, school report cards, or attendance records. Which source is the most reliable for a particular type of information, and how data should be obtained from that source, are key decisions in developing an outcome evaluation protocol. Each source type has its own built-in threats to reliability and validity. For instance, clients may misrepresent their feelings, views, or beliefs on self-report instruments for a variety of reasons. Clinicians' observations may be biased by their need to appear competent or by unacknowledged negative beliefs about families of children with serious emotional disorders. Independent observers, especially if they are well trained in applying the measures used, are thought to be the most reliable reporters; however, it is costly to hire and train independent observers.

Triangulation helps ensure reliability, as does simply *understanding* the threats to reliability posed by various data sources. For example, several studies have found that clinically depressed mothers tend to rate their children's behavior as significantly more problematic than teachers and independent observers rate them (Sachs & Hall, 1991; Schaughency & Lahey, 1985; Webster-Stratton & Hammond, 1988). If a high proportion of mothers in a home-based program exhibit clinical levels of depression, it might skew parental ratings of child psychosocial functioning.

The evaluator must select among various *data collection methods* as well. These include semi-structured interviews, surveys and questionnaires, standardized instruments, observational measures, and others. *Standardized instruments* are preferable because their psychometric characteristics have been rigorously tested, and this information is readily available. A review of the literature in a specific research area will soon identify which instruments are preferred. For example, a review of studies of family-focused interventions using a family systems approach reveals that most studies use one of the three standardized *self-report instruments* identified earlier in this chapter: the Family Assessment Device, the Family Environment Scale, or the Family Adaptability and Cohesion Scale. Similarly, there are a handful of instruments used to rate child behavior, the Child Behavior Checklist being the most prominent of these.

In recent years a number of books have been published that

summarize the most widely used assessment instruments and provide information on how to obtain them. *The Handbook of Family Measurement Techniques* (Touliatos, Perlmutter, & Straus, 1990), *Family Assessment* (Grotevant & Carlson, 1989), and *Measures for Clinical Practice, Vols. I & II* (Corcoran & Fischer, 1994) are examples of these summaries. Most standardized instruments are copyrighted and require permission from the author or his/her representative to use them. There is often a fee to purchase the printed instruments. Fees range from $25 upwards, depending on the amount of supporting material required to use the instruments as well as the purpose for which they will be used. Some authors also charge for handbooks and scoring devices necessary to accurately use their instruments. Many authors are extremely generous about sharing information about findings as well as references to other studies that have used the instrument.

In contacting authors of standardized instruments or their representatives, always ask for *normative data* on the instrument as well as whether it has been tested on *nontraditional populations*. Normative data provides the distribution of scores of subjects to whom the instrument has been applied. These data enable comparisons between the scores of families and/or children in an outcome evaluation and the scores of what is usually a large number of others. To adequately interpret these comparisons, however, it is necessary to have information about the subjects upon whom the norms were established: How representative are they of the population of the United States—or, more to the point, of the population being served in the home-based program being evaluated? If the population on which an instrument has been tested was drawn exclusively from middle-class Caucasian families, its application to poor people, Latinos, or African-Americans is questionable. It is simply not known how reliably such an instrument can garner the desired information in other populations. Cultural relevance of standardized assessment instruments is an important consideration. Unfortunately, there is not a great deal of work being done in this area. It *is* possible, however, to determine whether an instrument has been successfully used in studies of non-Caucasian and socioeconomically diverse populations. Fortunately, the most widely used standardized instruments have usually been tested on a variety of racial, ethnic, and socioeconomic groups.

If the program being evaluated serves Spanish-speaking families, it is important to find out if the instruments under consideration have been translated into Spanish. There is usually no additional charge to obtain a Spanish version of an instrument, if one exists. In the Pennsylvania home-based study, we used the Spanish version of the Family Assessment Device quite successfully with several families in which the parents spoke little English. Other language translations, while not as common, are sometimes available as well.

The Follow-Up Interview as Data Source

An essential component of any evaluation of treatment outcome is the follow-up interview. Since most evaluations will not include random assignment of treatment and control conditions, and therefore cannot control for other explanations for changes that take place during the treatment period, the follow-up interview allows for crucial comparisons between pre- and post-treatment events, such as psychiatric hospitalizations or emergency room treatment for mental health crises. Follow-up surveys or interviews lend themselves best to assessment of *functional outcomes*—which, as the name suggests, are those outcomes that indicate how the identified patient and/or family is functioning in day-to-day living. Children with serious emotional disorders have often experienced a great deal of instability in their school lives, suggesting that school-related indicators are obviously important. Asking a parent or other caregiver at follow-up about the nature of the child's current school placement, whether the child is functioning well in that setting, whether the parent/caregiver is satisfied with the placement and, if not, what kind of placement he/she believes would benefit the child, provides valuable information on school-related functioning. More specific questions on grades achieved, number of absences, or times expelled are obvious, additional indicators of school functioning.

Another functional area that might be addressed in a follow-up interview is post-treatment involvement with other child-serving systems, such as child protective services or juvenile court. In our study, the identified patient or other family member in about 28% of families was involved with the police for various reasons, including both misdemeanors and felonies, during the 12 months follow-ing termination of home-based treatment. These tended to be families with poorer treatment outcomes in terms of family and child functioning as well as higher rates of pre-treatment service system involvement for both parents and children. This percentage seems to represent a small subset of highly dysfunctional families exhibiting intergenerational antisocial and other problematic be-haviors.

Follow-up interviews also demonstrate the stability of treatment gains over time. One mechanism for assessing outcomes over time is *goal attainment scaling*, a type of individualized outcome assess-ment (Kiresuk & Sherman, 1968; Kiresuk, Smith, & Cardillo, 1994; Ogles, Lambert, & Masters, 1996). Most current legislation establishing children's mental health services requires the involve-ment of families in setting individualized treatment goals. Even when this is not mandated, contemporary clinical practice calls for clients' input in jointly defining treatment goals and objectives. Funders may even require submission of goal-directed individual-ized treatment plans. Embedding goal attainment scaling in the treatment process as an outcome measure is supported by such external accountability demands as these. Once case goals have been identified and operationalized with sufficient specificity so that they are measurable, periodic progress ratings can be easily carried out. Goal attainment scaling allows for rating progress quantitatively on each treatment goal and tracking that progress over time, at treatment termination, and at follow-up.

In the Pennsylvania study, we used the family's individualized treatment goals to assess post-treatment stability of the changes families had demonstrated at treatment termination at three, six, and 12 months. At each follow-up contact family members were asked to rate the current status of each treatment goal on a three-point scale indicating "no change," "some improvement," and "significant improvement." Level of goal attainment at treatment termination was highly associated with outcomes at 12 months post-treatment, particularly in regard to out-of-home placement of the child with serious emotional disturbance.

In addition to collecting data on a variety of functional outcomes, follow-up interviews are an excellent vehicle for obtaining data on consumer satisfaction with treatment—another dimension of

treatment outcome (Berger, 1983). Eliciting the views of participants about the services they have received is consistent with the
increasing emphasis in mental health policy on engaging the consumer in all aspects of service delivery, including its evaluation.
Although issues have been raised about the validity of consumer
evaluations of their treatment experiences—primarily centering on
the question of whether consumers can objectively evaluate and
accurately express their feelings about treatment—consumer satisfaction indices are widely employed in outcome evaluation efforts
(Ogles, Lambert & Masters, 1996; Sperry, 1996). These are most
often used in conjunction with other outcome indicators, as we
recommend here.

Measures of consumer satisfaction can range from a single question in a follow-up interview, such as, "Would you recommend
this program to a friend whose child was having problems like your
child?", to well-tested standardized measures of client satisfaction.
One widely-used measure in adult mental health services is the
Client Satisfaction Questionnaire, an eight-item self-report instrument (Attkisson & Zwick, 1982; Larsen, Attkisson, Hargreaves, &
Nguyen, 1979). Recent efforts have been made in children's services
to measure satisfaction of child and adolescent patients with the
treatment they have received. One such measure, the Youth Satisfaction Questionnaire (Stuntzer-Gibson, Koren, & DeChillo,
1995), contains five questions and a scale for grading service delivery and is designed to be used with children nine years of age
and older. As part of an evaluation of the Robert Wood Johnson
Foundation's Mental Health Services Program for Youth in Mult-
nomah County, Oregon, it has been tested on a sample of 165
children and found to be valid and reliable in eliciting children's
feelings about their experiences as service recipients.

Qualitative Methods for Assessing Treatment Outcomes

In our experience in assessing treatment outcomes, the most
useful data often come from the open-ended questions we imbed
in our follow-up questionnaires. These questions include:

> "What did you like best about the home-based program?"
> "What did you like least?"

"What suggestions do you have for making home-based services more helpful to families like yours?"

We have found that families often have very thoughtful responses to these questions and are willing to share useful ideas about improving home-based treatment with us. As mentioned previously, one of the most frequently heard suggestions for improving services is to increase efforts to develop supportive networks. Early in the program we also heard comments regarding clinicians who appeared to side with emotionally disturbed children against parents—behavior certainly *not* consistent with our treatment philosophy of parent empowerment! This indicated a need for additional training in this area, especially for young clinicians who often identified more with the struggles of the children in our families, particularly the adolescents, than with parents.

Another qualitative method for evaluating treatment outcomes is to create a *focus group*. This is a longstanding method in the social sciences that is increasingly used in program evaluation and outcome research (Piercy & Nickerson, 1996). Focus groups are small in size, usually composed of 6 to 12 randomly-selected individuals who share some common quality or experience, such as participation in home-based services. The purpose of the group is to enable participants to come together to discuss a topic in an open, supportive, and facilitating environment. Research shows that the interaction of individuals in focus groups generally leads to expression and exploration of a wealth of ideas not accessible when individuals are interviewed alone. The group process appears to stimulate thinking and engagement with the topic at hand.

Focus groups are led by a moderator whose job is to introduce questions for discussion and to guide the group process. The moderator should be someone who is skilled in group work, though not necessarily in group treatment. This not a therapy group and the leader should not let it drift into becoming one. It is equally important that the group not be dominated by a few individuals and that all points of view be heard.

Questions presented to a focus group in outcome evaluation should relate directly to the treatment model and its application. Questions similar to those noted above in the client satisfaction questionnaire are often used: "What did you like best about home-based services?", "What did you like least?", "What would you most like to change about home-based services?" Authorities on the use of focus groups recommend that the moderator have a prepared list of 8 to 10 questions for discussion. However, most also stress the need to be flexible and nonintrusive so that group members can generate relevant material on their own.

Focus group discussions are generally recorded on audiotape (with written permission of the participants, of course) and transcribed afterward for more thorough analysis. Various methods for analyzing the content of focus group discussions have been developed (Piercy & Nickerson, 1996), some quite complex. However, in our experience, the primary themes and issues are usually readily apparent in the transcription. These can be easily identified and used to support and provide context for findings from questionnaires, self-report instruments, and other quantitative data sources.

Analysis and Interpretation of Data

If the time and effort expended on collecting data regarding treatment outcomes in home-based services is to be meaningful, adequate arrangements must be made for analyzing the data and interpreting the findings. Most standardized instruments can be scored by hand; however, computer-assisted scoring makes the process much easier. If the agency or organization housing a home-based program does not have sufficient computer capacity for data analysis, it is sometimes possible to access needed resources through a local college or university. One way to do this is to inquire in a math department whether students in statistics courses could use the data to practice analytic methods or to complete requirements for a special project. Or, if the home-based program can pay for computer data entry and analysis, there are often graduate students willing to do this at minimal cost. A word of caution, however: If he/she is inexperienced in data management, be sure the student is well supervised. Cleaning, coding, and entry of quantitative data require know-how and close attention to detail.

Another possibility is to join with a junior faculty member in a family studies, counseling psychology, or social work department of a local university. Newly-hired faculty members are often eager to connect with community agencies for research and teaching purposes. They generally possess solid training in evaluation skills and have access to computer resources through their home institutions. Such collaborations can be very fruitful for all parties concerned, as long as agreements about roles and authority are made upfront. There should be clarity about who owns any data collected and how evaluation results will be disseminated. For example, an agreement that the program director's name, or those of other agency staff involved in the project, will appear on all publications resulting from the study ought to be established at the outset before issues about authorship arise.

If the home-based program has its own computer resources, so much the better. The issue then becomes one of allocation of program resources to the data management task. With direction and training, a skilled secretary can handle the data cleaning, coding, and entry tasks. Data analysis is another matter, however. An analytic program for the computer, such as SAS or SPSS, is necessary and generally quite costly. Another possibility is to enter the data on-site, then provide a disk containing the raw data and a directory of the variables to a statistician for analysis. Such a person would also require a list of questions or hypotheses guiding the evaluation to provide direction to the analysis.

Any analysis of outcome data generally begins with the frequency distributions of scores on each variable in the data set. This display answers basic questions like "How many children of each sex were served?" or "What proportion of our families are headed by single mothers?" This level of analysis allows for a description of the program, its services, and the clients served. It also begins to generate additional questions that can be explored in further analyses: "Is gender related to outcome?" or "Do two-parent families have better outcomes than single-parent families?" Once frequency distributions are available, it can be very productive to share them with clinicians and others involved in the home-based program, to see what additional questions are generated by the data themselves.

The second level of analysis, depending on the questions to be asked, is generally correlational. These are the "What is the relationship between . . . ?" questions. The statistical procedures appropriate for answering correlational-type questions depend on the structure of the data: *Categorical data* are analyzed using one analytic technique, while *continuous-response data* use another. It is at this point that knowledge of statistical probability and significance testing is crucial. If this expertise is not available in-house, then it must be sought elsewhere. There are many publications available to aid the lay person or those with a basic knowledge of statistics in analyzing evaluation data, of which *Statistics for Social Workers* (Weinbach & Grinnell, 1987) and *Reasoning with Statistics* (Williams, 1992) are just two examples. But keep in mind that even experienced researchers must hire statisticians to assist with data analysis and interpretation, which means that it is unlikely that any program would—or should—be able to manage everything in-house.

Presentation and Dissemination of Findings

Most current authorities on outcome evaluation suggest involving interested constituencies in interpretation and presentation of findings at every level in the process. Certainly clinicians should be part of each step, as their input in helping to understand findings regarding treatment outcomes is invaluable. The involvement of other constituents, such as clients and funders, can also provide important perspectives and is advocated strongly by some evaluators. We believe that the interpretation of outcome data is an ongoing endeavor that benefits from multiple inputs, often obtained through the presentation of findings in various forums. For example, while home-based clinicians and service recipients may have very valuable perspectives on outcomes, they also have a particular investment in the program that may affect their interpretations. Presenting findings at professional conferences and gatherings of home-based services providers from other states can provide critical perspectives and raise additional key questions for further data analysis.

Finally, preparing an article for publication is also to be encouraged. This allows for dissemination of results to a wider audience than a conference presentation and begins a process of building an empirical base for this treatment approach. It also engenders connections among those involved in programs across the country who are evaluating home-based outcomes and allows for sharing and exchange of evaluation ideas and methods. In designing the

Pennsylvania home-based evaluation, we benefited greatly from the advice and input of experienced evaluators whose articles we had read or whose conference presentations we had attended.

SUMMARY

Outcome evaluation is increasingly becoming a basic component of mental health services for children with serious emotional disturbances and their families. Funders and other constituencies are requiring that programs demonstrate empirically the results of treatment in addition to simply showing that services have been implemented as designed. Clinicians, too, are interested in knowing whether their methods and techniques for generating change are effective, for how long, and under what circumstances. Further, as the policy mandate for consumer involvement grows, families themselves want to be sure that their participation in home-based services will have a positive effect. As a result, home-based programs are actively seeking ways to evaluate the impact of their services.

Potential obstacles to implementing outcome evaluation in home-based programs *can* be overcome with preparation and foresight. Such obstacles are inherent in the structure and function of any organization. Some have their origins in the need of organizations, like families, to maintain a level of homeostasis, protecting themselves from unanticipated change in their external and internal environments (Scott, 1983). Others arise from the natural tendency of organizations to become more rigidly structured and less ideologically open to change over time (Hage & Aiken, 1970).

Anticipating these obstacles and actively working to surmount them enable researchers to implement successful methods for evaluating outcomes for families and their children. Several strategies for addressing potential obstacles and enhancing the evaluation endeavor have been described. Implementing outcome evaluation protocols must be viewed as tantamount to initiating organizational change. Engaging all levels of the agency system as collaborators in the evaluation process is central to its success. A number of methods (noted in this chapter) take into account the power structure of an organization and the resource needs of key organizational actors.

Once the contextual factors in implementing outcome evaluation protocols are understood and addressed in an ongoing process, the steps in designing and implementing the evaluation can proceed. Each of these steps requires knowledge of evaluation strategies and techniques as well as a mindfulness of the needs and resources of the home-based program and its various constituencies. These have been described in such a way as to enable the novice evaluator to implement an outcome evaluation protocol and to identify resources to aid in doing so.

Outcome evaluations are essential to the development of sound practice in home-based children's mental health services. As more programs evaluate the results of their services to families and children and disseminate their findings, we will be able to build a reliable and replicable treatment method with well-specified techniques that can be taught to beginning clinicians.

From talking with nearly 2,000 families from widely differing socioeconomic and racial groups, we already know that home-based services can provide the skills, knowledge, and support they need to more adequately care for a child with serious emotional disturbance. In our follow-up interviews, family after family told us that having clinicians come to their homes and communities to provide help meant something special to them—a sign that there was hope for the family and for their child. The home-based workers conveyed to families that they were important resources for their children and their special knowledge of their children's needs *was* recognized and respected. One mother, whose child was able to return home from a residential treatment program several hundred miles away, with the support of home-based services, told us a year later:

The home-based team joined with our family to help us make a life for Jason with us. That was all we had ever really wanted—to be able to have our child at home with his sisters and brother, where he belongs. Together we figured out how to make that happen. Things are not perfect. We still struggle to get through some days. But it is not impossibly chaotic now, thanks to the ideas that Bill and Carol [home-based clinicians] gave us about structuring things better. Jason has more and more good days and that gives us encouragement to go on. I just realized—we actually have a pretty happy family life now!

APPENDICES

Family-Based Services Satisfaction Survey*

Circle the number after each question that best answers the question

	Always	Usually	Sometimes	Never
Did your FBS team ask for your opinions about your problems and the kind of help you wanted?	4	3	2	1
Did your team work with you to set treatment goals that you felt were right for your family?	4	3	2	1
Did your team help you to see each family member's good points as well as problems?	4	3	2	1
Did the team explain to you what they were trying to do and why they were doing it?	4	3	2	1
Did your team help you feel that progress could be made on your problems?	4	3	2	1
Did your team try to help you understand your own feelings and behavior?	4	3	2	1
Was it easy for you to talk to your team?	4	3	2	1

Did you feel that your team understood you, even if they didn't agree with you?	4	3	2	1
Did your team help you talk about subjects that were not easy to talk about?	4	3	2	1
Did your team make you feel that everything was your own fault?	4	3	2	1
Did your team tell you when they thought you weren't working hard enough on your problems?	4	3	2	1
Did you feel that your team was open and "straight" with you?	4	3	2	1
Did you feel that you could express dissatisfaction about services?	4	3	2	1
Did you feel your team respected and cared about you and your child as unique people?	4	3	2	1
Did you have the feeling that you could depend on your team when you ran into a problem?	4	3	2	1

Did you feel that your team knew what they were doing?	4	3	2	1
Did the team visit you regularly and keep in touch with you?	4	3	2	1
Was your team available when you wanted or needed them?	4	3	2	1
Was the emergency on-call worker available when you wanted or needed this person?	4	3	2	1
Did the team help you work with schools, other agencies, or people to solve your problems?	4	3	2	1
Was there something your team could have done differently that you feel would have helped your working together? Name (optional):_____				

*Developed by Deanna Linn. Reprinted with permission.

Family Follow-up Information*

Family-Based Services is interested in events that have happened since ending with your family.

How have the children been doing in school? Please list your children's names and if school is better or worse. If there have been changes in the type of school program, please include this.

Has it been possible to continue family therapy with another therapist? If it hasn't succeeded, what were the problems that prevented this?

Has there been a need for psychiatric hospitalization or placement out of the home for any family member?

Has the family become involved with any additional services for any family member? Wraparound services, Office of Children and Youth, Juvenile Probation? Has this helped? Why did these services become involved?

When you think of the reasons for FBS working with your family, do you think the issues are better or worse than originally? Please list a couple of the problems and your feelings about the results.

Problem 1 _____

Completely better	Some better	No change	Worse
1	2	3	4

If *no change* or *worse*, what is happening now with this problem?

Problem 2 _____

Completely better	Some better	No change	Worse
1	2	3	4

If *no change* or *worse*, what is happening now with this problem?

Problem 3 _____

Completely better	Some better	No change	Worse
1	2	3	4

If *no change* or *worse*, what is happening now with this problem?

Problem 4 _____

Completely better	Some better	No change	Worse
1	2	3	4

If *no change* or *worse*, what is happening now with this problem?

*Developed by Deanna Linn. Reprinted with permission.

Agency Satisfaction Survey

Family-Based Services appreciates your services and collaboration in working with families. If you could complete the following survey, it will assist us in our continuous improvement process.

Circle the response that most closely approximates your experience. Please return this survey to FBS in the enclosed stamped envelope. If several staff members are interested in participating in this survey, please make additional copies as necessary.

1. Quality of response in referral to FBS:

Excellent	Good	Fair	Poor	Cannot Rate

2. Response time to referral to FBS:

Excellent	Good	Fair	Poor	Cannot Rate

3. Overall quality of collaboration provided by FBS:

Excellent	Good	Fair	Poor	Cannot Rate

4. Quality of communication with FBS:

Excellent	Good	Fair	Poor	Cannot Rate

5. FBS awareness of requirements/needs/goals of your agency:

Excellent	Good	Fair	Poor	Cannot Rate

6. Response time to your requests for information and/or assistance:

Excellent	Good	Fair	Poor	Cannot Rate

7. Completion of treatment plan objectives:

Excellent	Good	Fair	Poor	Cannot Rate

8. Clarity of FBS treatment plan goals:

Excellent	Good	Fair	Poor	Cannot Rate

9. FBS workers involved were professional:

Excellent	Good	Fair	Poor	Cannot Rate

10. Cultural sensitivity of service to client/family:

Excellent	Good	Fair	Poor	Cannot Rate

Additional comments/suggestions _____
_____
_____
_____
_____
_____
_____
_____

Name: _____   Title: _____
Agency: _____   Date: _____

*Developed by Deanna Linn. Reprinted with permission.

Permission for Videotaping during Home-Based Family Services

Agencies: 1. _____

_____

_____

_____

2. _____

_____

_____

_____

Patient: _____

Date: _____

I (we) authorize the two agencies: _____ and the
_____ Clinic to use any audio-
visual recordings made at said clinic of myself (us) and my (our) family,
for the purposes of:

1. Evaluation by the therapist, home-based family service's team, super-
    visor, and consultants
2. Supervision by the home-based family service's supervisor and con-
    sultant
3. Training home-based family service teams
4. Teaching to home-based family service professionals

Upon written notice, I (we) may have any or all audiovisual recordings
erased, and/or restrict their use to one or more of the above stated purposes.

I (we) understand that all audiovisual recordings are available for viewing
by me (us).

_____   _____

Father   Mother

_____   _____

_____   _____

This release must be signed by all family members 14 years old or over
(Patient's Copy)

Strength-Based Behaviors Checklist*

Complete the strength-based behaviors checklist for the IP and other household/natural family members. Use initials to indicate the household/family members who exhibit strength or need for each item. Add items as needed.

Indicate strength (s) or need (n) of household member or IP.

School Issues

_____ _____ learning new subjects
_____ _____ retaining information
_____ _____ reading ability
_____ _____ math ability
_____ _____ interest in achievement
_____ _____ appropriate school behavior
_____ _____ attendance
_____ _____ school goals
_____ _____ participation in activities
_____ _____ academic achievement
_____ _____ attention span
Other:_____
_____
_____

Developmental/Organic (explain if needed)

_____ _____ physical health_____
_____ _____ mental health_____
_____ _____ developmental milestones_____
_____ _____ language ability_____
_____ _____ neurological functioning_____
_____ _____ activity level_____
_____ _____ attention span (preschool)_____
_____ _____ learning ability (preschool)_____
Other:_____
_____
_____

Emotional Health

————— ————— ability to cope with change (new situations)
————— ————— ability to cope with losses
————— ————— ability to express angry feelings safely
————— ————— ability to express happiness
————— ————— ability to express sadness
————— ————— ability to express affection
————— ————— ability to adjust/accept new situations
————— ————— expresses appropriate self-esteem

Behavioral Health

————— ————— able to sleep through approximately eight hours
a night—————————————————
————— ————— has healthy eating habits—————————
————— ————— is able to stop dangerous or disruptive behaviors
————— ————— is respectful of others' privacy
————— ————— is respectful of adults
————— ————— is respectful of others' property
————— ————— accepts rules and limits set by family—————
————— ————— accepts rules and limits set by others (school and
community)————————————————
————— ————— acts safely with self—————————
————— ————— acts safely with others—————————
————— ————— is respectful and appropriate with siblings
————— ————— is sexually age-appropriate
————— ————— is able to take ownership for behavior
Other:————————————————————
————————————————————————
————————————————————————

Social Relations

————— ————— is able to make friends
————— ————— has more than one friend he/she can count on
————— ————— has a positive peer group and relations with them
————— ————— gets along well with peers in school
————— ————— enjoys interactions with peers
————— ————— gets along well with siblings
————— ————— is able to problem-solve with peers
————— ————— will take direction from adults

_____ _____ can play on a team
_____ _____ is active with others, has group activities
_____ _____ can take responsibility in a group
_____ _____ is able to negotiate and compromise
_____ _____ is able to share and take turns
_____ _____ looks out for others' needs
_____ _____ has an appropriate knowledge and/or regard for sex and sexuality

Other (note areas of conflict):_____

_____

_____

Medical

_____ _____ has a good energy level
_____ _____ has a healthy diet
_____ _____ has good toilet habits
_____ _____ has good (age-appropriate) elimination control
_____ _____ has good hygiene

Other (note use of substances: tobacco, alcohol, drugs, inhalants):____

_____

_____

Family Relationships

_____ _____ frequently sees members of extended family
_____ _____ family has ceremonies and rituals to celebrate rites of passage and other events
_____ _____ family has friends that they can rely on for support
_____ _____ family attends church together
_____ _____ family participates in community events or activities
_____ _____ parents attend children's school functions
_____ _____ family has routines for housekeeping
_____ _____ family has budget for spending
_____ _____ children have tasks for participating in housekeeping
_____ _____ tasks are mostly equally distributed among members, as appropriate
_____ _____ family enjoys activities and play together
_____ _____ family has rules that are known to all members

—————— —————— family has effective methods of discipline
—————— —————— family has safe methods of discipline
—————— —————— family members receive safe consequences for
                        rule violations
—————— —————— tasks are appropriate for age and status in family
Other:————————————————————————————————
——————————————————————————————————
——————————————————————————————————

*Developed by Helene M. Elko, M.S.S.A. Reprinted with permission.

Release of Information Form

Client Name _____ D.O.B. _____ S.S.# _____

I hereby authorize the _____

_____ to release to and/or receive from:

_____ County Mental Health   _____ Medical Provider _____
Office

_____ County Children & Youth   _____ Health Services
Services

_____ County Intermediate Unit   _____ Medical Center

_____ School District _____   _____ Base Service Unit

_____ County Mental Retardation   _____ Mental Health Provider
Office   _____

_____ County Juvenile Court

_____ Drug and Alcohol Provider

_____ Other _____

_____

confidential information on the above-named client pertaining to treatment on or about _____.

The specific information to be released is limited to the following:

_____ Psychological/Psychiatric   _____ Social Work Reports
Report

_____ Aptitude or Achievement   _____ Drug & Alcohol Treatment
Test Scores   Records

_____ Vocational Skills Assess-   _____ Progress Reports
ment

_____ Report Cards   _____ Medical Records

_____ Teacher Observations   _____ Neurological Reports

_____ Attendance Reports   _____ Other—specify_____

_____ Family Background Information

This information is needed for evaluation, treatment, and service planning for my child/family with the multiservice meeting participants. The service planning will formally take place at a multiservice meeting (MSM), where I will participate. I also understand and agree that reports developed at the Base Service Unit will be shared with any of the above designated agencies/services who will participate with me in the MSM meeting.

I understand and agree that my authorization shall remain valid from the date of my signature, beginning on _____ and for a maximum of 6 months, ending on _____, except drug and alcohol records for which this authorization expires in 60 days, ending on _____. I have been informed that I may revoke this authorization, except to the extent that action has been taken in reliance thereon, by written or oral communication. I have also been informed of my right subject to section 7100.111.3 of the Mental Health Procedures Act, 1976, to inspect the information to be released and that all information will be treated confidentially, in compliance with: the Juvenile Court Act (42 PA C.S.A. 6301 et. seq.); the Child Protection Services Act (11 P.S. 2201 et. seq.); the Federal Privacy Act (P.L. 93–575); the Federal Alcohol and Drug Abuse Act (P.L. 92–255); the Pennsylvania Drug and Alcohol Abuse Act (P.L. 221, No. 63); the Education Regulations (P.L. 94–142 and 22 PA. Chapters 12 & 341); Department of Public Welfare Regulations (55 PA Code 4225.21—4225.50) and in compliance with other applicable state and federal laws and regulations.

I certify that this form has been fully explained to me and that I understand and agree with its contents. I copy of this signed form shall have the same force and effect as an original document.

Signature of Client   _____ Date _____
Signature of Parent/   _____ Date _____
Legal Guardian/   _____ Date _____
Caretaker and   _____ Date _____
Relationship   _____ Date _____
Witnessed by: _____ Date _____

APPENDIX G

Attendance Confidentiality Statement

I acknowledge that by my attendance at the multisystem meeting (herein after MSM) for the _____ family on _____ *(date)*, I will obtain confidential information. I agree that I will not disclose this information without the appropriate written consent of the parent/guardian and/or the child or as permitted by state and federal laws and regulations.

I understand and agree that if any information is disclosed from Drug and Alcohol records during this MSM, that the confidentiality of such information is governed by Federal Regulation (42 C.F.R. Part 2). The federal rules prohibit me from making any further disclosure of this information unless disclosure is expressly permitted by written consent of the person to whom it pertains or is otherwise permitted by 42 C.F.R. Part 2. The Federal rules restrict any use of information to criminally investigate or prosecute an alcohol or drug abuse client.

Name	Agency/Relationship	Phone	Signature

1. _____
2. _____
3. _____
4. _____
5. _____
6. _____
7. _____
8. _____
9. _____
10. _____
11. _____
12. _____
13. _____
14. _____
15. _____

Note: This statement is signed prior to exchange of any information.

APPENDIX H

Orientation Training Checklist

Administrative Issues	I understand	Need more explanation
• Office memos		
• Formal structure		
• Informal structure		
• Green sheets/Mileage		
Computer Orientation Training (Initial)	I understand	Need more explanation
• Alfacom		
• Word Perfect		
• Care and Maintenance		
• Note Writing/Template Writing		
Agency Policy and Procedure Review	I understand	Need more explanation
• Counsel on Accreditation Standard Orientation		
Community Networking	I understand	Need more explanation
• Town tour		
• Human Services luncheon		
• Family Focus Policy and Procedure Review		
• Family Support Services Orientation		
• Multisystems meeting orientation		

Expected Skills Review	I understand	Need more explanation
• Mental status writing		
• Clinical impression writing		
• Critical life events timeline		
• Genogram		
Intake Procedure and Notes	I understand	Need more explanation
• Review of intake process		
• Review of intake criteria		
• Review of intake note		
• Review of eligibility		
Treatment Plan Writing	I understand	Need more explanation
• Review of training document		
• Construct a group treatment plan		
• Positive goal writing		
• Treatment plan as a therapeutic skill development		
• Content loop between presenting problem, intake notes, clinical impessions, and treatment plan		
Question/Answers	I understand	Need more explanation
• Review of each person's first case in context of training delivered		

Demonstration of Genogram and Critical Life Events Timeline		
• Role-play		
• Review of notes		
• Live supervision scheduled with staffer at intake process		
Team Issues Training	I understand	Need more explanation
• Use of team partners		
• Techniques to create a team		
• Expectations of team partners		
• Expectations of supervisor in team performance		
•Team boundaries		
Computer Training (Intermediate)	I understand	Need more explanation
•Windows 95		
• Office Pro		
Training Manual	I understand	Need more explanation
•Apply training to current cases		

*Developed by D. J. Dunlap

Clinical Case Presentation

I. Understanding and Working with Referral Source Issues
   1. Who referred the family?
   2. What was the referral source's relationship with the family?
   3. What kind of relationship did you establish?
   4. How were referral source issues dealt with in the family?
II. Presenting Problems and Symptoms
III. Genogram (at least three generations)
   1. Cross-generational similarities and relationships
IV. Timeline of Critical Life Events
   1. Your hypotheses regarding contributing life-cycle events to the presenting problems
V. Family Adaptations
   1. Stress created by presenting problem
   2. Environmental stressors
   3. Economic stressors
   4. Ethnicity/cultural factors
   5. Developmental family life-cycle factors
VI. Strengths of Each Family Member
VII. Risk Factors
VIII. Family Structural Maps Depicting:
   1. Current pattern
   2. Optimal future pattern

   Maps:
         a. Hierarchy
         b. Boundary Functioning
            (1) proximity/distance
            (2) coalitions
            (3) alliances and conflicts
         c. Affective Relationships
            (1) nurturant and emotionally close
            (2) unpredictable
            (3) estranged and emotionally distant

IX. Eco-maps Depicting: positive, neutral, or stressful relationships; possible services to explore
   1. Social services
   2. Support services
X. Description of Team Relationship and Family/Team Relationships

XI. Integration of Assessment Data
1. Hypotheses to be tested
2. Confirmed hypotheses
3. Family themes
XII. Treatment Plan
1. Treatment goals
2. Treatment objectives
3. Resource allocations (how will family support, case management, and informal resources be used?)
XIII. Consultation Questions

APPENDIX J

*Clinical Skill Competencies for In-home Therapists**

	A Great Deal		Some-what		Incon-sistent	Not at All
1. Forms a collaborative relationship as seen in how a mutual service plan and contract is achieved	5	4	3	2	1	0
2. Demonstrates a collaborative relationship during the therapeutic process	5	4	3	2	1	0
3. Develops collaborative relationship(s) with an outside agency, individual or individuals	5	4	3	2	1	0
4. Explores each person's view of the problem(s) he/she wants addressed	5	4	3	2	1	0
5. Explores scope of an assessment and adjusts the hypothesis based on family feedback	5	4	3	2	1	0
6. Conducts an adequate inquiry regarding the presenting problem(s)	5	4	3	2	1	0
7. Provides examples of dysfunctional patterns (three structural maps) when presenting cases	5	4	3	2	1	0

8. Provides example(s) of dysfunctional patterns between family and extrafamilial systems when presenting cases	5	4	3	2	1	0
9. Redefines problem(s) in interactional terms	5	4	3	2	1	0
10. Works with family's strengths to facilitate change in family interactive patterns	5	4	3	2	1	0
11. Uses enactment(s) to promote alternative behavior patterns in the family	5	4	3	2	1	0
12. Creates intensity to promote change	5	4	3	2	1	0
13. Changes family's belief system by altering perceptions	5	4	3	2	1	0
14. Promotes boundary-making (with family and/or agencies)	5	4	3	2	1	0
15. Demonstrates use of concrete assistance (family support services) to achieve family's goals and to change family patterns	5	4	3	2	1	0
16. Promotes affective changes among family members	5	4	3	2	1	0

17. Helps parent(s) to demonstrate effective parental control/discipline toward identified patient	5	4	3	2	1	0
18. Helps parent(s) to demonstrate appropriate nurturing behavior toward identified patient	5	4	3	2	1	0
19. Demonstrates change in family relationship patterns with regard to identified patient's problems	5	4	3	2	1	0
20. Demonstrates change in relationship patterns between family/ extrafamilial systems	5	4	3	2	1	0
21. Demonstrates how to help repower parent(s) to activate outside agency resources to assist the family	5	4	3	2	1	0
22. Helps family to prepare for termination	5	4	3	2	1	0
23. Demonstrates effective partnership with team member	5	4	3	2	1	0

*Developed by Marion Lindblad-Goldberg, Ph.D., 1993

REFERENCES

Aber, J. L., Allen, J. P., Carlson, V., & Cicchetti, D. (1989). The effects of maltreatment on development during early childhood: Recent studies and their theoretical, clinical, and policy implications. In D. Cicchetti & V. Carlson (Eds.), *Child maltreatment* (pp. 579–619). New York: Cambridge University Press.

Achenbach, T. M. (1991a). *Manual for the Child Behavior Checklist/4–18 and 1991 profiles.* Burlington, VT: University of Vermont, Department of Psychiatry.

Achenbach, T. M. (1991b). *Manual for the Youth Self Report Form and 1991 profile.* Burlington, VT: University of Vermont, Department of Psychiatry.

Adams, P. (1994). Marketing social change: The case of family preservation. *Children and Youth Services Review, 16*(5/6), 417–431.

Ainsworth, M. D. (1985). Attachments across the life span. *Bulletin of the New York Academy of Medicine, 61,* 792–812.

Alexander, J. F., Barton, C., Schiavo, R. S., & Parsons, B. V. (1976). Systems-behavioral intervention with families of delinquents: Therapist characteristics, family behavior, and outcome. *Journal of Consulting and Clinical Psychology, 44*(4), 656–664.

Alexander, J. F., & Parsons, B. V. (1973). Short-term behavioral intervention with delinquent families: Impact on family process and recidivism. *Journal of Abnormal Psychology, 81,* 219–225.

Amato, P. R., & Keith, B. (1991). Consequences of parental divorce for the well-being of children: A meta-analysis. *Psychological Bulletin, 110,* 26–46.

American Psychiatric Association. (1994). *Diagnostic and statistical manual of mental disorders* (4th ed.). Washington, DC.

Anderson, A. R., & Henry, C. S. (1994). Family system characteristics and parental behaviors as predictors of adolescent substance use. *Adolescence, 29*(114), 405–420.

Antonovsky, A. (1979). *Health, stress, and coping.* San Francisco: Jossey-Bass.

Aponte, H.J. (1970). The family-school interview: An eco-structural approach. *Family Process, 15* , 303–311.

Archacki-Stone, C. (1989). *Clinical case presentation outline.* Unpublished manuscript.

333

Archacki-Stone, C. (1991). *What is home-based family therapy?* Unpublished manuscript.

Attkisson, C. C., & Zwick, R. (1982). The client satisfaction questionnaire: Psychometric properties and correlations with service utilization and psychotherapy outcome. *Evaluation and Program Planning, 5,* 233–237.

Auerswald, E. H. (1968). Interdisciplinary versus ecological approach. *Family Process, 7,* 202–215.

Auerswald, E. H. (1971). Families, change and the ecological perspective. *Family Process, 10,* 263–280.

Bank, S., & Kahn, M. (1982). *The sibling bond.* New York: Basic Books.

Barber, B. L., & Eccles, J. S. (1992). Long-term influence of divorce and single parenting on adolescent family- and work-related values, behaviors, and aspirations. *Psychological Bulletin, 111*(1), 108–126.

Barkley, R. A. (1990). *Attention deficit hyperactivity disorder: A handbook for diagnosis and treatment.* New York: Guilford.

Barkley, R. A. (1997). *Defiant children: A clinician's manual for assessment and parent training* (2nd ed.). New York: Guilford.

Barth, R. P. (1988). Theories guiding home-based intensive family preservation services. In J. K. Whittaker, J. Kinney, E. M. Tracy & C. Booth (Eds.), *Improving practice technology for work with high risk families: Lessons from the "Homebuilders" social work education project* (pp. 91–114). Seattle: Center for Social Welfare Research, University of Washington.

Barth, R. P., Courtney, M., Berrick, J. D., & Albert, V. (1994). *From child abuse to permanency planning: Child welfare services pathways and placements.* New York: Aldine de Gruyter.

Bateson, G. (1972). *Steps to an ecology of mind.* New York: Ballantine Books.

Bateson, G. (1979). *Mind and nature: A necessary unity.* New York: Dutton.

Bath, H. I., & Haapala, D. A. (1993). Intensive family preservation services with abused and neglected children: An examination of group differences. *Child Abuse & Neglect, 17,* 213–225.

Bath, H. I., & Haapala, D. A. (1995). Evaluation outcomes of family preservation services and the way ahead: A reply to Littell. *Social Service Review, 69,* 351–358.

Bath, H. I., Richey, C. A., & Haapala, D. A. (1992). Child age and outcome correlates in intensive family preservation services. *Children and Youth Services Review, 14,* 389–406.

Baum, F. L. (1903). *The wizard of Oz.* New York: Grosset and Dunlap.

Beck, A., Ward, C., Mendelson, M., Mock, J., & Erbaugh, J. (1961). An inventory for measuring depression. *Archives of General Psychiatry, 4,* 53–63.

Belsky, J. (1979). The interrelation of parental and spousal behavior during infancy in traditional nuclear families: An exploratory analysis. *Journal of Marriage and the Family, 41,* 62–68.

Belsky, J. (1981). Early human experience: a family perspective. *Developmental Psychology, 17,* 3–23.

Belsky, J., Woodworth, S., & Crnic, K. (1996). Troubled family interaction during toddlerhood. *Development and Psychopathology, 8,* 477–495.

Benjamin, M. P. (1997, Spring). Overrepresentation of youth of color in the juvenile justice system: Culturally competent service system strategies. *Focal Point,* 12–15.

Berger, M. (1983). Toward maximizing utility of consumer satisfaction as an outcome. In M. J. Lambert, E. R. Christensen, & S. S. DeJulio (Eds.), *The assessment of psychotherapy outcome* (pp. 56–80). New York: John Wiley & Sons.

Bernard, J., & Goodyear, R. (1992). *Fundamentals of clinical supervision.* Needham Heights, MA: Allyn and Bacon.

Berry, M. (1997). *The family at risk: Issues and trends in family preservation services.* Columbia, SC: University of South Carolina Press.

Bickman, L. (1987). *Using program theory in evaluation.* San Francisco: Jossey-Bass.

Bird, H. R., Canino, G. J., Rubio-Stipec, M., & Ribera, J. C. (1987). Further measures of the psychometric properties of the Children's Global Assessment Scale. *Archives of General Psychiatry, 44,* 821–824.

Birmaher, B., Ryan, N., Williamson, D., Brent, D., Kauffman, J., Dahl, R., Perel, J., & Nelson, B. (1996). Childhood and adolescent depression: A review of the past 10 years. Part I. *Journal of the American Academy of Child and Adolescent Psychiatry, 35*(12), 1575–1583.

Blatt, S., & Homann, E. (1992). Parent-child interaction in the etiology of dependent and self-critical depression. *Clinical Psychology Review, 12,* 47–91.

Bogas, S. (1993). An integrative treatment model for children's attentional and learning problems. *Family Systems Medicine, II,* 385–396.

Borduin, C. M., Mann, B. J., Cone, L. T., & Henggeler, S. W. (1995). Multisystemic treatment of serious juvenile offenders: Long-term prevention of criminality and violence. *Journal of Consulting and Clinical Psychology, 63*(4), 569–578.

Borrine, M. L., Handal, P. J., Brown, N. Y., & Searight, H. R. (1991). Family conflict and adolescent adjustment in intact, divorced, and blended families. *Journal of Consulting and Clinical Psychology, 59*(5), 753–755.

Boss, P. G. (1988). *Family stress management.* Beverly Hills, CA: Sage.

Bowlby, J. (1983). *Attachment and loss, Vol. 1* (2nd ed.). New York: Basic Books.

Bowlby, J. (1988). *A secure base: Parent-child attachment and healthy human development.* New York: Basic Books.

Brager, G. & Holloway, S. (1978). *Changing human service organizations.* New York: Free Press.

Broderick, C. B., & Schrader, S. S. (1981). The history of professional marriage and family therapy. In A. S. Gurman & D. P. Kniskern (Eds.), *Handbook of family therapy* (pp. 5–35). New York: Brunner/Mazel.

Bronstein, P., Clauson, J., Stoll, M. F., & Abrams, C. L. (1993). Parenting behavior and children's social, psychological, and academic adjustment in diverse family structures. *Family Relations, 42,* 268–276.

Bureau of Children's Services. (1993). Family based mental health services for children and adolescents. *Pennsylvania Bulletin, 23*(18), 2127–2136.

Bureau of Children's Services. (1995). *Core principles: Child and adolescent service system program.* Harrisburg, PA: Pennsylvania Office of Mental Health.

Burr, W. R., Klein, S. R., & Associates (1994). *Reexamining family stress: New theory and research.* Thousand Oaks, CA: Sage.

Campbell, D. T. (1987). Problems for the experimenting society in the interface between evaluation and service providers. In S. Kagan, D. Powell, B. Weissbourd, & E. Zigler, (Eds.), *America's family support programs*. New Haven: Yale University Press.

Caputo, R. K. (1985). The role of research in the family service agency. *Social Casework*, 205–212.

Carl, D., & Jurkovic, G. (1983). Agency triangles: problems in agency-family relationships. *Family Process, 22*, 441–451.

Carlson, E. B., Furby, L., Armstrong, J., & Shales, J. (1997). A conceptual framework for the long-term psychological effects of traumatic child abuse. *Child Maltreatment, 2*(3), 272–295.

Carlson, G., & Cantwell, D. (1982). Suicidal behavior and depression in children and adolescents. *Journal of the American Academy of Child Psychiatry, 21*, 361–368.

Chen, H. (1990). *Theory-driven evaluations*. Newbury Park, CA: Sage.

Chiariello, M., & Orvaschel, H. (1995). Patterns of parent-child communication: Relationship to depression. *Clinical Psychology Review, 15*(5), 395–407.

Christensen, L. (1995). Therapists' perspectives on home-based family therapy. *The American Journal of Family Therapy, 23*, 306–314.

Churchill, M. (1995). I never wanted to live in New York City. *Focal Point, 9*(2), 19.

Cicchetti, D., & Nurcombe, B. (1993). Special issue: toward a developmental perspective on conduct disorder. *Development and Psychopathology, 5*, 1–144.

Claremont de Castillejo, I. (1974) *Knowing woman, a feminine psychology*. New York: Harper Colophon Books.

Cohen, E. (1996). *Devolution's missing link: Investing in family-centered front-line training*. Washington, DC: Family Impact Seminar.

Cohen-Sandler, R., Bermal, A., & King, R. (1982). Life stress and symptomatology: Determinants of suicidal behavior in children. *Journal of the American Academy of Child Psychiatry, 21*, 564–569.

Colapinto, J. (1983). Beyond technique: Teaching how to think structurally. *Journal of Strategic and Systemic Therapies, 2*, 12–21.

Colapinto, J. (1991). Structural family therapy. In A. S. Gurman & D. P. Kniskern (Eds.), *Handbook of family therapy, Vol. 2*. New York: Brunner/Mazel.

Colapinto, J. (1995). Dilution of family process in social services: Implications for treatment of neglectful families. *Family Process, 34*, 59–74.

Cole, E. & Duva, J. (1990). *Family preservation: An orientation for practitioners and administrators*. Washington, DC: Child Welfare League of America.

Combrinck-Graham, L. (1985). A developmental model for family systems. *Family Process, 24*, 139–150.

Combrinck-Graham, L. (1989). Family models of child psychopathology. In L. Combrinck-Graham (Ed.), *Children in family contexts* (pp. 67–89). New York: Guilford.

Combrinck-Graham, L. (1990). Developments in family systems theory and research. *Journal of the American Academy of Child and Adolescent Psychiatry, 29*(4), 501–512.

Combrinck-Graham, L. (Ed.) (1995). *Children in families at risk: Maintaining the connections*. New York: Guilford.

Comer, J. P., & Hill, H. (1985). Social policy and the mental health of Black children. *Journal of the American Academy of Child Psychiatry, 24*(2), 175–181.

Commonwealth of Pennsylvania (1997). *Health choices: Behavioral health ser-*

vices guidelines for behavioral health medical necessity criteria. Harrisburg, PA: Department of Welfare, Commonwealth of Pennsylvania.

Compher, J. (1989). *Family-centered practice: The interactional dance beyond the family system.* New York: Human Sciences Press.

Connell, G.M. (1984). An approach to supervision of symbolic-experiential psychotherapy. *Journal of Marriage and Family Therapy, 10,* 273–280.

Conners, C. K. (1969). A teacher rating scale for use in drug studies with children. *American Journal of Psychiatry, 126,* 884–889.

Cook, D. (1994). Racial identity in supervision. *Counselor Education and Supervision, 34,* 132–139.

Corcoran, K., & Fischer, J. (1994). *Measures for clinical practice* (Vols. 1–2) (2nd. ed.). New York: Free Press.

Cottrell, D. (1994). Family therapy in the home. *Journal of Family Therapy, 16,* 189–197.

Crittenden, P. M. (1985). Maltreated infants: Vulnerability and resilience. *Journal of Child Psychology and Psychiatry, 26,* 297–300.

Crnic, K. A., Friedrich, W. N., & Greenberg, M. T. (1983). Adaptation of families with mentally retarded children: A model of stress, coping and family ecology. *American Journal of Mental Deficiency, 88*(2), 125–138.

Dadds, M. (1995). *Families, children, and the development of dysfunction.* Thousand Oaks, CA: Sage.

Dadds, M., Barrett, P., Rapee, R., & Ryan, S. (1996). Family process and child anxiety and aggression: An observational analysis. *Journal of Abnormal Child Psychology, 24*(6), 715–734.

DeChillo, N., Koren, P. E., & Schultze, K. H. (1994). From paternalism to partnership: Family and professional collaboration in children's mental health. *American Journal of Orthopsychiatry, 64*(4), 564–576.

DeKemp, R., & Van Acker, J. (1997). Therapist-parent interaction patterns in home-based treatments: Exploring family therapy processes. *Family Process, 36,* 281–295.

Diamond, G. S., Serrano, A. C., Dickey, M., & Sonis, W. A. (1996). Current status of family-based outcome and process research. *Journal of the American Academy of Child and Adolescent Psychiatry, 35*(1), 6–16.

DiNicola, V. (1997). *A stranger in the family.* New York: Norton.

Dore, M. M. (1991a). Context and the structure of practice: Implications for research. In K. Wells & D. Biegel (Eds.), *Family preservation services: Research and evaluation* (pp. 121–137). Newbury Park, CA: Sage.

Dore, M. M. (1991b). Effectiveness of state-wide implementation of a family-based approach to children's mental health services. In A. Algarin & R. M. Friedman (Eds.), *A system of care for children's mental health: Expanding the research base* (pp. 31–37). Tampa, FL: Research and Training Center for Children's Mental Health, Florida Mental Health Institute.

Dore, M. M. (1993). Family-based services in children's mental health care. *Child and Adolescent Mental Health Journal, 3,* 175–189.

Dore, M. M. (1994). *Annual research report on family-based services.* Harrisburg, PA: Bureau of Children's Services, Pennsylvania Office of Mental Health.

Dore, M. M. (1996). *Annual research report on family-based services.* Harrisburg, PA: Bureau of Children's Services, Pennsylvania Office of Mental Health.

Dore, M. M., & Guberman-Kennedy, K. (1981). Two decades of turmoil: Child welfare services, 1960–1980. *Child Welfare, 60,* 371–382.

Dore, M. M., Kauffman, E., Nelson-Zlupko, L., & Granfort, E. (1996). Psychosocial functioning and treatment needs of latency-age children from drug-involved families. *Families in Society, 77*(1), 595–604.

Dore, M. M., & Pereira, L. M. (in press). Family systems theory and serious emotional disturbances in children. In D. A. Sabatino & B. L. Brooks (Eds.), *Current research on educational and clinical treatment approaches with emotionally and behaviorally disturbed children*. Durham, NC: Carolina Academic Press.

Dore, M. M., Wilkinson, A. N., & Sonis, W. A. (1992). Exploring the concept of a continuum of care in children's mental health services. *Hospital and Community Psychiatry, 43*(1), 44–55.

Downey, G., & Coyne, J. C. (1990). Children of depressed parents: An integrative review. *Psychological Bulletin, 108*(1), 50–75.

Duhl, B. (1983). *From the inside out and other metaphors*. New York: Brunner/Mazel.

Dunlap, D. J. (1996). *Orientation training checklist*. Unpublished document. Catholic Charities Diocese of Harrisburg, Pa., Inc.

Dunlap, D. J. (1997, April). *Teams and team formation*. Pennsylvania family-based mental health training workshop. Philadelphia Child Guidance Center, Philadelphia, PA.

Early, B. P., & Hawkins, M. J. (1994). Opportunity and risks in emerging family policy: An analysis of family preservation legislation. *Children and Youth Services Review, 16*(5/6), 309–318.

Eckenrode, J., & Gore, S. (1981). Stressful events and social supports: The significance of context. In B. Gottlieb (Ed.), *Social networks and social support*. Beverly Hills, CA: Sage.

Edens, J. F., & Otto, R. K. (1997, Spring). Prevalence of mental disorders among youth in the juvenile justice system. *Focal Point, 1*, 6–7.

Edna McConnell Clark Foundation. (1985). *Keeping families together: The case for family preservation*. New York: Edna McConnell Clark Foundation.

Elko, H. (1997). *Strength based behaviors checklist*. Unpublished document. Coudersport, PA: Charles Cole Memorial Hospital.

Epstein, N. B., Baldwin, L. M., & Bishop, D. S. (1983). The McMaster Family Assessment Device. *Journal of Marital and Family Therapy, 9*(2), 171–180.

Epstein, W. M. (1997). Social science, child welfare, and family preservation: A failure of rationality in public policy. *Children and Youth Services Review, 19*(1/2), 41–60.

Evans, M. E., Armstrong, M. T., Thompson, F., & Lee, J-K. (1994). Assessing the outcomes of parent- and practitioner-designed systems of care for children with emotional and behavioral disturbances. *Psychiatric Quarterly, 65*(4), 257–272.

Evans, M. E., & Boothroyd, R. A. (1997). Family preservation services for families with children who have mental health problems. In S. W. Henggeler & Santos, A. B.(Eds.), *Innovative approaches for difficult-to-treat populations* (pp. 27–46). Washington, DC: American Psychiatric Press.

Faber, A., & Mazlish, E. (1987). *How to talk so kids will listen and listen so kids will talk*. New York: Avon Books.

Falicov, C. J. (1988). Learning to think culturally. In H. A. Liddle, D.C. Breulin, & R. C. Schwartz (Eds.), *Handbook of family therapy training and supervision*. New York: Guilford.

Falicov, C. J., & Brudner-White, L. (1983). The shifting family triangle: The issue of cultural and contextual relativity. In C. J. Falicov (Ed.), *Cultural perspectives in family therapy*. Rockville, MD: Aspen.

Family Resource Coalition. (1993). *Building strong foundations: Evaluation strategies for family resource programs*. Chicago. Family Resource Coalition.

Famularo, R., Kinscherff, R., & Fenton, T. (1992). Psychiatric diagnoses of maltreated children: Preliminary findings. *Journal of the American Academy of Child and Adolescent Psychiatry, 31*(5), 863–867.

Fanshel, D., & Shinn, E. B. (1978). *Children in foster care: A longitudinal investigation*. New York: Columbia University Press.

Fauber, R., Forehand, R., Thomas, A. M., & Wierson, M. (1990). A mediational model of the impact of marital conflict on adolescent adjustment in intact and divorced families: The role of disrupted parenting. *Child Development, 61*, 1112–1123.

Fauber, R., & Long, N. (1991). Children in context: The role of the family in child psychotherapy. *Journal of Consulting and Clinical Psychology, 59*(6), 813–820.

Figley, C., & McCubbin, H. (Eds.) (1983). *Stress and the family: Coping with catastrophe, Vol. 2*. New York: Brunner/Mazel.

Fine, G., & Borden, J. R. (1989). Parents Involved Network project: Support and advocacy training for parents. In R. M. Friedman, A. J. Duchnowski, & E. L. Henderson (Eds.), *Advocacy on behalf of children with serious emotional problems* (pp. 68–77). Springfield, IL: Charles C. Thomas.

Flisher, A. J., Kramer, R. A., Hoven, C. W., Greenwald, S., Alegria, M., Bird, H. R., Canino, G., Connell, R., & Moore, R. E. (1997). Psychosocial characteristics of physically abused children and adolescents. *Journal of the American Academy of Child and Adolescent Psychiatry, 36*(1), 123–131.

Forsythe, P. (1992). Homebuilders and family preservation. *Children and Youth Services Review, 14*, 37–47.

Friedman, A. S., Tomko, L. A., & Utada, A. (1991). Client and family characteristics that predict better family therapy outcomes for adolescent drug abusers. *Family Dynamics of Addiction Quarterly, 1*(1), 77–93.

Friedman, D., & Kaslow, F. J. (1986). The development of professional identity in psychotherapists: Six stages in the supervision process. In F. J. Kaslow (Ed.), *Supervision and training: Models, dilemmas, and challenges*. New York: Hawthorne Press.

Friedrich, W. N., Wilturner, L. T., & Cohen, D. S. (1985). Coping resources and parenting mentally retarded children. *American Journal of Mental Deficiency, 90*(2), 130–139.

Friesen, B. J., & Koroloff, N. M. (1990). Family-centered services: Implications for mental health administration and research. *Journal of Mental Health Administration, 17*(1), 13–25.

Fristad, M. A., & Clayton, T. L. (1991). Family dysfunction and family psychopathology in child psychiatry outpatients. *Journal of Family Psychology, 5*(1), 46–59.

Gardner, F. E. M. (1989). Inconsistent parenting: Is there evidence for a link with children's conduct problems? *Journal of Abnormal Child Psychology, 17*(2), 223–233.

Garmezy, N. (1987). Stress, competence, and development: Continuities in the study of schizophrenic adults, children vulnerable to psychopathology, and the search for stress-resistant children. *American Journal of Orthopsychiatry, 57*(2), 159–174.

Ge, X., Best, K., Conger, R., & Simons, R. (1996). Parenting behaviors and the occurrence and co-occurrence of adolescent depressive symptoms and conduct problems. *Developmental Psychology, 32*(4), 717–731.

Gelfand, D. M., & Teti, D. M. (1990). The effects of maternal depression on children. *Clinical Psychology Review, 10,* 329–353.

Gilbert, R., Christensen, A., & Margolin, G. (1984). Patterns of alliances in nondistressed and multiproblem families. *Family Process, 23*(1), 75–87.

Gilgun, J. F. (1996). Human development and adversity in an ecological perspective. Part 1: A conceptual framework. *Families in Society, 77*(7), 395–402.

Gingerich, W. J. (1984). Generalizing single-case evaluation from classroom to practice. *Journal of Education for Social Work, 20,* 74–82.

Goldberg, S. (1982). *Special education law: A guide for parents, advocates and educators.* New York: Plenum.

Goldenthal, P. (1996). *Doing contextual therapy.* New York: Norton.

Goldman, A. (1990). Basic rules of writing treatment goals and objectives. *Practical Communications, 4*(3), 1–2.

Goldner, V. (1988). Generation and gender: normative and covert hierarchies. *Family Process, 27,* 17–31.

Goodman, S. H., & Brumley, H. E. (1990). Schizophrenic and depressed mothers: Relational deficits in parenting. *Developmental Psychology, 26*(1), 31–39.

Goodyer, I. M. (1990). Family relationships, life events and childhood psychopathology. *Journal of Child Psychology and Psychiatry, 31*(1), 161–192.

Gordon, D. A., Arbuthnot, J., Gustafson, K. E., & McGreen, P. (1988). Home-based behavioral-systems family therapy with disadvantaged juvenile delinquents. *The American Journal of Family Therapy, 16*(3), 243–254.

Gordon, D., Burge, D., Hammen, C., Adrian, C., Jaenicke, C., & Hiroto, D. (1989). Observations of interactions of depressed women with their children. *American Journal of Psychiatry, 146*(1), 50–55.

Gorman, P., Lockerman, G., & Giffels, P. (1995). Conversations outside the clinic: Video-reflecting teams for in-home therapy and supervision. *Journal of Systemic Therapies, 14,* 1–15.

Green, R. J., & Werner, P. D. (1996). Intrusiveness and closeness-caregiving: Rethinking the concept of family "enmeshment." *Family Process, 35,* 115–136.

Greenspan, S. I. (1992). *Infancy and early childhood: The practice of clinical assessment and intervention with emotional and developmental challenges.* Madison, CT: International Universities Press.

Greenspan, S. I. (1997). Developmentally based psychotherapy. Madison: International University Press.

Greenspan, S. I., & Salmon, J. (1995). The challenging child. New York: Addison-Wesley.

Grotevant, H. D., & Carlson, C. I. (1989). *Family assessment: A guide to methods and measures.* New York: Guilford.

Gummer, B. (1978). A power-politics approach to social welfare organizations. *Social Service Review, 52*(3), 349–361.

Haber, R. (1996). *Dimensions of psychotherapy supervision: Maps and means.* New York: Norton.

Hage, J., & Aiken, M. (1970). *Social change in complex organizations.* New York: Random House.

Hampson, R. B., Hulgus, Y. F., Beavers, W. R., & Beavers, J. S. (1988). The assessment of competence in families with a retarded child. *Journal of Family Psychology, 2*(1), 32–53.

Hansen, M. (1995). *Guide to professional behavior for therapeutic staff support workers.* Harrisburg, PA: CASSP Training and Technical Assistance Institute.

Harrison, A. O., Wilson, M. N., Pine, C. J., Chan, S. Q., & Buriel, R. (1990). Family ecologies of ethnic minority children. *Child Development, 61,* 347–362.

Hardy, K. V. & Laszloffy, T. A. (1994). Deconstructing race in family therapy. In R. V. Almeida (Ed.), *Expansions of feminist family therapy through diversity* (pp. 5–33). Binghamton, NY: Haworth Press.

Hazenfeld, Y. (1992). Theoretical approaches to human service organizations. In Y. Hazenfeld (Ed.), *Human services as complex organizations* (pp. 24–44). Newbury Park, CA: Sage.

Heflinger, C. A., & Bickman, L. (1996). Family empowerment: A conceptual model for promoting parent-professional partnership. In C. A. Heflinger & C. T. Nixon (Eds.), *Families and the mental health system for children and adolescents* (pp. 96–116). Thousand Oaks, CA: Sage.

Henggeler, S. W., Burr-Harris, A. W., Bordiun, C. M., & McCallum, G. (1991). Use of the Family Adaptation and Cohesion Evaluation Scales in child clinical research. *Journal of Abnormal Child Psychology, 19*(1), 53–63.

Henggeler, S. W., Melton, G. B., & Smith, L. A. (1992). Family preservation using multisystemic therapy: An effective alternative to incarcerating serious juvenile offenders. *Journal of Consulting and Clinical Psychology, 60*(6), 953–961.

Henggeler, S. W., Melton, G. B., Smith, L. A., & Schoenwald, S. K. (1993). Family preservation using multisystemic therapy: Long-term follow-up to a clinical trial with serious juvenile offenders. *Journal of Child and Family Studies, 2*(4), 283–293.

Henggeler, S. W., Rowland, M. D., Pickerel, S. G., Miller, S. L., Cunningham, P. B., Santos, A. B., Schoenwald, S. K., Randall, J., & Edwards, J. E. (1997). Investigating family-based alternatives to institution-based mental health services for youth: Lessons learned from the pilot study of a randomized field trial. *Journal of Clinical Child Psychology, 26*(3), 226–233.

Heying, K. R. (1985). Family-based, in-home services for the severely emotionally disturbed child. *Child Welfare, 64*(5), 519–527.

Hobbs, D. (1965). Parenthood as crisis: A third study. *Journal of Marriage and the Family, 27,* 677–689.

Hobbs, D., & Wimbish, J. (1977). Transition to parenthood by black couples. *Journal of Marriage and the Family, 39,* 677–689.

Hobfoll, S. E., & Spielberger, C. D. (1992). Family stress: Integrating theory and measurement. *Journal of Family Psychology, 6*(2), 99–112.

Hodas, G. (1992). *In your face.* Unpublished manuscript. Philadelphia Child Guidance Center, Philadelphia, PA.

Hodas, G. (1995). *Pitfalls in writing treatment plans.* CASSP Training and Technical Institute, Harrisburg, PA.

Hodas, G. (1996a). *What makes wraparound special: Understanding and creating a unique experience for children and their families.* Harrisburg, PA: CASSP Training and Technical Assistance Institute.

Hodas, G. (1996b). *Listen to their story.* Unpublished song. Philadelphia Child Guidance Center, Philadelphia, PA.

Hodas, G. (1997). *Guidelines for best practice in child and adolescent mental health services.* Harrisburg, PA: Pennsylvania Department of Public Welfare.

Hodas, G., & Sargent, J. (1983). Psychiatric emergencies. In G. Fleisher & S.

Ludwig (Eds.), *Textbook of pediatric emergency medicine*. Baltimore: Williams and Wilkins.

Holahan, C. J., & Moos, R. H. (1987). Risk, resistance, and psychological distress: A longitudinal analysis with adults and children. *Journal of Abnormal Psychology, 96*(1), 3–13.

Holloway, E. L. (1995). *Clinical supervision: A systems approach*. Newbury Park, CA: Sage.

Hooper, S. R., & Tramontana, M. G. (1997). Advances in the neuropsychological bases of child and adolescent psychopathology. In T. H. Ollendick & R. J. Prinz (Eds.), *Advances in clinical child psychology, vol. 19* (pp. 133–175). New York: Plenum Press.

Horne, A. M. & Sayger, T. V. (1990). *Treating conduct and oppositional defiant disorders in children*. New York: Basic Books.

Houser, J. (1995). *Family based mental health procedure manual*. Unpublished manuscript. Family Therapy Center, Williamsport, PA.

Isaacs, M. B., Montalvo, B., & Abelsohn, D. (1986). *The difficult divorce: Therapy for children and families*. New York: Basic Books.

Itzkowitz, A. (1992, December). *Adolescent Depression*. Family Therapy Training Center lecture. Philadelphia Child Guidance Center, Philadelphia, PA.

Itzkowitz, A. (1995, January). *Working with Adolescents*. Family Therapy Training Center lecture. Philadelphia Child Guidance Center, Philadelphia, PA.

Jensen, P. S., Bloedau, L., Degroot, J., Ussery, T., & Davis, H. (1990). Children at risk: I. Risk factors and child symptomatology. *Journal of the American Academy of Child and Adolescent Psychiatry, 29*(1), 51–59.

Johnson, H. L., Glassman, M. B., Fiks, K. B., & Rosen, T. S. (1990). Path analysis of variables affecting 36-month outcome in a population of multi-risk children. *Infant Behavior and Development, 10*(4), 451–465.

Jones, W. C. (1986). Frame cultivation: Helping new meanings take root in families. *The American Journal of Family Therapy, 14*, 57–68.

Jones, W. C. (1991, December). *Teaching parenting skills in context*. Family Therapy Training Center lecture. Philadelphia Child Guidance Center, Philadelphia, PA.

Jones, W. C. (1992, September). *Linking systems*. Family Therapy Training Center lecture. Philadelphia Child Guidance Center, Philadelphia, PA.

Jones, W. C. (1997, April). *Oppositional-defiant children and their families: A bio-developmental-systems approach*. Family Therapy Training Center workshop. Philadelphia Child Guidance Center, Philadelphia, PA.

Jordan, J., Kraus, D., & Ware, E. (1993). Observations on loss and family development. *Family Process, 32* (4), 425–440.

Jouriles, E. N., Pfiffner, L. J., & O'Leary, S. G. (1988). Marital conflict, parenting, and toddler conduct problems. *Journal of Abnormal Child Psychology, 16*, 197–206.

Kagan, R., & Schlossberg, S. (1989). *Families in perpetual crisis*. New York: Norton.

Kashani, J. H., Daniel, A. E., Dandoy, A. C., & Holcomb, W. R. (1992). Family violence: Impact on children. *Journal of the American Academy of Child and Adolescent Psychiatry, 31*(2), 181–189.

Kaslow, F. J. (1986). Themes and patterns. In F. J. Kaslow (Ed.), *Supervision and training: Models, dilemmas, and challenges*. New York: Hawthorne Press.

Kazak, A. E. (1986). Families with physically handicapped children: Social ecology and family systems. *Family Process, 25*, 265–281.

Kinney, J. C., Haapala, D., & Booth, C. (1991). *Keeping families together: The Homebuilders model.* New York: Aldine de Gruyter.

Kiresuk, T. J., & Sherman, R. E. (1968). Goal attainment scaling: A method for evaluating comprehensive community mental health programs. *Community Mental Health Journal, 4*(6), 443–453.

Kiresuk, T. J., Smith, A., & Cardillo, J. E. (1994). *Goal attainment scaling: Applications, theory, and measurement.* Hillsdale, NJ: Earlbaum.

Klein-Walker, D., & Crocker, D. (1988). Measuring family systems outcomes. In H. Weiss & F. Jacobs, Eds., *Evaluating family programs.* New York: Aldine de Gruyer.

Knitzer, J. (1989). *Collaborations between child welfare and child mental health: Emerging patterns and challenges.* New York: Bank Street College of Education.

Kreppner, K., Paulsen, S., & Schuetze, Y. (1982). Infant and family development: From triads to tetrads. *Human Development, 25,* 373–391.

Kuhns, L., & Witt, R. (1994). *Homekeepers program.* Unpublished manuscript.

Kutash, K., & Rivera, V. R. (1995). Effectiveness of children's mental health services: A review of the literature. *Education and Treatment of Children, 18*(4), 443–477.

L'Engle, M. (1972). *A circle of quiet.* New York: Harper Collins.

Landau-Stanton, J., & Stanton, D. M. (1985). Treating suicidal adolescents and their families. In M. Pravder-Merkin & S. L. Koman (Eds.), *Handbook of adolescents and family therapy.* New York: Gardner Press.

Larsen, D. L., Attkisson, C. C., Hargreaves, W. A., & Nguyen, T. D. (1979). Assessment of client/patient satisfaction: Development of a general scale. *Evaluation and Program Planning, 2,* 197–207.

Leadbetter, B. J., Bishop, S. J., & Raver, C. C. (1996). Quality of mother-toddler interactions, maternal depressive symptoms, and behavior problems in preschoolers of adolescent mothers. *Developmental Psychology, 32*(2), 280–288.

Leonard, G. (1987, May). Playing for keeps. *Esquire,* 116.

Lehr, R. F., & Fitzsimmons, G. (1991). Adaptation and cohesion: Implications for understanding the violence-prone system. *Journal of Family Violence, 6*(3), 255–265.

Liddle, H. (1995). Conceptual and clinical dimensions of a multidimensional multi-systems engagement strategy in family based adolescent treatment. *Psychotherapy, 32*(1), 39–58.

Liddle, H., Breunlin, D. C., Schwartz, R. C., & Constantine, J. (1984). Training family therapy supervisors: Issues of content, form and context. *Journal of Marriage and Family Therapy, 10,* 139–150.

Liddle, H., & Saba, G. (1983). On context replication: The isomorphic relationship of training and therapy. *Journal of Strategic and Systemic Therapies, 2,* 3–11.

Lindblad-Goldberg, M. (1989). Successful minority single-parent families. In L. Combrinck-Graham (Ed.), *Children in family contexts: Perspectives on treatment* (pp. 116–134). New York: Guilford.

Lindblad-Goldberg, M., & Dore, M. M. (1989, November/ December). Home-based services widely used in the USA. *Family Therapy News, 7,* 26.

Lindblad-Goldberg, M., & Dukes, J. (1988). Stress in black, low-income single parent families: Normative and dysfunctional patterns. *American Journal of Orthopsychiatry, 58,* 104–120.

Linn, D. (1991). *Family-based services programs.* Unpublished manuscript.

Littell, J. H. (1995). Evidence or assertions? The outcomes of family perservation services. *Social Service Review, 69*, 338–351.

Loganbill, C., Hardy, E., & Delworth, U. (1982). Supervision: A conceptual model. *Counseling Psychologist, 10*, 3–42.

Lourie, I. S., & Katz-Leavy, J. (1991). New directions for mental health services for families and children. *Families in Society*, 277–283.

Malinosky-Rummell, R., & Hansen, D. J. (1993). Long-term consequences of childhood physical abuse. *Psychological Bulletin, 114*(1), 68–79.

Manly, J. T., Cicchetti, D., & Barnett, D. (1994). The impact of subtype, frequency, chronicity, and severity of child maltreatment on social competence and behavior problems. *Development and Psychopathology, 6*, 121–143.

Mann, B. J., Borduin, C. M., Henggeler, S. W., & Blaske, D. M. (1990). An investigation of systemic conceptualizations of parent-child coalitions and symptom change. *Journal of Consulting and Clinical Psychology, 58*(3), 336–344.

Maybanks, S., & Bryce, M. (1979). *Home-based services for children and families: Policy, practice and research*. Springfield, IL: Charles A. Thomas.

McCloskey, L. A., Figueredo, A. J., & Koss, M. P. (1995). The effects of systemic family violence on children's mental health. *Child Development, 66*, 1239–1261.

McCroskey, J., & Nelson, J. (1989). Practice-based research in a family-support program: The Family Connection Project example. *Child Welfare, 68*(6), 573–587.

McGoldrick, M. (1988). Ethnicity and the family life cycle. In B. Carter & M. McGoldrick (Eds.), *The changing family life cycle: A framework for family therapy* (2nd ed.). New York: Gardner Press.

McGowan, B. G., & Meezan, W. (1983). *Child welfare: Current dilemmas, future directions*. Itasca, IL: Peacock.

McIntyre, A., & Keesler, T. Y. (1986). Psychological disorders among foster children. *Journal of Clinical Child Psychology, 15*(4), 297–303.

Meehan, K. (1994). *The multi-system service planning meeting*. Unpublished manuscript.

Meisels, S. J. (1989). Meeting the mandate of public law 99–457: Early childhood intervention in the nineties. *American Journal of Orthopsychiatry, 59*(3), 451–460.

Melton, B. (1989, winter/spring). Overcoming stigma. *Focal Point, 3*(2), 11.

Miller, G. E., & Prinz, R. J. (1990). Enhancement of social learning family interventions for childhood conduct disorder. *Psychological Bulletin, 108*(2), 291–307.

Minuchin, S. (1970). The use of an ecological framework in the treatment of a child. In E. J. Anthony & C. Koupernik (Eds.), *The child in his family*. New York: Wiley.

Minuchin, S. (1974). *Families and family therapy*. Cambridge, MA: Harvard University Press.

Minuchin, S., & Fishman, H. C. (1981). *Family therapy techniques*. Cambridge, MA: Harvard University Press.

Minuchin, S., & Nichols, M. P. (1993). *Family healing*. New York: Free Press.

Mones, A. G. (1998). Oppositional children and their families: An adaptational dance in space and time. *American Journal of Orthopsychiatry, 68*, 147–153.

Montalvo, B. (1982). Interpersonal arrangements in disrupted families. In F. Walsh (Ed.), *Normal family processes*. New York: Guilford.

Montalvo, B., & Gutierrez, M. (1988). The emphasis on cultural identity: A developmental-ecological constraint. In C. J. Falicov (Ed.), *Family transitions: Continuity and change over the life cycle*. New York: Guilford.

Moos, R. (1974). *Family environment scale (form R)*. Palo Alto, CA: Consulting Psychologists Press.

Morton, E. S., & Grigsby, R. K. (Eds.). (1993). *Advancing family preservation practice*. Newbury Park, CA: Sage.

Mutschler, E. (1984). Evaluating practice: A study of research utilization by practitioners. *Social Work, 29*, 332–337.

National Center for Clinical Infant Programs. (1987). *Charting change in infants, families and services: A guide to program evaluation for administrators and practitioners*. Arlington, VA: National Center for Clinical Infant Programs.

Nelson, K. E. (1997). Family preservation—what is it? *Children and Youth Services Review, 19*(1/2), 101–118.

Oetting, E. R. (1982). Program evaluation, scientific inquiry, and counseling psychology. *The Counseling Psychologist, 10*(4), 61–70.

Ogles, B. M., Lambert, M. J., & Masters, K. S. (1996). *Assessing outcome in clinical practice*. Boston: Allyn & Bacon.

Olson, D., Portner, J., & Lavee, Y. (1985). *Faces-III*. Minneapolis: Family Social Science, University of Minnesota.

Ooms, T. (1990). *Implementation of P.L. 99–457: Parent/professional partnership in early education*. Background briefing report, Family Impact Seminar. Washington, DC: American Association for Marriage and Family Therapy.

Ooms, T., & Beck, D. (1990). *Keeping troubled families together: Promising programs and statewide reform*. Background briefing report, Family Impact Seminar. Washington, DC: American Association for Marriage and Family Therapy.

Parsons, B. V., & Alexander, J. F. (1973). Short-term family intervention: A therapy outcome study. *Journal of Consulting and Clinical Psychology, 41*, 195–201.

Patterson, G. R. (1982). *Coercive family processes*. Eugene, OR: Castalia.

Pearlin, L. I., & Schooler, C. (1978). The structure of coping. *Journal of Health and Social Behavior, 19*, 2–21.

Pecora, P. J., Fraser, M. W., & Haapala, D. A. (1991). Client outcomes and issues for program design. In K. Wells & D. Biegel (Eds.), *Family preservation services: Research and evaluation* (pp. 3–32). Newbury Park, CA: Sage.

Pecora, P. J., Fraser, M. W., & Haapala, D. A. (1992). Intensive home-based family preservation services: An update from the FIT project. *Child Welfare, 71*(2), 177–188.

Pecora, P. J., Fraser, M. W., Nelson, K. E., McCroskey, J., & Meezan, W. (1995). *Evaluating family-based services*. New York: Aldine de Gruyter.

Pettit, G. S., Bates, J. E., & Dodge, K. A. (1997). Supportive parenting, ecological context, and children's adjustment: A seven-year longitudinal study. *Child Development, 68*(5), 908–923.

Piercy, F. P., & Nickerson, V. (1996). Focus groups in family therapy research. In D. H. Sprenkle & S. M. Moon (Eds.), *Research methods in family therapy* (pp. 173–190). New York: Guilford.

Piercy, M. (1982). *Circles on the water: Selected poems of Marge Piercy*. New York: Alfred A. Knopf.

Powell, D. (1987). Methodological and conceptual issues in research. In S. Kagan, D. Powell, B. Weissbourd, & E. Zigler, (Eds.), *America's family support programs*. New Haven: Yale University Press.

Prigogine, I. (1973). Time, irreversibility, and structure. In J. Mehra (Ed.), *The physicist's conception of nature*. Boston, MA: D. Reidel.

Radke-Yarrow, M., Nottelmann, E., Martinez, P., Fox, M. B., & Belmont, B. (1992). Young children of affectively ill parents: A longitudinal study of psychosocial development. *Journal of the American Academy of Child and Adolescent Psychiatry, 31*(1), 68–77.

Reid, W. J., & Crisafulli, A. (1990). Marital discord and child behavior problems: A meta-analysis. *Journal of Abnormal Child Psychology, 18* (1), 105–117.

Richman, J.(1979). The family therapy of attempted suicide. *Family Process, 18*, 131–142.

Rinkin, M. (1995, Fall). My son taught me to keep fighting and to keep my head raised high. *Focal Point, 9*(2), 20.

Rossi, P. (1992). Strategies for evaluation. *Child and Youth Services Review, 14*(1/2), 167–191.

Rossi, P., & Freeman, H. E. (1993). *Evaluation: A systematic approach*. Newbury Park, CA: Sage.

Rotenberg, S. (1997, Spring). Responding to the mental health needs of youth in the juvenile justice system. *Focal Point, 1*, 3–5.

Russell, C. (1974) Transition to parenthood: Problems and gratifications. *Journal of Marriage and the Family, 36*, 294–301.

Rutter, M. (1987). Psychosocial resilience and protective mechanisms. *American Journal of Orthopsychiatry, 57*, 316–331.

Rutter, M., & Quinton, D. (1984). Parental psychiatric disorder: Effects on children. *Psychological Medicine, 14*, 853–880.

Ryan, A., & Hendricks, C. (1989). Culture and communication: Supervising the Asian and Hispanic social worker. *The Clinical Supervisor, 7*, 27–40.

Sachs, B., & Hall, L. A. (1991). Maladaptive mother-child relationships: A pilot study. *Public Health Nursing, 8* (4), 226–233.

Saleeby, D. (1979). The tension between research and practice: Assumptions of the experimental paradigm. *Clinical Social Work, 7*, 267–284.

Salend, S. (1990). *Effective mainstreaming*. New York: Macmillan.

Sawin, K. J., & Harrigan, M. P. (1995). *Measures of family functioning for research and practice*. New York: Springer.

Schalock, R. L. (1995). *Outcome-based evaluation*. New York: Plenum Press.

Schaugnency, E. A., & Lahey, B. B. (1985). Mothers' and fathers' perceptions of child deviance: Roles of child behavior, parental depression, and marital satisfaction. *Journal of Consulting and Clinical Psychology, 53*(5), 718–723.

Schilling, R. F., Gilchrist, L. D., & Schinke, S. P. (1984). Coping and social support in families of developmentally disabled children. *Family Relations, 33*, 46–53.

Schoenwald, S. K., Scherer, D. G., & Brondino, M. J. (1997). Effective community-based treatments for serious juvenile offenders. In S. W. Henggeler & A. B. Santos (Eds.), *Innovative approaches for difficult-to-treat populations* (pp. 65–82). Washington, DC: American Psychiatric Press.

Schuerman, J. R., Rzepnicki, T. L., & Littell, J. H. (1994). *Putting families first: An experiment in family preservation*. New York: Aldine de Gruyter.

Schulberg, H. C. (1981). Outcome evaluations in the mental health field. *Community Mental Health Journal, 17*(2), 130–141.

Schwartz, I. M., AuClaire, P., & Harris, L. J. (1991). Family preservation services as an alternative to the out-of-home placement of adolescents: The Hennepin County experience. In K. Wells & D. Biegel (Eds.), *Family preservation services: Research and evaluation* (pp. 33–46). Newbury Park, CA: Sage.

Schwartz, I. M., Jackson-Beeck, M., & Anderson, R. (1984). The "hidden" system of juvenile control. *Crime & Delinquency, 30*(3), 371–385.

Schwartz, R. C. (1988). The trainer-trainee relationship in family therapy training. In H. A. Liddle, D. C. Breunlin, & R. C. Schwartz (Eds.), *Handbook of family therapy training and supervision.* New York: Guilford.

Schwartzman, J. (Ed). (1985) *Families and other systems.* New York: Guilford.

Scott, W. R. (1983). The organization of environments: Network, cultural, and historical elements. In J. W. Meyer & W. R. Scott (Eds.), *Organizational environments: Ritual and reality.* Beverly Hills: Sage.

Sederer, L. I., & Dickey, B. (Eds.). (1996). *Outcomes assessment in clinical practice.* Baltimore: Williams & Wilkins.

Seelig, W. R., Goldman-Hall, B. J., & Jerrell, J. M. (1992). In-home treatment of families with seriously disturbed adolescents in crisis. *Family Process, 31,* 135–149.

Seifer, R., & Dickstein, S. (1993). Parental mental illness and infant development. In C. H. Zeanah, Jr. (Ed.), *Handbook of infant mental health* (pp. 120–141). New York: Guilford.

Shaw, D. S., & Emery, R. E. (1987). Parental conflict and other correlates of the adjustment of school-age children whose parents have separated. *Journal of Abnormal Child Psychology, 15,* 269–281.

Simon, G. (1995). A revisionist rendering of structural family therapy. *Journal of Marital and Family Therapy, 21,* 17–25.

Smith, E. (1981). Cultural and historical perspectives in counseling Blacks. In D. W. Sue (Ed.), *Counseling the Culturally Different.* New York: John Wiley and Sons.

Spaccarelli, S., Sandler, I. N., & Roosa, M. (1994). History of spouse violence against mother: Correlated risks and unique effects in child mental health. *Journal of Family Violence, 9*(1), 79–98.

Sperry, L. (1996). *Treatment outcomes in psychotherapy and psychiatric interventions.* New York: Brunner/Mazel.

Stanton, D. M. (1992). The time line and the "why now?" question: A technique and rationale for therapy, training, organizational consultation and research. *Family Process, 18,* 331–343.

Stehno, S. (1986). Family-centered child welfare services: New life for a historic idea. *Child Welfare, 65,* 231–240.

Stein, E., Evans, B., Mazumdar, R., & Rae-Grant, N. (1996). The mental health of children in foster care: A comparison with community and clinical samples. *Canadian Journal of Psychiatry, 41*(6), 385–391.

Stern, L. (1993). *Family-based mental health services quality assurance standards: Supervision.* Harrisburg, PA: Office of Mental Health, Bureau of Children's Services.

Stockdill, J. (1991). The NIMH in relation to state and local mental health administrators and policymakers: CASSP as a prototype. *Administration and Policy in Mental Health, 18*(6), 455–459.

Stroul, B. A., & Goldman, S. K. (1990). Study of community-based services for children and adolescents who are severely emotionally disturbed. *The Journal of Mental Health Administration, 17*(1), 61–77.

Stuntzner-Gibson, D., Koren, P. E., & DeChillo, N. (1995). The Youth Satisfaction Questionnaire: What kids think of services. *Families in Society, 76*(10), 616–624.

Sudia, C. (1986, November/December). Preventing out-of-home placement of children: The first step to permanency planning. *Children Today,* 4–5.

Suelzle, M., & Keenan, V. (1981). Changes in family support networks over the life cycle of mentally retarded persons. *American Journal of Mental Deficiency, 86,* 267–268.

Sugarman, S., & Masheter, C. (1985). The family crisis intervention literature: What is meant by "family"? *Journal of Marital and Family Therapy, II,* 167–177.

Swire, M. R., & Kavalar, F. (1978). The health status of foster children. In S. Chess & A. Thomas (Eds.), *Annual progress in child psychiatry and child development* (pp. 626–642). New York: Brunner/Mazel.

Taffel, R. (1991, July/August). How to talk with kids. *Family Therapy Networker,* 41–45, 68–70.

Tarico, V. S., Low, B. P., Trupin, E., & Forsyth-Stephens, A. (1989). Children's mental health services: A parent perspective. *Community Mental Health Journal, 25*(4), 313–326.

Teyber, E. (1983). Structural family relations: Primary dyadic alliances and adolescent adjustment. *Journal of Marital and Family Therapy, 9*(1), 89–99.

The American Heritage Dictionary (2nd ed.). (1985). Boston, MA Houghton Mifflin.

Theiman, A. A., & Dail, P. W. (1992). Family preservation services: Problems of measurement and assessment of risk. *Family Relations, 41,* 186–191.

Thomas, A., Chess, S., & Birch, H. (1968). *Temperament and behavior disorders in children.* New York: New York University Press.

Thompson, A. H., & Fuhr, D. (1992). Emotional disturbance in fifty children in the care of a child welfare system. *Journal of Social Service Research, 15*(34), 95–112.

Tingley, S. (1995, Fall). Chuck: My younger brother. *Focal Point, 9*(2), 17.

Tomm, K., & Wright, L. (1979). Training in family therapy: Perceptual, conceptual and executive skills. *Family Process, 18,* 227–250.

Toprac, M. G., & Rouse, L. W. (1993, February). *Home-based services for children with serious emotional disturbance: An analysis of consumer and program variables associated with positive outcomes.* Paper presented at the sixth annual research conference of the Florida Mental Health Institute, Tampa, FL.

Touliatos, J., Perlmutter, B. F., & Strauss, M. A. (Eds.). (1990). *Handbook of family measurement techniques.* Newbury Park, CA: Sage.

Tracy, E. M., Bean, N., Gwatkin, S., & Hill, B. (1992). Family preservation workers: Sources of job satisfaction and job stress. *Research on Social Work Practice, 2,* 465–479.

Trupin, E. W., Tarico, V. S., Low, B. P., Jemelka, R., & McClellan, J. (1993). Children on child protective service caseloads: Prevalence and nature of serious emotional disturbance. *Child Abuse & Neglect, 17,* 345–355.

Trute, B. (1990). Child and parent predictors of family adjustment in households containing young developmentally disabled children. *Family Relations, 39,* 292–297.

Trute, B., & Hauch, C. (1988). Building on family strengths: A study of families with positive adjustment to the birth of a developmentally disabled child. *Journal of Marital and Family Therapy, 14*(2), 185–193.

Tuma, J. M. (1989). Mental health services for children. *American Psychologist,* 44(2), 188–199.

Tuttle, G. (Ed.). (1995). *Practice strategies.* Washington, DC: American Association for Marriage and Family Therapy.

Umbarger, C. (1983) *Structural family therapy.* New York: Grune & Stratton.

Unger, D. G., & Powell, D. R. (1980). Supporting families under stress: The role of social networks. *Family Relations, 29,* 566–574.

Urquiza, A. J., Wirtz, S. J., Peterson, M. S., & Singer, V. A. (1994). Screening and evaluating abused and neglected children entering protective custody. *Child Welfare 73*(2), 155–171.

Verwaaijen, A. A. G., & Van Acker, J. C. A. (1993). Family treatment for adolescents at risk of placement. I: Theory and treatment process. *Family Therapy, 20,* 103–132.

Watzlawick, P., Weakland, J., & Fisch, R. (1967). *Pragmatics of human communication: A study of interactional patterns, pathologies and paradoxes.* New York: Norton.

Watzlawick, P., Weakland, J., & Fisch, R. (1974). *Change: Principles of problem formation and problem resolution.* New York: Norton.

Webster-Stratton, C., & Hammond, M. (1988). Maternal depression and its relationship to life stress, perceptions of child behavior problems, parenting behaviors, and child conduct problems. *Journal of Abnormal Child Psychology, 16,* 299–315.

Webster-Stratton, C., & Herbert, M. (1994). *Troubled families/problem children.* New York: Wiley.

Weinbach, R. W., & Grinnell, R. M. Jr. (1987). *Statistics for social workers.* New York: Longman.

Wells, K., & Freer, R. (1994). Reading between the lines: The case for qualitative research in intensive family preservation services. *Children and Youth Services Review, 16*(5/6), 399–415.

Werner, E. (1989). High-risk children in young adulthood: A longitudinal study from birth to 32 years. *American Journal of Orthopsychiatry, 59*(2), 72–81.

Werrbach, G. B. (1992). A study of home-based services for families of adolescents. *Child and Adolescent Social Work Journal, 9*(6), 505–523.

West, M. O., & Prinz, R. J. (1987). Parental alcoholism and childhood psychopathology. *Psychological Bulletin, 102*(2), 204–218.

Westendorp, F., Brink, K. L., Roberson, M. K., & Ortiz, I. E. (1986). Variables which differentiate placement of adolescents into juvenile justice or mental health systems. *Adolescence, 21,* 24–37.

Whyte, D. (1994). *The heart aroused.* New York: Doubleday.

Williams, F. (1992). *Reasoning with statistics* (4th ed.). Fort Worth: Harcourt Brace Jovanovich.

Williams, S., Anderson J., McGee, R., & Silva, P. A. (1990). Risk factors for behavioral and emotional disorder in preadolescent children. *Journal of the American Academy of Child and Adolescent Psychiatry, 29*(3), 413–419.

Williams-Murphy, T. (1995). My brother James. *Focal Point, 9*(2), 15–17.

Wolf, E. (1990) *Northumberland county's Homekeepers program.* Unpublished manuscript.

Wood, B. (1985). Proximity and hierarchy: Orthogonal dimensions of family interconnectedness. *Family Process, 24,* 487–507.

Woody, R. H., Woody, J. D., & Greenberg, D. B. (1991). Case management for the individual family service plan under public law 99–457. *The American Journal of Family Therapy, 19*(1), 67–76.

Young, T. M., Dore, M. M., & Pappenfort, D. M. (1988). Residential group care for children considered emotionally disturbed, 1966–1981. *Social Service Review, 62*(1), 158–170.

Yuan, Y. T., & Struckman-Johnson, D. L. (1991). Placement outcomes for neglected children with prior placements in family preservation programs. In K. Wells & D. Biegel (Eds), *Family preservation services: Research and evaluation* (pp. 92–120). Newbury Park, CA: Sage Publications.

Zarski, J. J., & Fluharty, L. B. (1992). Treating emotionally disturbed youth: A comparison of home-based and outpatient interventions. *Contemporary Family Therapy, 14*(4), 335–350.

Zarski, J. J., Pastore, C. A., Way, L. A., & Shepler, R.N. (1988). Families at risk and home-based intervention: A therapist training model. *Contemporary Family Therapy, 10*, 53–62.

INDEX

351